DATE DUE

SEP 1 1994	
SEP 1 2 1994	
SEP 2 0 1994	
OCT 1 8 1994	
NOV 3 1994	
NOV 2 3 1994	
DEC 2 7 1994	
JAN 1 8 1995	

BRODART   Cat. No. 23-221

UNDER OBSERVATION

OTHER BOOKS
BY LISA BERGER

Feathering Your Nest

We Heard the Angels of Madness:
One Family's Struggle with Manic Depression
(with Diane Berger)

The Healthy Company (with Robert Rosen)

Cashing In (with Donelson Berger and C. William Eastwood)

UNDER
OBSERVATION

Life Inside a Psychiatric Hospital

Lisa Berger and
Alexander Vuckovic, M.D.

Ticknor & Fields   NEW YORK 1994

W

For information about permission to reproduce selections
from this book, write to Permissions, Ticknor & Fields,
215 Park Avenue South, New York, New York 10003.

Library of Congress Cataloging-in-Publication Data
Berger, Lisa.
  Under observation : life inside a psychiatric hospital /
Lisa Berger and Alexander Vuckovic.
    p. cm.
  Includes index.
  ISBN 0-395-63413-X
  1. McLean Hospital. 2. Psychiatric hospital care. 3. Mental
illness — Popular works. 4. Belmont (Mass.).   I. Vuckovic,
Alexander. II. Title.
  RC445.M4B448 1994
  362.2'1'097444 — dc20   94-5051
                        CIP   r94

Printed in the United States of America

MP 10 9 8 7 6 5 4 3 2 1

Book design by Melodie Wertelet

In Memory of Catharine Raynolds Berger
— L.B.

To My Wonderful Wife, Lisa
— A.V.

CONTENTS

ACKNOWLEDGMENTS

THIS BOOK could not have been written without the extraordinary cooperation of McLean Hospital. From top administrators to hospital staff, the people at McLean gave us not only unprecedented access but also were enormously generous with their time and knowledge. Special thanks to Dr. Bruce M. Cohen, Dr. Paul Howard, Dr. Pierre Mayer, Dr. Steven M. Mirin, Joyce Quigley, Arnold R. Saitow, Sandra Talanian, L.I.C.S.W., and Paulette A. Trudeau, R.N. The staff members of the Unit, who have to remain unnamed, also deserve our appreciation for their remarkable courage and professionalism in welcoming a writer into their world.

Reporting and writing comprise just part of the making of a book. Credit is due to our agent, Gail Ross, who not only suggested writing about McLean but then provided encouragement and support over the next three years. Thanks also to Diane and David Stoner, whose thoughtful hospitality provided a Boston base for research and writing. Once the writing was finished, we had the great good fortune to have Jane von Mehren as our editor. Her unstinting attention, plus exceptional narrative craftsmanship, ensured that this book had the finest editorial guidance.

AUTHOR'S NOTE

THE IDEA for a book about life inside McLean Hospital
evolved following the publication of my book *We Heard the
Angels of Madness,* about my nephew's battle with manic depression. At the end of that book he finally connected with a
doctor and a hospital that offered caring, up-to-date treatment.
The doctor was a psychiatrist specializing in medication, a psychopharmacologist named Alexander Vuckovic, and the hospital was McLean Hospital in Belmont, Massachusetts. While
visiting my nephew at McLean and writing about his treatment,
I became intrigued by the place. My idea of what went on in
psychiatric hospitals had been shaped by movies like *One Flew
over the Cuckoo's Nest* and characters like Nurse Ratched. But
McLean was nothing like this. Not only were patient units
clean, modern, and spacious, but staff was experienced in the
latest advances in psychiatric research and care. Furthermore,
the hospital complex included a separate facility called the
Mailman Research Center, and its scientists, I discovered from
medical journals, were leaders in neuroscience. A book about
McLean, its exceptional care and groundbreaking research, was
impelling.

When I began the book, I met a number of times with Alex

Vuckovic. As we talked about his work, it became obvious that his medical knowledge and personal experiences offered a rich source of material. We decided to collaborate. The book we mapped out had many parts, some easier to assemble than others. The heart of the book was to be an account of a patient unit and how doctors and staff combated specific illnesses. At first glance, such a book seemed simple enough, but it raised numerous ethical issues for me as a writer, Alex as a doctor, and McLean as a private hospital.

In its 180-year history, McLean had never let a working writer inside its treatment units. And for good reason. Confidentiality and privacy are essential to patient care. But McLean is more than a private hospital — it is also a teaching hospital, and researchers and students from Harvard Medical School are a regular part of its operations. So when Alex and I proposed to the hospital's Institutional Review Board, which must approve and monitor any activity involving patients, that McLean allow me to observe and write about a unit, it was cautiously receptive. The IRB solved its dilemma — how to maintain confidentiality while allowing someone to write about it and educate the general public about its work — by granting me access to a unit but with strict limits.

Before any contact with unit staff members, I had to meet with them as a group, explain my project, and secure their written consent to interview them and watch them work. I had to keep names and identities confidential. Before I talked to the patients, the Unit's psychiatrist-in-charge had to explain my project and secure their written consent. My notes could include no patient names (I used numbers) and I could attend unit meetings only if all participants agreed. Furthermore, I had to meet every few months with the hospital ethics committee, which monitored my presence on the Unit and made sure my patient contacts were appropriate and within the limits set by the IRB. Lastly, the IRB read the final manuscript to ensure that patient confidentiality had been maintained.

Alex's ethical dilemma was not one of access but of maintaining personal and professional integrity. First and foremost, he is a doctor who provides superb care, and that could not be compromised by our writing. To avoid even the appearance of a conflict of interest, we decided that I should not observe on the unit where Alex is the psychiatrist-in-charge. Our book writing and his psychiatry were kept separate.

My ethical quandary involved trying to find the middle ground between accuracy and honesty on one end, and honoring patient privacy on the other end. As a nonfiction writer, I need my subjects to be accountable and accessible; if they are not, I begin to doubt their credibility and I think readers do, too. I had met some McLean patients through Alex. His private practice includes former McLean patients, and a number of them agreed to talk with me and to let me sit in on their meetings with him. These were not intensive psychotherapy encounters but relatively brief sessions to discuss medication. In turn, I readily agreed not to write about them by name, or in any way that might identify them.

Usually, when I write about people whose names or likenesses cannot be revealed, I give them a new name and alter telltale personal details. But for this book, the identity shield had to be impenetrable. The best option was to create composite characters. Alex and I added another layer of anonymity by assembling these composites together, with each of us drawing characteristics from patients and staff whom the other person did not know. Similarly, the incidents and conversations on the Unit are not verbatim accounts, but are amalgams of encounters I witnessed and Alex gleaned as a psychiatrist-in-charge at McLean.

Writing about people and activities off the Unit was much easier. The researchers and doctors working at the labs in the Mailman Research Center and elsewhere in the hospital were remarkably accessible. The difficulty in writing about these people was not confidentiality, for each agreed to be named, but accuracy, especially when describing complicated scientific or medical activities. These scientists and doctors, who appear in the book with their real names — Francine Benes, Ross Baldessarini, Alexander Campbell, Mauricio Tohen, Philip Levendusky, Martin Teicher, Paul McLean, and James Chu — gave me enormous chunks of their time and extensive interviews so that I could understand their work.

The research and writing for this book required about three years, and McLean underwent many changes during that time. Alex and I did not want a modern history of the hospital but a portrait of its present treatment. So we decided to contain the events described in the book, which we garnered from my observations and Alex's ten years of treating McLean patients, within the average length of a patient's stay. When we began the book, that stay was twenty-two days; when we wrote the final draft, that stay had dropped to thirteen days. Thus, the story in the book takes place over about two weeks in the spring of 1993, when I spent the most time inside the Unit.

Spring 1993 turned out to be a pivotal time for McLean Hospital, and I was lucky to be there while it was going through unprecedented changes. In today's climate of a health care crisis, psychiatric hospitals, perhaps more than any other type of medical institution, are undergoing major upheavals. Economic pressures from managed care, coupled with treatment controversies, such as those surrounding psychotropic medication and the role of psychotherapy, have put psychiatric hospitals and mental illness on the front lines in the crisis over health care.

As a result, *Under Observation* is about more than patients and treatment on a psychiatric unit; it's also about how forces outside the hospital are shaping that care.

LISA BERGER

MARCH 1994

Under Observation

CHAPTER ONE

Welcome to the Unit

ALEXANDER VUCKOVIC, the psychiatrist-in-charge of the Unit, jogs down the stairs from his third-floor office, slips through a side door marked ESCAPE RISK — DO NOT ENTER, and heads for the poolroom. In this long sunny place, patients and staff, whether in therapy groups, arts and crafts, or treatment meetings, do hand-to-hand combat with mental illness. Every Tuesday and Thursday morning, the pool table is shoved to one end of the room and seven Scandinavian-style chairs are arranged in a ring for family issues therapy.

Vuckovic gives a crisp, cheerful hello to the waiting patients. On the tall, lanky side with short, dark brown hair and a round, boyish face that makes him seem younger than his thirty-six years, he settles into a lounge chair positioned slightly back from the ring. On one side of him sits a middle-aged man in a starchy sport shirt who looks like he's in an elevator, studiously avoiding eye contact with anyone. Beside him is a fiftyish woman dressed in blue jeans and a sweatshirt, her hair a thick hat of pink sponge rollers; she is watching Vuckovic expectantly. The chair on the other side of Vuckovic is occupied by a young man, an MIT student, with a Celtics cap pulled low over his eyes, who seems to be dozing. The group waits quietly, except for two patients across from Vuckovic.

"You just don't understand, Kiesha," a thin, girlish woman with a tired face informs a young black woman who's smiling sweetly.

Vuckovic scans what he considers "his" group, although he's not a natural or especially enthusiastic leader. For him, leading group is unrewarding. He's uncomfortable with the wrestlings of the amorphous thoughts and emotions of these lost souls. And although his role is necessary, he doesn't like the feeling that he may be invading their closely guarded privacy. He prefers the tangible, more concrete rules and rewards of psychopharmacology, the hands-on clinical medicine. And this group is harder than most because it places in one room a hodgepodge of patients with conflicting needs: grandiose manic patients, the delusional, the depressed, and the occasional borderline personality.

Vuckovic sees his role as a sort of psychiatrist-cum-trail guide, pointing out what is real in the multiple perceptions of their treks, while gently leading his charges away from false paths. Sometimes he finds himself thrust into the role of a contentious or abusive parent or spouse through some subtle dynamic that neither he nor the group members can control. He tries not to lose his temper, but some days he is grateful just to avoid fistfights between patients. Occasionally he isn't so lucky.

"A pound cake is much more suitable for the hall," Julie continues to lecture. "We had it all the time on AB-II. Everyone loved it. Not everybody likes chocolate. It's too sweet for some." Although thirty-three, Julie Swoboda dresses like a teenager. She wears a short cotton shift, sandals with socks, and an oversized cardigan she wraps tightly around herself with firmly crossed arms. Her waifish appearance and five-foot frame are at odds with her booming, confident voice, itself incongruous in this locked, somber place.

Kiesha Thomas, her sweat suit bulging with early signs of pregnancy, wears socks but no shoes, and snorts at Julie's argument. "Anybody who doesn't like brownies is crazy crazy, needs a mattress in the quiet room, needs a shot of Thorazine." Her laughter fills the room. "Brownies, the breakfast of champions, the sacrament of the sacred, are just what this group needs!"

She leans to within an inch or two of Julie's face. "That's why they're so *boring* on AB-II — not enough chocolate!" Beaming, delighted with her powers of logic, she turns to Vuckovic. "Isn't that so, doctor?"

"We should get started, although I thought there were going to be two more people here."

He notes the patients' various degrees of alertness and dress, unconsciously doing "mini mental status exams," looking for possible signs of trouble in the group members' demeanor. He can't sort out why he's particularly ill at ease with this group.

"Let me explain the family issues group," Vuckovic begins, sliding his six-foot frame and double-breasted gabardine into a casual slump. Although the group is a regular feature of unit life, he lays out the ground rules almost every week because of the rapid turnover, exacerbated in recent months by continuing pressure from insurers and the hospital administration to shorten the length of patient stays.

His remarks also reinforce his position as the senior psychiatrist on the Unit. Despite eight years' experience running things here, Vuckovic occasionally feels the need to assert himself. Every so often, a new arrival to the Unit, usually a wizened, toothless veteran of years in the Massachusetts state hospital system, refuses to be treated by "that kid." His hair, free of any gray strands, along with his downright cherubic cheeks, produces what he calls "my Dorian Gray look."

It is a mix of the resulting diffidence, professional pride, and personal taste which compels him to look and sound like a seasoned physician. He dresses well — Armani ties, Boss suits, tasseled loafers — and conducts himself like a no-nonsense businessman. Sharp and efficient, eschewing long-winded dissertations for snappy, practical answers and quick action, he could be a chief financial officer.

"This group is for talking about things that may not seem relevant to your illness but have an impact on you and the people around you. Your illness stirs up a lot of anger. Sometimes that anger is misplaced, sometimes it's not. You may use it, as we all may be prone to doing when we're scared, as a weapon. And so may your families. They may lash out at you, getting angry for good reasons or bad.

"Talking about your anger may not prevent it, or even immediately change the impulse. But it may give you insight so you can cope with it and control it better. Sometimes it's perfectly appropriate to be angry, but even then you have a choice of how to deal with it. I'm sure all of you have been angry recently."

A murmur of assent, along with a chuckle or two, rises from the group as Vuckovic shifts in his chair; restless energy keeps some part of him constantly in motion.

"In this group, we're not going to talk about wounds inflicted in the past; those are sensitive issues, matters for you and your therapist. Please understand: this is *not* psychotherapy."

Julie mutters to Kiesha, "The only thing he understands is pills and shots. On AB-II, they listen to you."

"He doesn't know shit," Kiesha declares. Then, with a strange and distant look in her eye, she loudly demands, "You must let me out. I can't be here. I have to buy a lottery ticket. I saw the numbers last night in a dream. You're keeping me from winning millions!"

Vuckovic replies, warily, "That may be, or it may not, Kiesha, but such ideas could be symptoms of your illness."

He shifts quickly to the other patients. "Let's start by thinking of times when your family gets angry for no reason. You do something you can't help, or maybe you don't do anything at all, and they blow up anyway." As he waits for a response, there is a timid knock on the door. A young man in a black studded leather vest, with matching wristbands, enters the room, followed at some distance by a hunched, wispy, weather-beaten woman wearing a terry cloth dressing gown and tattered matching slippers.

"You looking for the family issues group?" Vuckovic asks in an inviting voice, recognizing them as new admissions. "Come on in."

Patients admitted at night are first seen by the resident psy-chiatrist on call, who does an initial work-up and prescribes medication if necessary. The admissions office then assigns the patient to a unit based on an initial sense of the diagnosis and severity of illness, as provided by families or treating clinicians, and on the availability of beds. Once ensconced in a unit, the psychiatrist-in-charge takes over a patient's treatment.

The family issues group isn't compulsory, but any patient considered stable enough to sit and talk for an hour or so is strongly encouraged to attend. Nevertheless, of the Unit's ap-proximately twenty-one patients, no more than five or six usu-ally make it to the 9:30 sessions.

"I'm Dr. Vuckovic. I'm the PIC here. And you're . . . ?" If the patients are confused by the acronym, they won't be for long. Newcomers to McLean Hospital quickly acquire the local shorthand and can string together abbreviations and medical terms as glibly as a third-year resident.

"My name's Glenda. I want to go home." The frizzy, gray-haired new arrival stares defiantly at Vuckovic, adjusting her robe to cover her hospital gown, perhaps her only possession at the moment.

"Matt. Matt Mullany." The young man's eyes comb over the other patients, and he sits beside the neatly pressed middle-aged man, who still seems oblivious to his fellow sufferers.

In a tired voice, Vuckovic repeats the gist of his introductory remarks, his eyes drifting beyond the windows to a bricked patio and two patients leisurely smoking at a picnic table. The morning sun floods the poolroom with a soft light. If one looks closely, the entire expanse of the window and door are covered by a thick and unyielding steel mesh. The patients stir uneasily in their seats, some wary of the brittle silence and others absorbed by the smokers, or maybe the spring garden outside.

"David," Vuckovic nudges, "do you remember a time your wife got angry with you for no reason?"

Fifty-six-year-old David Seltzer, an out-of-work salesman hailing from Newton, an upper middle-class Boston suburb, listens intently to the question but doesn't respond. Perhaps he's hearing the staccato clicking of his wife's heels as she walks across the kitchen floor and halts in the doorway. She has caught him waking from a nap. She glowers, not asking if he's been out, knowing he hasn't, and marches, click-click, back to the kitchen to make a drink. The slamming of cupboards and cracking of ice cubes screams louder than any voice. David curls deeper into his afghan, bewildered that she doesn't understand, that he is so tired he can barely get dressed in the mornings.

"Yeah," he finally says. "I felt smothered by this fatigue, this sleepiness. Some days I couldn't even talk, it was so hard. My wife, she thought it was all an act, that I was lazy and just didn't care. As if I wanted her to go back to work! That was the blackest day of our marriage. After twenty-one years, she brings home the paycheck." He lets out a sigh, his eyes watery.

Matt, one of the newcomers, chimes in, surprising Vuckovic. "She was outta line. You supported her for how many years? Come on, get real. You hit a slow patch, it happens to everybody. She should carry you for a while. Not bust your balls just because you want to take it easy for a while." Matt shoves his leather bracelets up his arms, as if readying for a fight.

"What do you think, Glenda?" Vuckovic asks, and receives an icy stare in return. The psychiatrist deciphers the blank, stormy look; it's the face of someone whose mind has been occupied for decades by warring voices.

"You don't know shit," Kiesha scolds Matt, who glowers back.

"Bitch." He smiles.

Vuckovic marvels at how quickly the young man in black leather has caught the pulse of the group.

"Don't listen to her," Julie warns Matt. "She's one of the low-functioning patients. You know, sees angels, hears voices. She even thinks she knows the lottery numbers. Clearly delusional, in my opinion," she adds haughtily, and beams at the psychiatrist. "Don't you agree, Dr. Vuckovic?"

Vuckovic doesn't respond, partly bemused but mostly disdainful of the transparent manipulations of a so-called "borderline personality," the name he prefers to use for Julie's diagnosis rather than its historical tag, grand hysteria.

Julie continues, "I don't think this petty demonstration of obviously limited vocabularies is what we're here for. David, I know your problem is serious, but I have to deal with my abusive husband every day, and I don't know how to deal with him, and I get so angry I do this. That's really why I'm here." She shoves up the sleeves of her shift to reveal a collection, more like a pattern, of latticed bruises, healed cuts, and concentrically arranged cigarette burns, and thrusts her arms out.

"Big deal," Matt declares, rotating his arms to expose a mass of what appears to be homemade tattoos, crude black-and-white stick drawings of daggers, serpents, and bleeding valentine hearts underneath the leather bracelets. Julie recoils.

"I want to go home," Glenda insists to no one in particular. "Grandmother's waiting for me." She half rises from her chair, pauses as if encountering an invisible force, then sits.

"You hurt yourself because the Devil has hold of your soul," Kiesha announces, a distant look overtaking her. "God loves me, and I will speak with him on your behalf. He loves me so, that he hath given me the secrets of the lottery."

Matt rolls his eyes and shakes his head, smiling again. "What a dweeb you are, lady."

Kiesha turns to him with her unfocused look.

After a pause, he leans over, less suspicious, conspiratorial. "Just the daily number, or the Megabucks?"

Vuckovic decides it's time to intervene; the atmosphere of the meeting continues to disturb him.

"Enough of this. We're getting away from family issues." He wishes David would say more. While the psychotic and character-disordered patients can be irritating, the quiet depressed patient worries the psychiatrist far more. David is harder to read than someone acting out; he leaves volumes unspoken.

Knowing David's background, Vuckovic feels a kinship. Both grew up in academic surroundings. Vuckovic's father was a professor at the University of Notre Dame; David's father had been a dean at a small eastern college. Silent, deadly depression runs in both families: Vuckovic's mother suffers bouts of depression, David's grandmother was a suicide at forty-nine, and David's father killed himself at the same age. Vuckovic remembers the fear that rippled through his house when his mother was having one of her "cloudy days," and the games he made up to comfort his little sister on those days. He wants now to somehow protect David Seltzer from the consuming clouds. Try as Vuckovic might to will David to voice his feelings, the morose man says nothing.

"Glenda, please sit down," Vuckovic commands her as she shuffles toward the door. A schizophrenic with a long history of alcohol abuse and spells of homelessness, Glenda has been at McLean before. This time she was admitted strapped to a gurney in a fit of temper — she had tried to stab her roommate. Her violent episodes are usually triggered by what her treaters call "recurrent noncompliance" with medication therapy, meaning she stops taking her pills. Once back in the hospital, it takes about two weeks for the medication to begin working and her scrambled thoughts and irritability to subside.

"If you leave, Glenda, you can't come back," Vuckovic cautions.

Although the other patients are momentarily entertained, Julie ignores this exchange, unable to take her eyes off Matt's tattoos. She smiles sweetly. "Kiesha is very psychotic, Matt. She lies too." She turns to the black woman.

"Why don't you tell us the numbers, dear, and we'll split it with you. For that matter, where're your winnings from last week?"

Before Vuckovic can react, Kiesha shoves Julie's chair. As she tips backward, Julie swings out at Kiesha, clipping her on the shoulder. Though thin and pale from lack of exercise and sunshine, Julie knows how to punch. She is standing, poised to take another swing at Kiesha, who's cringing in her chair as Vuckovic takes two giant strides to the door and yells into the hall, "Staff!"

Thirty seconds later, two mental health workers and a nurse rush into the poolroom. As they push in, most of the patients are shoving to get out. Vuckovic is gently talking to Julie, persuading her to back away from Kiesha.

"This isn't going to help your situation, Julie. Why don't you sit down and think about this for a minute."

The mental health workers and nurse surround her, pressing in close. The nurse, Nancy, speaks sternly.

"Julie, you're going to have to go into the quiet room if you don't settle down right now."

Julie hesitates, as the staff and Vuckovic brace for a confrontation. "You're right, this is not a good thing to do," she concedes, her voice and shoulders relaxing. "I'm very sorry. I must apologize to Kiesha."

Vuckovic suspects this concession is for his benefit but doesn't argue with any motive that defuses a violent confrontation. To Julie, he is the Keeper of Privileges. If she doesn't wish to spend the rest of her day in a bare room, observed every five minutes, she has to convince the PIC that she is in control and won't hurt anyone.

By now, the poolroom is empty except for Julie and staff. Vuckovic and the staff agree that Julie will probably behave herself and doesn't need to be restricted to her room. But her group grounds privilege, which allows her to go to the cafeteria or other parts of the hospital with a few patients and a staff escort, is revoked for the day.

With the family issues group in a shambles, Vuckovic heads to the nurses' station to meet with the treatment team, feeling like the parent to a group of wayward children who hurt a lot.

McLean Hospital sits at the top of Belmont Hill, eight miles outside of Boston, surrounded by 240 acres of grassy slopes and thick woods. It has occupied these grounds since 1895, a time when the insane were either imprisoned, locked away in attics by frightened relatives, or kept in "madhouses," boarding houses for the insane, or almshouses. Only a small fraction lived in insane asylums, so called because they were meant to be caring shelters. When it opened its doors, 160 patients inhabited the McLean Asylum for the Insane, which gradually became famous for its radical "moral treatment." Patients at McLean generally came from educated, well-to-do families who could afford the minimum $80 a month for its unusual humanitarian approach to mental illness.

Instead of applying the accepted ministration of the times — housing patients in large wards, mixing men and women, paying scant attention to their hygiene and clothing, letting curiosity seekers in to watch their bizarre behavior, and treating their illness with bloodletting and purging — the McLean practitioners avoided physical remedies. Its moral treatment emphasized the importance of a safe environment and a calm mental state. Its doctors offered gentle, individualized care and soothed patients' minds rather than physically controlling their behavior. They practiced a kind of intuitive psychology, given that their methods were not a recognized scientific discipline. Attendants, who spent the most time with the patients, were hired for their sensitivity and kindness. Patients were never left alone, except for a brief time after meals. At the end of each day, attendants collected and cleaned patients' clothing.

A number of brick buildings on the McLean campus today date to the time of moral treatment, giving the grounds a genteel, somewhat antiquated look. But dotted among the ivy-covered facades and gabled roofs are concrete and glass structures with sharp angles. The pastoral, rambling McLean grounds, even with the mishmash of architecture, not only shelter the hospital from curiosity seekers but also mask its identity as one of the country's oldest and largest private psychiatric hospitals.

The entrance road to McLean climbs up a hill past a three-story, brick and sandstone building, Proctor House, then flattens out and continues around to the circular driveway fronting the Admissions Building. Completed in 1986, the Admissions Building is a showpiece. The foyer of the admitting area, with its deep green marble veneer, elegant mahogany reception counter, and waiting room furnished with contemporary upholstered chairs, TV and VCR, and the day's *New York Times*, feels like an expensive club. The first floor treats psychiatric patients and the second floor, AB-II, specializes in patients with mental illnesses related to trauma and abuse, namely post-traumatic stress disorder and dissociative disorders, such as multiple personality and hysterical neurosis. Admissions is typical of most buildings at McLean: the first two floors are occupied by patient units and the third floor by offices.

The Unit is one of three twenty-one-bed units at McLean for patients with severe psychosis. In medical terms, "psychosis" covers schizophrenia, forms of mania or depression, and schizoaffective disorders. In human terms, it means a person has delusions, hallucinations, scrambled thoughts, and may be impulsive and very out of touch with reality. A person who is psychotic usually has great difficulty with normal daily activities — getting dressed, going to work, interacting with family.

This is not the world of the worried well, nor an ashram-style retreat for those afflicted with an existential crisis or a troubled relationship. These are patients with confused thoughts and unchecked emotions that have made them dangerous to themselves or those around them. Frequently they arrive at McLean on a gurney in four-point restraints — arms and legs strapped down for the protection of the patient or people nearby. In the language of the psychiatric hospital, most new inpatients on the Unit are "safety risks."

The doors of the Unit, like those to most patient units at McLean, are locked; the only way in or out is with a key or by pushing a buzzer to summon someone to unlock the door. Visitors are warned that not all patients accept their confinement. Doors are posted with small signs reading, SPLIT RISK or ESCAPE RISK, telling visitors that a patient may try to run out when the door is opened.

The Unit is led by two psychiatrists-in-charge who prescribe medication and other treatments, such as electroshock therapy. It is staffed by psychiatric nurses and mental health workers, and has at least two full-time social workers, an occupational therapist, a recreational therapist, and a steady stream of students, residents, attending physicians, and consultants, such as psychologists and researchers.

As usual after group, Vuckovic slips into the nursing station, working his way through the small clutch of patients hovering outside, waiting for the hourly cigarette break. The usual low hum of morning routine courses through the halls with most patients groggily appearing at the nurses' station for medication, indifferent to Julie's outburst. Patients move as if underwater, and even Philip, the MIT freshman so manic he paces the halls for hours, has not yet revved up.

The nurses' station snakes half the length of the wing, a string of rooms crammed with worktables and filing cabinets, its walls covered by chalkboards and hung with clipboards. Vuckovic winds past the kitchen nook, around two large desks hogging the open space at the heart of the station, and goes into a conference room crammed with furniture, where Jack Springer, the clinical nurse supervisor, sits flipping through a fat binder of treatment plans. Vuckovic grabs a binder marked with his name which lists each patient's medications.

Jack smiles slightly at Vuckovic. "I hear you had a wild group this morning. Count on a borderline to stir things up."

"It's almost inevitable when you mix the psychotics with the character disorders," Vuckovic notes sourly. He, like many professionals in his field, tends to use diagnostic labels as nouns rather than adjectives, as if the essence of the patient can be reduced to an official disease. The space in the nurses' station flows, with few doors and little distance in the way, so conversations are rarely private and usually open to anyone within earshot. Nancy Nicholson, the charge nurse, enters the room just at the right moment to counter Vuckovic.

"I don't think that's the problem," she states emphatically. "The problem is letting new admissions attend groups. They're too unstable, too labile. They need a day or so for some of the meds to kick in and to get used to it here."

Vuckovic shakes his head. "Look, Glenda's been here before. She knows the routine. And the sociopath, Mullany, he'll be antagonizing people until the day he leaves." While he's talking, Nina Lehmann, a social worker, squeezes in at the conference table.

"I agree with Nancy. It's too much for someone just out of restraints and still on five-minute checks to participate in a group." She looks to Jack, hoping that the Unit's staff leader sides with her. Jack grins benignly, knowing that Vuckovic enjoys this give-and-take, also knowing that his colleague has a streak of stubbornness.

"A dose of controlled tension is useful. The entrenched patients don't know how the new ones are going to react. Having to deal with unpredictable personalities is healthy. They're going to have to learn sometime. Here they have a safe place to try out what works and what doesn't." Vuckovic doesn't add that in his experience, many patients never do learn and they will be discharged as destructive in their relationships as when they entered.

Leaning against the doorframe of the conference room, idly twirling a rubber chicken, the Unit's standing gag mascot, is Frank Wilson, a mental health worker.

"Yeah, but Julie's interpersonal skills need more than a tryout. They could use an entire season at the Leona Helmsley Charm School," he chimes in.

"The Leona Helmsley what?" Nancy wonders.

"Sure, you know, the course she's taking compliments of the Internal Revenue Service. Learning to Live with the Little People." Everyone chuckles, and Frank drives home his point: "Julie'll either end up in jail like Leona or knifed by another borderline. Or by a multiple." He pauses, now on a roll. "I wonder if AB-II worries about one multiple doing in another. You'd have the mass murder of the century! I can see the headlines now, 'Hundreds Die as . . .' "

Vuckovic laughs, though he feels he shouldn't. Nursing staff occasionally has a hard time curbing angry reactions to the provocative behavior of some patients; so, for that matter, does he. Humor helps channel these emotions away from patients, and each other.

A phone ringing on the wall abruptly hushes the group.

"Nina speaking. Oh yes, Mr. Thomas. Hold on for a minute, will you, while I move to a quieter phone." The conversation resumes as the social worker exits to speak with Kiesha's husband.

"Alex, controlled tension is a great idea, but unless it's really controlled, it erupts into chaos, and a mess like today. These groups where we're mixing the floridly ill new admissions with the more functional, calmer patients are always going to end in disaster. We're going to accomplish nothing." As Nancy weighs in, she jots notes on the assessment flow sheets, the shift-by-shift report on each patient.

Vuckovic scans the room, wondering if the entire staff opposes his approach. Nancy tends to have a by-the-book attitude toward treatment and she has objected before. But Vuckovic feels she's doing this more to pin on him the responsibility for the busted group than to persuade him to change. The group fracas doesn't bother Vuckovic; he readily admits that he's not a very adept leader. But he does mind feeling like the heavy, the contentious doctor who always argues and objects. He knows that his strong opinions sometimes get the better of him, compelling him to speak up and butt heads when it's really not necessary.

"That's a little extreme," Frank interjects. "I think even the fights are therapeutic. As long as I don't get decked!" He tosses the rubber chicken in the air and, with a schoolboy flourish, catches it behind his back.

Nancy smiles at his antics. Only Frank, six foot two with wavy brown hair, huge brown eyes with long lashes, and a dimpled smile that never seems to go away, can make her lighten up.

Nina has returned, shaking her head. "Poor Kiesha. That husband is a real trip. Wants her home *now*. Afraid his family and neighbors are going to find out she's in here."

She studies the chalkboard that covers an entire wall. Patient names and room numbers scroll down the left-hand column. Going across in rows along the top of the board are the names of their primary staff, hall doctor, attending doctor, admission date, and legal status (whether voluntary patients or under guardianship or a commitment order). Upcoming discharge dates are noted in red chalk at the bottom. She sees that Kiesha was admitted a few days earlier, which means she will probably be in the hospital for at least a couple of more weeks. Although each patient's stay depends on treatment response and, to an extent that makes treaters uncomfortable, insurance coverage, the average length of stay for psychotic patients is about two weeks.

"I agree with Nancy, Alex," Nina goes on. "These groups seem to be very poorly focused and get caught up in secondary issues. They really need to focus on their families. What Kiesha's going through with her husband — his demands and pressure to leave — is hindering her recovery. She's very conflicted about whether to go home to take care of him or stay here and get better. Not to mention that she doesn't think she's sick."

Vuckovic nods, muttering, "I hear you, thanks for sharing." He brings himself up short, sensing that when he tries to check his opinions and be receptive to others, he sounds condescending. Still, Nina's freshly minted expertise, emanating from a master's degree in social work barely six months old, grates on him.

Silence signals that the treatment team meeting is over; it ends as casually as it began. Despite the off-the-cuff tone, the meeting has been constructive. Vuckovic resumes scribbling in the doctor's order book and Nancy writes her flow sheet notes as the rest of the staff drifts out.

"I'm upping Matt's pemoline to seventy-five milligrams and leaving some p.r.n. Ativan for Julie." Adjusting the patients' medications — increasing the dosage on Matt's hyperactivity drug and adding an antianxiety drug, as needed, to Julie's regime — is Vuckovic's way of acknowledging that the dynamics of the family issues group are shaky.

He restrains voicing his doubts about mixing volatile new patients with calmer, seasoned ones. He holds back because the nursing staff usually assumes his objections are based on his personal aversion to leading group. In truth, he has little faith in group therapy regardless of who is orchestrating it. He considers it a watered-down treatment compared with other psychiatric remedies. Mix patients or separate them, he doesn't believe it makes a whole lot of difference in terms of whether or when they get better. But some staff members put great faith in group therapy, and their conviction is the primary reason therapy is sometimes helpful. So Vuckovic swallows his cynicism, knowing his views can be bleak.

"While you're at it," Nancy offers, "we need to back off on Hector's trazodone. He may have had an episode of priapism yesterday."

"He *may* have? You waiting to flip a coin to decide whether he did or not?" Vuckovic's smirk signals that he's teasing Nancy about her cautious diagnosis. He rarely challenges her maybes, knowing they are nurse diplomacy for an astute observation. Priapism is a drug side effect that causes a painful erection that lasts for hours and sometimes days, and can result in permanent inability to obtain erection if not treated quickly.

"Well, he had a problem for at least a couple of hours before saying something to Frank, and by the time the doctor on call saw Hector it was gone. He held last night's dose. He was very embarrassed."

Vuckovic shakes his head. "Well, discontinue it. I'll talk to the patient later."

Little dignity accompanies a psychiatric inpatient. A patient on "five-minute checks" — visual look-sees twelve times an hour by a staff member to make sure the patient is safe — is virtually never alone. When in the throes of illness, patients often need help dressing or bathing, and modesty goes out the window when a person's mind is occupied by demons. Manic patients are especially prone to episodes of "denudation" while high and hypersexual, and are often mortified at their behavior later. For staff, keeping patients clean and dressed, as efficiently and thoughtfully as possible, comes with the territory.

Vuckovic finishes his scribbling. "You know," he comments, still hoping to patch up the therapy argument, "group would have gone better today if Art had been there. He's good at steering the dynamics and not letting things go off on a tangent. When's he finished with jury duty?"

Art Wiggins is legendary at McLean for his savvy skills with prickly groups and testy patients. Families of new patients ask specifically that Art Wiggins be assigned to their relatives.

"Soon. I thought today or tomorrow. He should be at your group Thursday."

The smell of baked goods floats into the room, and Vuckovic and the nurse simultaneously rise to seek out the source. Across the two desks in the center of the main area of the nurses' station are platters of homemade cookies, cheesecake, mud pie, and a rose-bordered sheet cake with the inscription "Good Luck, Terese."

Half a dozen staff members lurk around the table, eyeing the victuals, which are being carried into the poolroom.

"Where's Terese?" Frank ventures.

"She's still doing meds," Jack answers. "I'll go see how long she'll be." Around the corner from the main area is a Dutch door where the medication nurse for the shift dispenses pills and occasionally gives injections, usually around 9:00 A.M. and bedtime, and for many patients, more often. A nurse assigned to meds doesn't have to do checks or vital signs, and has relatively little interaction with patients. It's an assignment nurses volunteer for when they're feeling burnt out and need a low-stress, no-hassle day.

Jack finds Terese talking to a hysterical, insistent woman on the verge of either tears or a temper tantrum. The young patient is pleading with the nurse.

"You *gotta* give me more Xanax. I feel like I'm going to die.

Can't you see? I feel like shit, I can't take this much longer. You gotta help me." Obese and pale, she clings to the doorframe, as if holding herself up with great effort. Her long, pale brown hair has not been combed in days, and, though dressed, the buttons on her blouse don't match up and her stomach hangs over the stretch band of her pants.

"Donna," Terese says soothingly, "don't you remember what happened with the higher dose? You slept most of the day?"

"I know, I remember. But I can handle it now. I'm better. You *gotta* give me more." Her tone has become menacing, and she presses herself into the bottom half of the Dutch door. "I gotta have it," she declares, then continues shrilly, "you're just trying to torture me. You don't care about me, you're nothing but a pill-pusher. You're not a nurse, you're a sadist." Donna leans over the split door, spraying spittle on the nurse as she ventilates.

Terese steps back. "Donna, why don't you wait a bit and see how you feel on the three milligrams? If you still feel angry and uncomfortable this afternoon, we'll talk to Dr. Vuckovic. Right now, you have to let the other patients get their meds. You're blocking their way." In fact, while two patients have hung back during Donna's outburst, another has crowded into the Dutch door for his pills.

Terese resumes handing out small paper cups with the pre-measured medications, along with small cups of water. Meds are swallowed right there, and occasionally a patient is asked to remain in the lounge area to make sure the medication isn't spit out.

"When you're finished," Jack tells Terese, "you're wanted in the poolroom."

Except for a skeleton staff of the checks nurse and a mental health worker, the entire staff congregates in the poolroom to say good-bye to Terese Bailey. Terese, people often remark, has an affection for psychotic patients, and at times it seemed as if she could read their minds. She has been a nurse on the Unit since the early days when it occupied the Bowditch building, and will be missed.

The Bowditch days, in McLean folklore, make the Unit and its staff special. Bowditch is a small, white frame building along the edge of the campus. Today, it is a quarter-way house for adolescents; eighteen years ago it was the site of a revolution in psychiatry at McLean, the first inpatient unit at the hospital offering treatment based on a biological model of mental illness. It treated schizophrenia and affective illnesses like diseases of the body, not of the mind. Instead of relying on psychotherapy as the primary treatment, with medication considered as a sort of adjunct, Bowditch psychiatrists reversed the emphasis and styled themselves as internists of the brain. They believed that most severe mental disorders, especially the psychoses, were caused not by bad parenting or childhood trauma but by skewed genetics and faulty brain chemistry. Instead of psycho-analytically oriented psychotherapy, they offered antipsychotic and antidepressant medication combined with a "psychoeduca-tional" approach to therapy. Patients received rehab or support-ive therapy: that is, help in managing their daily lives. Today, the biological model reigns supreme not only throughout McLean but in most psychiatric hospitals. In 1986, the Bow-ditch unit moved from its tight quarters to its more roomy current space. A few of the staff from its heyday, including Terese Bailey, joined it.

When Terese enters the room for her farewell party, people don't know whether to applaud or commiserate. There's a smattering of both before Vuckovic, as the senior physician, declares, "You can't retire. It's time to eat." The ritual of cake cutting and passing plates and cookies fills the awkward social vacuum.

"Before we all get to stuffing our faces and losing our heads," Jack takes over, "I'd like to give Terese this small gift." He pulls out the standard McLean white T-shirt available at the gift shop and emblazoned with the green "McL" hospital logo. But something has been added: across the chest is stenciled, "I've Been Shrunk by the Best."

Everyone cheers and claps, Terese laughs and smiles, and people resume eating and talking in small groups. Vuckovic doesn't linger — he has an outpatient waiting at his third-floor office — but before he dashes out, he draws Terese aside.

"We're going to miss you," he begins. Although not given to casual touching, Vuckovic puts his hand on her shoulder. "But I think you're doing the right thing, retiring early. This place is changing so fast, no one feels secure. We're looking like a MASH unit working from temporary quarters. With little more to offer than crisis intervention. But you know this, so don't look back. You're getting out with your livelihood intact. I don't know about the rest of us." He smiles grimly and squeezes her shoulder.

"Thanks, Alex. But don't say too much or I'll start bawling." Her eyes water up, then she catches herself. "Any news on whether we're moving? I heard that AB-II is going to East House. There's so much talk, no one knows what to believe."

Throughout the winter of 1992, McLean was rife with rumors of units closing or shifting to smaller quarters. The rumblings started the summer before when the hospital census plummeted, then did not recover robustly in the fall, as it had historically. Psychiatric hospitals have seasons, predictable times of the year when they're full or overflowing, and times when beds go empty. The peak seasons tend to be spring and fall, which correspond to long-observed peaks in the severity of depressions and manias. Seasonal depression is well documented. Though most people suffering from seasonal affective disorder (SAD) usually aren't sick enough to warrant hospitalization, the moods of the severely ill are similarly affected by the duration and intensity of the sun's light. Also, for many psychotic or clinically depressed people, seasonal change may represent either, in the spring, a rebirth of the world around them which they feel unable to share, or, in the fall, a reminder of death and human finality. In younger patients, the academic calendar tends to create additional stress in autumn and spring. April and October are peak suicide months.

But during the late 1980s, a curious paradox was observed. While demand for admissions rose as expected in September, the number of filled beds began slipping from a high of 328 down to around 220. The dramatic change in the hospital's census occurred because the average number of days a patient stayed at McLean plummeted from 81 days in 1988 to 24 days in late 1992 — with no end in sight.

The unit staff, accustomed to juggling rooms for new patients and refusing potential admissions not diagnosed as psychotic, found itself admitting a wide assortment of patients. Many of these patients were difficult to treat, yet the Unit was pressured to discharge them quickly, so while the census remained low, the staff felt overworked, underappreciated, and unable to make meaningful changes in the lives of their patients. Nurses felt like valet parking attendants and some of the more experienced ones, including Terese Bailey, were taking early retirement.

What is happening at McLean is being repeated across the country: dramatically rising health costs coupled with managed care practices are forcing patients out of psychiatric hospitals. As hospital expenses soar, insurance carriers have tightened guidelines for the mental illnesses that justify lengthy hospitalization. Many carriers refuse to pay for hospitalization without a patient meeting stringent commitment criteria: a patient must be acutely suicidal or homicidal or so disorganized as to be unable to feed himself or herself.

Other carriers are turning to a system of "capitation," creating contracts with specific hospitals and alloting a sum of money for the total care of a patient. When the money runs out, the hospital is obliged to continue providing for the patient out of its own pocket. McLean has entered into several such contracts, and thus there is enormous internal pressure on units to shorten the length of stay in order to leave a pool of funds to treat the patient later in the year if necessary. Medicare has used such a system, a cap on the annual amount it pays for a patient's psychiatric hospitalization, since 1983, and this has gradually added to the pressure. As a result, the total number of patients arriving yearly surged from just under 2,000 in 1988 to almost 3,500 in 1992, with little change in the staffing on the units.

The realities of the health care cost crisis have stunned everyone at the hospital, including the McLean Corporation itself. As the population has dropped and the length of stay shortened, the revenue stream has thinned, and the only recourse has been to shut down units and consolidate others. The shrinking of McLean began with the closing of a twenty-bed unit in the building called South Belknap which treated patients with affective disorders, mainly the clinically depressed. Next to go was a unit in the North Belknap building which treated psychotic disorders. To merge remaining units, the hospital reorganized its treatment programs. It created a twenty-bed women's unit in East House, which quickly filled with abuse victims and characterologically ill patients from other units who had become self-mutilating or suicidal. AB-II was slated to move to the floor above the women's unit.

News of these changes has put the staff on edge. Rumors about units either moving or being shut down spread through the campus like a rampant virus. The downsizing of McLean has been a new experience and no one knows what to expect. Clearly, economics are driving the changes, but it's hard to say at what point empty beds will be removed and units permanently shrunk. The staff is especially worried because the Unit's expansive layout makes it desirable real estate for any unit or department.

Thus, Terese Bailey's retirement party is as much a chance for staff to say good-bye as it is another opportunity for people to swap rumors and theories about the hospital upheavals.

"Who knows what's going to happen," Vuckovic opines. "Between the politics of this place and the socialists on Capitol Hill talking national health care, we could all end up dispensing aspirin at clinics."

Vuckovic's occasionally phlegmatic views, which in politics swing between conservative and libertarian, stand out in his liberal profession. He loathes the idea of nationalized medicine, which he considers an intrusion into his professional life and an assault on his pocketbook, and never hesitates to take a swipe at Washington.

"Not you, Alex," Terese says with a chuckle, having heard Vuckovic's tirades before. "You'll always have a gadzillion patients and somehow manage to keep them all happy."

Vuckovic's private practice is legendary at McLean. In addition to being a senior PIC, which requires thirty-plus hours per week, his roster of private patients, some who visit him regularly for medication or therapy, and others who stop by only once or twice a year to renew their prescriptions, reach into the hundreds at any given time. His workday is so demanding — starting around 8:00 A.M. and ending after 7:00 P.M., with no time for lunch — that he has a difficult time persuading anyone to cover for him when he is unexpectedly out.

Vuckovic smiles weakly. He doesn't like staff talking about his private practice; he feels it dilutes his position at the hospital, making him sound like a part-timer.

"And that's my cue, I've got to run. Good luck." He dashes out the door, past the chalkboard where patients sign in and out, and heads for the stairwell. Just as he reaches it, a hand tugs at his sleeve.

"Dr. Vuckovic, I need to talk to you."

Vuckovic looks at his sleeve, then at the patient. "Boundaries, Rusty. No touching."

A middle-aged woman wearing tights, pink socks, and a large Harvard sweatshirt is pressing close to Vuckovic. At his chiding, she steps back, saying quietly, "I was afraid you'd leave without talking to me."

"Can it wait until rounds?" he asks weakly.

"That's up to you," the woman responds, sounding more aloof now. "I simply want you to know that I'm putting in a three-day notice. I think it's best. I'm as good as I'm going to get here. I want out."

A three-day notice is a patient's legal notification to the hospital that he or she intends to leave in three working days regardless of whether the doctors recommend staying. The only way the hospital can keep such a patient is through a formal commitment procedure to show that the person is a danger to herself or others. However, a patient can retract a three-day notice at any time before a commitment hearing, which often takes a week to schedule.

Three-day notices are also a gambit between patient and doctor. Patients use them as a way of voting with their feet, showing doctors that their magic elixirs aren't working or that they don't agree with their treatment. Of course, a patient suffering from a mental illness is not always the best judge of what is working and what isn't. Patients also use the notices to get the physician's or the staff's attention, sometimes in pursuit of the seemingly trivial, such as privileges or passes. However, these privileges, Vuckovic reminds himself, are not trivial to the patient.

From Vuckovic's perspective, three-day notices are a potential nuisance and a source of great frustration. The nuisance is the possibility of a court hearing. Vuckovic resents the legal rigmarole he has to go through simply to be able to treat someone who has a potentially lethal illness. The frustration surfaces with patients like Rusty who use three-day notices to force treatment decisions that only time can make.

Usually severely depressed, at other times manic, this housewife and mother from Cambridge tried to kill herself by jumping in front of the T, the Boston subway, then assaulting the fast-acting passenger who saved her. During her first day on the Unit, she tore apart her room and hurled things out the door, and was put in restraints for a day.

That was two weeks ago, and Vuckovic can tell that the initial electroshock therapy, then a combination of antidepressant and mood-stabilizer medication has doused her anger and cleared her thinking.

"You're better, Rusty, but we can do more." The woman's slumping posture and downcast eyes indicate to Vuckovic that her depression has not lifted sufficiently. He is concerned that she still might harbor suicidal thoughts. "I'd like to titrate up your nortriptyline."

Rusty shakes her head. "I don't like the tricyclics. They make me sleepy and give me the sweats. I'm putting in the notice this morning."

Vuckovic assumes his most doctorly manner, trying his hardest to persuade her to stay. He is reasonably certain that in one more week her gray veil of sadness and self-loathing will lift significantly. And he wants to keep her at McLean for another reason: her husband routinely boxes her ears, and she has lost about sixty percent of her hearing in one and forty percent in the other. Maybe she would fight the abuse or even leave her husband if her depression were sufficiently erased. But so far she refuses to leave him, fearing the loss of the security he provides. Her stance contributes to the frustration of her social worker and doctor.

"I advise against it, Rusty. The negativism and unhappiness you're feeling are part of the illness. The side effects get better with time. Stay for one more week, and I know you'll feel better." This is as close as Vuckovic comes to begging, or promising results. He feels for this too-sad woman.

She pauses. "I'll think about it," then counters, "can I have 'unescorted towns'?" This privilege allows her to walk or take a taxi to Belmont Center or nearby Waverley Square by herself.

Vuckovic purses his lips. He hates the constant negotiation and wrangling between staff and patients for various levels of freedom. Patients act as if privileges are a system of rewards for good behavior, and in truth, for line staff that is often the case. Vuckovic believes privileges should be solely a matter of safety, a patient's ability to go to and fro without getting lost or hurt, to interact with strangers without altercation, to be alone and be able to resist destructive impulses.

"Do you think you're up to it? You promise no leaps in front of buses, no close encounters with subways?" Vuckovic has learned over the years that patients are quite candid about their plans and intentions. A patient contemplating suicide typically says something about not feeling comfortable outside or not wanting to be alone. In this particular case, the juxtaposition between the request and the three-day threat can mean either that she has been angling for the privilege all along, or, ominously, that both are made with dark purposes in mind.

Rusty nods repeatedly. Vuckovic decides to run her request past the nurses to buy himself a bit more time so he can find out more about her state of mind. He sends her to Nancy and promises a decision by the end of the day.

Glancing at his watch, Vuckovic grits his teeth: fifteen minutes late, assuming his patient kept the appointment. Striding down the hall toward his office, he immediately notices that the straight-backed chair outside it is empty. He makes his way down the hall to the secretaries' office, an open space where his secretary, Joyce, and two other women manage the flow of patients and paper.

"Diane canceled. Something about losing her car keys," Joyce informs him as he grabs up a stack of phone messages from the corner of her desk.

"It's always something," Vuckovic says flatly, as if repeating an old story.

"Oh, and someone from the IRB called. They want a revised proposal and copies for everybody on the committee — that's twelve, I think — at least two weeks before the meeting," Joyce tells him.

Vuckovic groans. Any research project involving patients has to get the approval of the hospital's Institutional Review Board, and Vuckovic is applying for a grant to investigate the stigma of mental illness. "That makes revision number four. By the time they make a decision, psychosis will be cured."

Vuckovic heads to his office; he has fifteen minutes until his next appointment, enough time to make a dent in the fifty-odd calls he has received so far that day.

Vuckovic's office is an anomaly for a psychiatrist or doctor. No couch, no expensive Oriental rug, no sterile chrome surfaces, no wall charts of body parts. The mint green room is a jumble of papers, books, magazines, and objects, and clearly the natural habitat of someone who doesn't linger on any one task, who jumps readily from problem to decision, from patient to patient. The desk, angled in a corner beside the window, bears a mound of manila files, phone slips, and forms. Fighting for space at the end of the desk are pictures of his family, paperweights, a Kleenex box, and a jelly bean dispenser. Framed degrees from Notre Dame and Harvard Medical School hang permanently askew on the wall. The two chairs in front of the desk are straight-backed fabric-covered office furniture intended for function, not leisurely comfort.

Vuckovic's first call is to a third-floor corner office of the Mailman Research Center, a contemporary brick building at the center of the McLean grounds and home of the largest private psychiatric research facility in the country. This laboratory is home base to about sixty-five scientists and clinical investigators exploring the brain. A rarefied world of renowned Ph.D.s, Harvard Medical School professors, and skilled technicians, Mailman is both a laboratory engaged in basic research and a contributor to the clinical operations of the hospital. Many of its scientists are involved in scientific discovery and patient treatment. While much of their brain research may have little practical application, these investigators are also pursuing knowledge about psychiatric drugs and brain chemistry that may someday help the patients at McLean.

Mailman consists of several departments — the Laboratories for Psychiatric Research, the Ralph Lowell Laboratories, and the Brain Tissue Resource Center, also known as the brain bank and one of three such depositories in the country. Its three floors of offices, laboratories, computers, imaging machines, and brain tissue samples are connected by what the staff calls the Slowest Elevator in the World. Here, scientists experiment with new psychiatric drugs such as clozapine, a revolutionary medication for psychotic patients. They dissect brain cells to see how they grow, communicate with each other, and respond to certain chemicals; they sift through layers of the brain using microscopes as well as modern scanning technology, such as magnetic resonance imaging.

Vuckovic's call goes to the celebrated director of the Laboratories for Psychiatric Research, Ross Baldessarini. This neuroscientist and psychiatrist has devoted years to exploring the pathways of the brain which deliver the neurotransmitter dopamine. Baldessarini also has a knack for insightful diagnostic evaluation, as well as a remarkable feel for the human cost of psychiatric disorders. Baldessarini, as head of the psychotic disorders program, which includes the three psychotic disorders units, is also Vuckovic's boss. But today Vuckovic needs neither his boss nor the brilliant scientist; he needs to tap the expertise of one of the most knowledgeable practicing psychopharmacologists in the world.

"Ross, it's Alex Vuckovic. Got a couple of minutes?" Vuckovic treads a fine line between the familiarity of a colleague and the deference of a junior medicine man.

"Sure." In truth, he's probably due in the lab, has a meeting with his postdoctoral fellow in twenty minutes, is trying to complete a grant application, and wants to finish analyzing the data in a stack of computer printouts that just landed on his desk. But Vuckovic is always succinct and calls him only about truly perplexing situations.

"When you do your monthly consult on my unit next week, I'd like you to look at a very sick thirty-three-year-old lady. Julie Swoboda. Long history of depression, superficial suicide attempts. She's had spontaneous affective swings up and down, has positive family history for both affective and character disorder, and can't tolerate SSRIs, MAOIs, tricyclics, lithium, Tegretol, or valproate. Thoughts?"

Although Vuckovic's description takes less than thirty seconds, his choice of details gives the senior psychiatrist enough clues to construct a fuller picture. Despite her mood swings, she isn't responding to any of the usual medications known to control them. This suggests a large psychological element in her illness. From Vuckovic's sketch, Baldessarini surmises the patient not only presents a treatment challenge but also is probably wreaking havoc on the Unit with other patients and staff.

"Um, any reason she's not on AB-II?"

"Well, they transferred her to us. They said she needs to deal with her manic depression first."

This sounds unusual to Baldessarini. Either this patient's illness is unusually unresponsive to treatment or she has burned out a treatment team. Bad news in either case.

"Alex, can you hold for a minute? Francine just walked in. She's got that worried look. I'd better talk to her."

Francine Benes, director of the center's structural neuroscience lab, has an office down the hall from Baldessarini. Although their investigations are entirely different — Benes ventures into brain anatomy and Baldessarini into brain chemicals — they wrestle with the same research politics, competing for grants, lab resources, and attention, via publication, from colleagues. Very likely her interruption has to do with money.

Baldessarini comes back on the line after about a minute.

"Sorry about that, Alex."

"Ross, is Francine still there? I've been meaning to talk to her." Benes's research specialty is extreme psychosis, which usually centers on schizophrenia, but also includes manic depression and acute mania. She, too, provides consults for doctors and medical students.

"Yeah, sure. I'll put her on the speaker phone." With the touch of a button, Vuckovic is conversing with two of the most knowledgeable psychiatric researchers in the country. He silently marvels at his access; not many clinical psychiatrists can tap into such erudite advice.

"Francine, hi, it's Alex Vuckovic. I've got a student, John Graybill, who's doing the casework on the Swoboda woman I'm talking to Ross about — a borderline with an affective overlay. And I want to give him a chance to work another patient who's totally different. It's a woman named Kiesha Thomas — manic, delusional, refusing medication, and pregnant. Would you mind doing the case review with him?"

"Sure, Alex, be glad to."

"Thanks a lot, Francine. I appreciate it." Vuckovic hears her leave Baldessarini's office, then the speaker phone being clicked off.

"Getting back to Swoboda," Baldessarini continues. "Who's her attending?" Most patients are also seen regularly by attending physicians, psychiatrists not on the Unit's staff who provide another treatment opinion, and often individual psychotherapy. The question is a gentle reminder to Vuckovic that Baldessarini values the role of psychotherapy in complex cases.

Vuckovic knows very well that psychotherapy is useful to patients trying to put their fractured lives back together, but he has never seen it successfully treat someone with a severe borderline personality.

"Whelan. The family heard about him and signed him up." Vuckovic is trying to explain the unusual choice of Dr. Sean Whelan, an extensively published research psychiatrist with a strong biological leaning and a strong preference for a medical, pharmacological approach over psychodynamic methods.

Baldessarini grunts noncommittally. He isn't going to get into a discussion of a colleague's methods.

"Sounds like fun. I'll put her down for next week's conference and see her the day before. Will you have a case report?"

"Of course." Vuckovic laughs. "I have a student."

Case reports have a long history at McLean Hospital. In the days of several-month stays, residents and students interviewed patients for tens, sometimes hundreds of hours, then dictated a ten-to-twenty-page history worthy of a biographer, with another several pages of psychodynamic formulation, followed by a treatment plan that usually called for more hours of interviews. But psychiatry is being dragged from the era of ruminative case reports and rambling interviews into the modern era of touch-and-go medicine. Lately, the resident's admission note and the PIC's discharge summary serve as the only detailed record of a patient's brief stay. Nonetheless, Baldessarini believes it is a useful discipline for clinicians to do the reports and insists that one be prepared if he consults. Usually staff doctors assign residents and students to write these reports.

Vuckovic makes a note to call John Graybill, then turns to the stack of phone messages. With each completed call, he wads up the pink slip and flips it toward the wastebasket. As he dials and talks, he fiddles with a Lucite paperweight engraved with the word "Prozac" and thinks about Julie Swoboda. Her case bothers him, especially her potential for wrecking the fragile atmosphere on the Unit. He is glad he had gotten a hold of Baldessarini; reaching Benes is a bonus.

CHAPTER TWO

The Heavenly
Lottery Commission

KIESHA THOMAS: ADMISSION NOTES

- *Chief Complaint:* This 22yo mbf, 20-week gravida, presents for her
1st McLean and psych hosp in an acutely delusional, agitated state,
saying, "Leave me, he is the chosen one."
- *History of Present Illness:* Historians are pt. (unreliable), husband
(distraught), and Mass. Mental [a psychiatric hospital in Boston] evaluation note. Pt. has no formal psych history, has been at home with her
husband, an MBTA driver. While not complaining of major symptoms,
she had told husband she felt "anxious" for several days, accompanied by "tossing and turning" at night, without latency insomnia or
early morning waking. She was perfectly fine this morning according
to husband, and they went to mass, as is their custom. During the
service, the pt. became acutely agitated and began yelling that God
had come to her in a host with the College of Cardinals, they had all
impregnated her, and her child was the Messiah. She apparently ran
to the priest and attempted to wrestle away the communion chalice,
when she was overpowered by her husband and other churchgoers.
She was taken to Mass. Mental by ambulance, but husband insisted

she be brought to McLean because he feared for her safety "in that hellhole." He insisted that she not be medicated, and became belligerent when I stated I could not guarantee that. Dr. Vuckovic was called and persuaded him to leave her in our care. However, the pt. refused to sign in, and Dr. Vuckovic agreed that I should admit her involuntarily because of concern for her safety and her lack of insight.

■ *Past Psychiatric History:* None.

■ *Social, Family, and Developmental History:* Pt. is the youngest of three female children. Parents are divorced. Father was alcoholic; no other family history of psychiatric illness is known. She graduated from high school, and married immediately afterward. Her husband immigrated to the U.S. from St. Croix several years ago. Pt. and husband deny marital conflict; she denies a history of sexual or physical abuse. She acknowledges social use of alcohol, though not while pregnant, and denies recreational drug use. Husband denies psychiatric or drug history, and seems supportive, though he is quite upset. Remote and developmental history are unavailable.

■ *Past Medical History:* Pt. denies medical illness, is s/p T & A, allergic to PCN. No hx head trauma or seizures. Menarche age 12, normal periods, but unable to conceive for several years. (Neg. endocrine w/u, incl TFTs). Pregnancy uncomplicated.

■ *Mental Status Exam:* Pt. is intermittently cooperative, paces, often screams spontaneously, able to stop when asked. She is dressed in a torn white dress, white stockings, and pumps. Speech is rapid, tangential, with occasional clang associations. She is alternately giddy and irritable, tho denies any mood disturbance, saying, "I am one with the Lord. The lottery is mine." She denies suicidality and homicidality, and denies delusions or hallucinosis but her thoughts are preoccupied with apparent religious and grandiose content. She did not cooperate with cognitive testing but appears oriented to three spheres and her memory and fund of knowledge seem unimpaired. I estimate her intelligence as average, but her insight and judgment are grossly impaired.

■ *Physical Exam:* Refused.

■ *Provisional Diagnosis:* Axis 1: Bipolar Disorder, Manic, Severe, with

Mood-Congruent Psychotic Features. R/O Organic Delusional Syndrome

Axis 2: None

Axis 3: None. Other Medical Condition: Pt. is 20 weeks pregnant

Axis 4: Psychosocial Stressors: 4 (Pregnancy)

Axis 5: GAF: 20. Highest GAF in past year: 80

■ *Treatment Plan:* Admit to the Unit. Unit restrict, 5' checks, routine VS, regular diet, full neuro/med w/u, evaluate for meds, offer Conditional Voluntary when less agitated, family intervention, supportive/psychoeducational Rx.

Heather Pollard, M.D.
Resident in Adult Psychiatry

KIESHA CAN'T SIT STILL. She crosses and uncrosses her legs, props her hands on her protruding stomach, sits on her hands, wraps her arms around her chest. Gazing out from the poolroom, Vuckovic's voice droning in the background, she watches two patients in the garden beyond the bricked terrace, one hoeing intently and the other spreading seeds as if rolling dice. The scene reminds her of nuns and the movie *Lilies of the Field*, and she starts to hum "Amazing Grace."

Art Wiggins, the social worker who has been on jury duty, has suggested that the family issues group share foster home stories; three of the patients have spent most of their childhood in such places. Vuckovic admires Wiggins's strategy for steering patients toward common experiences and away from dramatic accounts of personal suffering, the purpose of which is often to elicit sympathy. Frequently, the result is an informal but intense game of one-upmanship: "You think *you* had it bad? Well, listen to this."

"I didn't think the curtains would catch on fire," Matt says, smiling. "Doesn't stuff like that have to be fireproof? Like kids' pajamas? So anyhow, Jean gets real pissed and starts whaling on me. With a flyswatter. Those things can hurt. She's lucky I took off instead of slugging her," he concludes, his smile broader.

Vuckovic's face is, he hopes, expressionless, though he's conscious of resisting his own violent impulses toward this unpleasant young man who smiles too much. Although on the Unit only a few days, this black-leather punk is flaunting behavior and attitudes that most experienced patients keep to themselves.

"Why didn't you hit her?" Vuckovic asks in a neutral tone.

Matt chuckles as if he and Vuckovic are sharing a private joke. "Yeah, shoulda, shouldn't I? Well, the bitch was huge. Not that I couldn't have wrecked her bad, but I wanted out of there anyhow."

Vuckovic can think of nothing to say that might make a difference to Matt. He surveys the circle of patients. Julie looks angry, the lines of her forehead fiercely compressed, her glare skipping across everyone; she probably wishes she was still on AB-II. Glenda, the weathered mental-illness veteran who arrived with Matt, seems to be dozing, and although David has perked up from his earlier depression and images of his unhappy wife, he is still detached, as if watching a play.

"Being a foster parent is obviously a tough job. Why do you think people do it?" Wiggins tosses out the question as if it were a new piece of clothing he wants them to try on.

Kiesha halts her humming. "God's going to punish you," she announces cheerfully, then resumes her tune more loudly.

"Did God say when he would do this?" Vuckovic inquires.

The pregnant woman smiles broadly and shakes her head. "Dr. Vuckovic." She speaks as if lecturing a child. "Do I look *that* loony? We both know that God doesn't share his plans with *anybody*." She smiles sweetly, and continues humming.

"Then I don't understand," Vuckovic responds. "How do you know God's going to punish Matt?"

Kiesha acts as if she doesn't hear. She simply sits smiling, then breaks into a soft rendition of the chorus, "I used to be lost, but now I'm found . . ." Vuckovic thinks her voice is a soothing contrast to the fire in her eyes.

"This is stupid," Julie interjects. "Do we have to sit here listening to this demented woman? My stepfather was worse than any of your foster mothers." She gestures at Matt. "You think a flyswatter hurts, try a lamp cord."

Vuckovic groans to himself. The contest is on. At this point, meaningful questions or insights about behavior patterns would float over the patients' heads like loose balloons.

Kiesha is now singing in a full voice and rocking in her chair. A startled Glenda, fully awake, snarls a command at Kiesha to stop. Julie joins in the chorus to muzzle Kiesha, telling her to cut it out, but Matt seems above it, shaking his head in seeming disgust but saying nothing.

Vuckovic watches the group turn on Kiesha. Usually patients are fairly tolerant when one of them acts bizarrely. They accept pacing through the halls, ranting and raving, even banging against walls and furniture, as long as there is no intrusion into their own space, an unpredictable composite of physical distance and private vulnerability. Wildly psychotic or manic patients are oblivious to those around them, and fights break out when such patients don't heed a saner patient's warning to stay away. These group sessions are a special situation, physically compressing the patients, leaving little room for escape tactics.

"Kiesha, please stop singing. You're bothering us," Wiggins declares. In the space of a few minutes, her mania has advanced on her like a relentless blizzard. She is deaf to those around her, unaware of all but her own singing and the accompanying choir in her head. She smiles, her lips move, her eyes are unfocused.

"Kiesha!" Vuckovic's voice is forceful and loud. "Please leave if you can't be quiet." He looks at the white-faced clock hanging on the wall above. Only ten minutes more for this session. He glances at Wiggins, who dips his eyes in agreement. "All right. I guess that's enough for today."

Vuckovic watches the patients amble back to their rooms, and wonders about the thorny issue of medicating Kiesha. Her pregnancy and her husband's distrust of psychiatry are serious complications. Normally, psychiatry is more forgiving than other medical specialties, with more room for harmless error. Its medications and noninvasive treatments don't fatally nick arteries or put people in comas. Prescribing a medication is an inexact science. A psychopharmacologist like Vuckovic, when deciding which agent to use, balances his knowledge of a drug's side effects with an imperfect estimate of a patient's vulnerability to those effects. All antipsychotic drugs carry the potential of causing a variety of discomforts: oversedation, stiffness, muscle spasms that can twist the patient into a human pretzel, and an intolerable restlessness called akathisia. Given a patient unconvinced she has *any* problem requiring attention, a single twitch might be enough to prove to her that her doctor is doing the devil's work.

Sometimes the first medication is a good fit and the patient improves immediately; in other cases, it takes weeks or months of trial and error to find the right drug or mixture of drugs. While the consequences of an ineffective drug are usually minimal, the damage to a patient's fragile trust and the continuing terror of the disorder's symptoms make the doctor's initial approach crucial.

Kiesha's pregnancy complicates the picture. A second life would be affected by both the treatment (medicine taken by the mother easily makes its way into the bloodstream of the fetus) and the illness as it whips up behavior as dangerous to the child as to the mother.

The day after the mass that precipitated Kiesha's arrival at McLean, Vuckovic went to her room to administer a mental status examination. Although the admitting resident had concluded that she was manic and psychotic, and her weird behavior would have been obvious to anyone, a senior doctor had to make a formal diagnosis. Some symptoms could be initially subtle, or a patient might be guarded and tell an incomplete or false story. In other cases, symptoms disappear overnight. Vuckovic had seen many variations on this unfolding, and so began the exam with an open mind.

The mental status exam is the psychiatrist's primary tool for evaluating a patient, the equivalent of an internist's physical exam. However, unlike the latter, it is usually woven into a consultation or history-taking session, allowing the psychiatrist to relax the depressed or fearful patient, or reassure the wary paranoid. To an unschooled listener, the examiner might be engaging in casual chitchat or offering general emotional support. Psychiatrists in training, all too conscious of the imposing list of vital information they need for a diagnosis, despair of ever relaxing.

Vuckovic had been no different. As a neophyte psychiatric resident, he conducted the exam cookbook-style, moving laboriously down the list, frustrated at the time and effort it took. Now, he glided seamlessly through the salient points. He consulted no papers and took no notes; later he would dictate the results into the patient's file.

The exam takes about twenty minutes and consists of a series of observations and exchanges, beginning with a patient's appearance and behavior — style of dress, whether he makes eye contact, his distance from the interviewer, if he leans forward or shies away. The psychiatrist notices less subtle signs: inappropriate laughter, inattention to personal hygiene, tremors, wild gesticulations, or twitches that may indicate a reaction to medication.

After the obvious points, the psychiatrist wends through less conspicuous, more psychological symptoms. He listens to speech — does the patient talk to or past the examiner, are the tone and rate normal? Does he make sense, or are there subtle disturbances of syntax, not quite meaningful associations or elisions, made-up words, gibberish?

Vuckovic assesses mood by both what the patient says and does. Does the patient say he's happy or sad? If happy, is he crying or irritable, thus displaying "inappropriate affect"? Suicidal thinking is explored. Wishing to be dead is not unusual; most teenagers have had such moments. But does it intrude continuously, wiping out any thoughts of the future? Is there a plan, and is it realistic? Have preparations been made — a gun purchased, pills secreted? Has the patient already tried and told no one? Is there a drug or alcohol history, making impulsive acts more likely? Conversely, is the suicidal thinking chronic but seemingly trivial, emerging when the garbage needs to be taken out, characterized by "cries for help," such as superficial slashes and burns, dramatic falls? And is there homicidal thinking?

Vuckovic examines a patient's thought process by scrutinizing its form and content. Are the patient's thoughts grossly disorganized, making sense to no one else? Or, as is more common, is there a spooky internal consistency, a persuasive logic, though from a premise unrooted in reality? These beliefs are called delusions, and range from grandiosity (I am God's chosen) to paranoia (Kennedy's killers know I know and have bugged the room). There may be a disturbing undercurrent of reality (is the ex–defense worker who did, after all, wipe out the company computer's memory, so off base to think the Defense Intelligence Agency is watching him?). Or the ideas may be so bizarre (No, Mr. Jones, the MRI conclusively shows the absence of multiple radio transmitters in your temporal lobe) that the doctor has no idea what the source of the belief is.

Another consideration is whether the beliefs reflect the patient's mood. The grandiose manic believes he will be elected president; the psychotically depressed patient thinks he deserves to die for imagined sins against his family. The mood-incongruent or overtly off-the-wall delusion (such as Mr. Jones's transmitters) often accompanies a grim prognosis of chronicity or poor response to treatment.

Hallucinations, another symptom, often but not always accompany delusions. They may appear without any other psychotic symptoms. They can involve any of the five senses. Voices commanding a person to hurt herself, or others, are the most dangerous hallucination. Olfactory hallucinations — the smell of burnt rubber, for instance — frequently indicate physical damage to the temporal lobe of the brain; tactile hallucinations, often associated with withdrawal from drugs or alcohol, can cause a patient to feel as if insects are crawling over her body.

To test a patient's cognitive status, Vuckovic notes the level of alertness, then evaluates three types of memory. He asks the patient to repeat a series of numbers to test immediate recall. Short-term memory is assessed by how many words out of three the patient can recall after five minutes. Finally, the patient's ability to relate details from past weeks, months, or years indicates his long-term memory. Vuckovic also tests general information, making allowances for education and social background. He gauges the patient's ability to engage in abstract reasoning by asking him to interpret proverbs. Vuckovic thinks this the most useless portion of the exam; to his chagrin, students and residents latch on to it with a vengeance. The psychiatrist also estimates the patient's intelligence, and while it may sound pejorative, an entire class of diagnoses — retardation or subnormal intelligence — rests on it.

Finally, Vuckovic considers the patient's insight and judgment. He first determines whether the patient knows he's ill. Psychosis leaves a person with a wide variety of degrees of acknowledgment, from straightforward acceptance and a desire to be helped to a total lack of insight, as seen in patients with severe paranoid disorders. Nonpsychotic patients may lack insight as well: the alcoholic slurring his denial of a problem or the character-disordered person unable to accept responsibility for beating his wife. Determining "judgment" requires applying the concept of "insight" to a patient's behavior. Irrespective of his beliefs, is the frightened paranoid patient able to resist the impulse to slug his tormentor? Or, evincing even more judgment, does he blandly deny symptoms to someone who can lock him up, thus demonstrating that he is aware of consequences?

By the end of the interview, Vuckovic pieces together a distinct symptom picture and gives it a name, based both on the *Diagnostic and Statistical Manual,* Third Edition, and on an informal comparison to the thousands of patients he has examined.

Following this interview, a psychotic patient is classified as manic, psychotically depressed, schizophreniform (unless the patient has been sick for a full six months, in which case he is labeled schizophrenic), or, if the doctor is puzzled, psychotic NOS, for Not Otherwise Specified. While establishing the diagnosis is crucial in determining treatment, it predicts neither the course of an illness nor how a patient will respond. Though nine out of ten patients diagnosed with schizophrenia, for instance, retain that diagnosis for a decade, many go on to relatively normal lives while others require institutionalization.

Midway through his veiled exam of Kiesha, Vuckovic concluded that the resident had done a good job the night before. Vuckovic had left the most important question for last. "Mrs. Thomas — may I call you Kiesha?"

She nodded.

"Kiesha, is there any chance at all you would act to hurt yourself or your baby? Does anything make you afraid you might do that?"

Kiesha giggled, in an almost patronizing way, as if Vuckovic had no idea of the importance of her mission. "No sir." She smiled. "No chance at all."

The next day, Vuckovic presented Kiesha's case in rounds, which are held twice a week in the poolroom. The entire staff involved with a patient's treatment — PIC, nurse, social worker, rehab or occupational therapist, and sometimes nursing and medical students — attends. It is the only time the entire treatment team comes together for an update on a patient.

Many McLean patients are regulars who have been checking in and out of the hospital for years, and staff talks about them as if they are distant cousins whose triumphs and tragedies are a continuing source of news and concern. First-timers, like Kiesha, are an unknown quantity, so the discussion is less personal, more lengthy, and more cautious. The patient without a history on the Unit is, simply, unpredictable.

Vuckovic opened the blue binder with Kiesha's name on the spine and began talking. Rather than reading the admission note, Vuckovic presented the salient points.

"Mrs. Thomas is delusional and twenty weeks pregnant. She has no history prior to the explosive onset of her symptoms in church. She believes the father of her child is the Pope and/or a cardinal or three; the child will apparently be the new Messiah.

"On Sunday, while she and her husband were attending mass, she began dancing in the aisle and singing about the coming of the new Messiah. While agitated on arrival here, she was not assaultive and accepted being placed in the quiet room. The resident was hesitant to order meds, given her condition, and she has made it clear she wants none.

"Her sleeping is erratic. She's been up and down at night, slept a total of two hours since arriving. Her mania hasn't escalated even when provoked in family issues group, and she tolerated a move to the convertible quiet room. Her husband hates us and thinks she's all cured. Any questions?" He looked around the room brightly, as if he had just delivered the weather report.

Nina Lehmann let out a sigh and sank her head on her arms, crossed on the table in front of her. As the social worker, she would be working with the family, in this case an obstreperous husband. Nancy Nicholson, the charge nurse, chuckled wryly. "He's been calling about every fifteen minutes asking for the doctor."

Vuckovic gestured expansively to Nina. "Your case, Mrs. L. Feel free to give him my extension."

She smiled at him through crossed fingers and remarked brightly, "I *certainly* will, Dr. V." General laughter, and the team moved to the next case.

As the family issues group dissolves and patients scatter, Kiesha lowers her singing to a moderate hum and retreats to her room. The so-called convertible room is furnished sparsely with a bed, night table, and small dresser, all in the blond Scandinavian style used throughout the hospital, all with rounded edges and drawers bolted in. Kiesha's assignment to this room so quickly after admission is partially a result of the arrival of an even more agitated patient the same night and partially her ability to respond to, in the parlance of nursing notes, "verbal limit-setting," to stop yelling.

Vuckovic has few medical qualms about offering antipsychotic medication to Kiesha. The neuroleptic drugs aren't a risk to the fetus, especially one past the first trimester. What he worries about is his ability to convince Kiesha and her husband of the greater risks of not treating her. She might induce a miscarriage through inadvertently traumatizing the baby, especially if she becomes more agitated. Her cardiovascular system might not be able to tolerate the stress of the baby plus the rush of neurotransmitters and steroids circulated by an out-of-balance central nervous system. Lack of sleep itself might damage the mother and baby. As he reviews the unpleasant alternatives, John Graybill, a medical student, comes up to him.

"Dr. Vuckovic, is this a good time for me to interview Kiesha Thomas?"

Graybill, a twenty-six-year-old who looks like a linebacker, is in his fourth year at Harvard Medical School. Psychiatry is his last month-long rotation as a student before he plunges into internship and specialty training. Medical students are regularly assigned to Vuckovic not only because he is a senior PIC and experienced psychiatrist, but also because students like him. Old enough to have authority and standing, but young enough to understand their anxieties and insecurities, Vuckovic is a natural mentor.

"Have you reviewed her file — the admission notes, the nursing assessments, lab work?" Medical students, Vuckovic has surmised, fall into two camps. The first camp bury themselves in the minutiae of a patient's story, losing track of the larger issues between doctor and patient. They sublimate their anxiety in a numbing flow of detail. The second group tends to move more naturally past the barrier of historical facts and EEG results, to diagnosis, treatment, and, in this field above all, sharing pain and helplessness. While Vuckovic enjoys teaching the second group of students more, he never forgets that he had been of the first camp during his student days. Time, effort, and exposure to patients are, he feels, the tonic for the most obsessive of his charges.

Another reason for his attention to students is his knowledge that outside his specialty, many physicians regard psychiatric disorders as wastebasket diagnoses, either inexplicably mysterious or trivial and immune to intervention. Even among psychiatrists, it is easy for practitioners to become lazy and inattentive to new developments. Vuckovic cautions his students: "There's a greater tolerance of sloppiness in psychiatry because there are fewer immediate consequences to misdiagnosis and mismanagement. No one bleeds on the operating table or keels over with the wrong heart medication, but patients may suffer silently."

The senior PIC likes to give his students as much freedom as they can manage, another reason he is a popular tutor. He lets fourth-year students actively manage cases and carry out treatments. Thus, students sign their own orders, which nurses follow after Vuckovic cosigns. While this procedure is routine in general hospitals, where the students rotate through medicine and surgery, it is uncommon in psychiatric settings, a disparity that Vuckovic believes is typical of the second-class status of psychiatry. He thinks that a student will take the responsibility of providing for a helpless patient's care much more seriously if the chain of decisions clearly begins with the student's signature. A student is more likely to establish a relationship with a patient, to transform a term in medical textbooks into a person with a name and a family and a personality.

Graybill shows a talent for psychiatry, and Vuckovic wants to encourage him. Despite the assumption by his classmates and professors that he will become a tree surgeon, a half-affectionate medical school term for orthopedist, Graybill has a natural empathy with the mentally ill. Comfortable and unafraid around patients, he is quiet, frank, and mature.

By opting for an advanced clerkship in his fourth year, Graybill is signaling that he's seriously considering psychiatry as his specialty. The fourth year of medical school is both a time for students to recuperate from rigorous clerkships in medicine and surgery and an opportunity to explore potential fields of specialization. An advanced clerk is usually diligent, presumably because he has an interest in the field, but also because he knows he is being watched for suitability in a residency program.

Though Kiesha's door is open, Graybill knocks quietly to announce his entrance. Her room is a mess. Clothes are strewn across the bed, floor, and dresser. The pregnant woman is standing at her window and apparently looking at the cloudless morning sky, tapping her feet, her voice a serenade. "Amaaazing grace, how sweet the sound . . ."

"Hello, Mrs. Thomas, I'm Mr. Graybill, a medical student assigned to your case. If you don't mind, I'd like to ask you a couple of questions." He smiles and sidles over to a chair. A stethoscope sticks self-consciously from his coat pocket. Virtually everyone on hospital staff — doctors, nurses, social workers, and rehabilitation staff — wears street clothes without identifying medical paraphernalia. Savvy students quickly learn to prominently display their laminated McLean ID. Graybill has not yet picked up the technique.

She shakes her head in friendly exasperation. "You people keep working on me. You're not going to persuade me, you know. This baby's special, and nothing's going to interfere with its destiny."

"Mrs. Thomas, what is your understanding about your situation here?" the young man begins.

"I was hoping you could tell me that," Kiesha replies. "I guess Henry brought me here to protect our baby."

"From what?"

"Doubters, disbelievers, I don't know. All I know is that I have been chosen to bear this child, and so I must."

"Chosen by whom, Mrs. Thomas?" he presses.

"The Heavenly Lottery Commission," Kiesha replies, and smiles again.

"Tell me: how do you feel about being here?" He scowls and gestures at their surroundings. A tone of sympathy can't hurt.

"I hate it, and I want to leave," she says sweetly. Then, in a near screech: "Immediately!" She pounds her fist on the windowsill and opens her eyes wide, showing white all around. "Right now!"

Graybill gapes. "I'm afraid that's not possible, Mrs. Thomas. You need treatment, and that takes time. I know this place must seem a little weird. Try to be patient."

"I already told the others," she continues angrily. "I won't take your drugs, and you can't make me. My baby's going to be a perfect Messiah and no poisons are going to come near it." She closes her eyes. "Lamb of God, take away the sins of the world."

"It's not just the medicine, Mrs. Thomas. Your treatment includes other things, groups like family issues. Patients seem to like groups. It gives them a chance to talk about why they're here and what they can do to get out."

Kiesha pulls up at the last phrase and smiles a rich, genuine smile. "Well, come on in, junior doctor. Let's talk!"

When John Graybill leaves Mrs. Thomas, he's pleased with his interview. After his shock at her frightening, lightning swings of mood from holy terror to perfect hostess, he collected enough clinical data to convince him that the patient fulfilled the full set of criteria for a manic episode with mood-congruent psychotic features. Further, the normalcy that preceded the sudden eruption of her symptoms points to a good chance for a full recovery. All she needs is what Vuckovic calls "a touch of the salt" in their supervision sessions — lithium carbonate, psychiatry's first wonder drug.

Graybill feels added excitement at the patient's wary acceptance of the drug as soon as he brought it up as a "natural" alternative to the chemical poisons she has been offered. Even patients out of touch with reality to the extent they don't perceive they are ill can still accept treatment for their own idiosyncratic reasons. Thus, a paranoid patient might take medication if convinced it will somehow ward off the FBI.

"Can I go home if I take it?" she had asked, and Graybill had nodded his smiling assent.

Eager to get started, he trots to the nursing station, fills out a medication order sheet with the cryptic instructions Li_2CO_3, *300 mg po bid x31d, routine levels,* and places it on the large pile of orders, lab reports, and dictated progress notes awaiting Vuckovic's signature in his mailbox.

Later in the day, before leaving, Vuckovic visits the Unit and goes through his usual routine. First, he scans the "doctor's pad," a list of reminders from nurses about unsigned telephone orders, needed constipation medicine, renewals of privileges and restrictions, and the like. He sighs; tonight's list is half a page long. The night nurse taking the new orders will probably leave a nasty message for the morning charge nurse, urging her to *make* the doctor take care of things earlier in the day. He then plows through his mailbox, absent-mindedly signing progress notes, lab slips, and incident reports. Finally, he goes looking for Nancy, the charge nurse.

Charge nurse is a rotating role — every three weeks, someone else is assigned the job. It is an enormous responsibility, and the nursing staff looks forward to it with a degree of dread. At the beginning of each shift, the charge nurse delegates various tasks for the next eight hours. In addition to checks and meds, she taps staff members for escort assignments to individual and group activities off the Unit, such as cafeteria groups and medical clinic visits, and "specials," continuous observation of the sickest patients, some free to move about the Unit, some behind a locked door in a quiet room, and the most severely disturbed, lying facedown on a mattress in leather wrist and ankle restraints, the frightening "four points."

Nurses hate sitting with patients in such dire straits. The patient begs to be let out, swearing he will be "good," asking for one more chance. No nurse, even remembering that the patient had attempted to bite someone's ear off fifteen minutes earlier, is immune to a frustrated ambivalence about the assignment. The charge nurse is often the target of staff's irritability in the face of such pressure: "How come us MHAs do more specials than you R.N.s?"

The charge nurse is also the chief troubleshooter. Vetting patient privileges, organizing admissions and discharges, mediating staff and patient disagreements, dealing with broken appliances in the kitchen — it all falls to the charge nurse.

Vuckovic finds Nancy in the back conference room having a cigarette, recording her end-of-shift patient notes for the night crew. Crammed with a microwave, file cabinets, table and chairs, the room is barely large enough to turn around in. An air freshener and dead spider plant crowd half the table. The far wall is covered by a blackboard, where the staff scribbles musings about life in a mental hospital. One reads, "Inverse Paranoia: the feeling that everybody's out to help you." Another, "99 percent of what Freud said was true, but of no practical use."

"I'm thinking about putting Glenda on clozapine," Vuckovic remarks as he munches his late substitute for breakfast and lunch, a bag of potato skins.

"Well, the Prolixin isn't working that well. She still thinks the CIA and KGB are after her. This afternoon, she was walking around with a pile of hats on her head to protect it from laser beams." Nancy wearily rubs her eyes, adding, "I think she's taken accessorizing too far."

Vuckovic smiles, surprised at his serious charge nurse's out-of-character witticism. She must be tired.

"Glenda lives from shelter to shelter, so I'm concerned about follow-up. Does she seem organized enough to you to go to her weekly blood tests?"

"You know what she's like, Alex. Your chronic schizophrenic street person. But since she's been here, she's made friends with Paul. They go on walks together, over to the music room or the library. Her hygiene's improved, and he's shed a lot of the denial we saw at first. He's getting discharged tomorrow, and I know they've exchanged phone numbers."

Vuckovic shakes his head in wonderment. "Go figure. College professor meets bag lady. Bag lady helps heal professor. The trouble with the clozapine is the tug of war with the Medicaid people." He leaves the issue unresolved.

Vuckovic frequently seeks out Nancy as a sounding board, even though they often disagree. She thinks him too lax, and her intermittent rigidity on occasion drives him to the edge. But they respect each other's professionalism, and neither harbors resentments. Their frequent spats feel like the well-worn commonplaces of an originally ill-matched, now comfortable, marriage.

Vuckovic is an unusual PIC. This is his eighth year in a position usually occupied by a psychiatrist fresh out of residency. Most doctors regard the PIC spot as transitional, a necessary trial by fire they endure before ascending to full-time research or administrative careers. To these psychiatrists, after the first year or so, the PIC position loses its allure, having evolved into a series of mundane clinical duties and repetitive patient, family, and staff crises. A PIC spends much of his or her day on the phone, arguing with insurance companies about a patient's admission and length of stay. So as the job grows more routine, the ambitious PIC tends to veer toward full-time research or administration, or takes a less strenuous job doing similar work for more pay in a community or smaller psychiatric hospital.

But not Alexander Vuckovic. He loves the work: seeing the very sick get better, working with an experienced treatment team that prides itself on handling the toughest cases, setting families' minds at ease with the knowledge that their sons, daughters, and spouses are receiving the finest care.

Another attraction of the position is that it allows Vuckovic to develop an outpatient practice. Psychiatry, next to pediatrics and family practice, is the lowest-paying medical specialty. With PIC salaries starting at $43,000, barely higher than a fourth-year resident's, fees from private practice raise Vuckovic's income closer to that of other specialists in full-time clinical work. Yet, remaining a PIC is regarded as a poor career choice. It means that his climb up the academic ladder, dependent on his output of research articles, proceeds slowly. His PIC assignments and practice don't leave time for the intensive grantsmanship and drudgery involved in a research career. And while he professes indifference to the choice he has made, he remains a trifle defensive about only now being up for an assistant professorship, the second-lowest tenured rank, at Harvard Medical School.

Vuckovic aspires to be an exceptional clinician, a psychiatrist so skilled at diagnosing and treating psychotic disorders that he is asked to consult on the most puzzling and intractable cases. He wants to be psychiatry's equivalent to the Massachusetts General Hospital cardiologist Roman DeSanctis, a man whose clinical expertise brings him baffling cases from around the world.

Psychiatry's reputation as a profession involving little night or weekend duty is regarded with envy and condescension by other specialists. While Vuckovic carries a beeper, and signs it over to colleagues when he is unavailable, most calls he receives after hours are routine prescription refills or questions about nonlethal medication side effects. Every several days, however, a patient calls in a crisis, or a family needs immediate help hospitalizing a relative, or, most dreaded and most rare, the cold voice of a policeman or morgue attendant calls to let him know of a body, just found, ". . . and your appointment card was in the wallet, doctor, and we can't reach the relatives."

Calls from the Unit are relatively routine. The escaped patient isn't uncommon, but often as not, the eloper is not dangerous to himself or others, just determined to be free of the hospital. Barely abnormal lab results sometimes alarm staff and generate a telephone call but rarely cause an emergency. Thus, when he arrives home after just talking with the charge nurse, and his wife tells him that Nancy has called, Vuckovic is more curious than concerned.

"Nancy, it's Alex. What's up?" This better be serious, he thinks. No nitpicky squabble about privileges. The legendary energy that drives Vuckovic twelve hours a day is draining quickly, and he is already envisioning the languid comfort of his reclining leather armchair, a sweating Johnnie Walker Black on the rocks at his side.

"Alex, I'm sorry to bother you, but I've just been going through your orders, and there's one here for lithium for Kiesha."

"No there's not," he replies, irritated.

"Alex, it's sitting in front of me. The student wrote it, you cosigned it. Um, you *do* remember Kiesha's pregnant?"

The pile of papers, so hurriedly signed, reappears like a wraith in front of Vuckovic. "Well, did you give her any?"

A part of Vuckovic knows he is being unfairly unpleasant to the nurse. She has saved him from an error for which he is fully responsible; if a chimpanzee signs an order and he cosigns it, he is the physician of record. His better self reminds him to slow down; his student was a human, just an inexperienced one, and he has not reached the chapter of the textbook that warns against using lithium in pregnancy for fear of a disastrous heart defect known as Ebstein's anomaly of the tricuspid valve. Blue babies, surgery, premature death — unlikely after the first trimester, but there it is, and here he is, naked in front of the charge nurse.

"*Of course* I didn't," she replies, the receiver chilly in his hands.

"Well, let's d/c the order. And thanks."

"You're welcome," she replies, her voice warmer. "Now what *can* we give her? She's more or less tearing down the wallpaper; we're afraid she's going to hurt the baby."

"Geez, I don't want to give her anything till I talk to her husband. You know the problem, Nancy. Can you keep her settled till the morning?"

"We'll try, but she's escalating, and I'm short-staffed. If you order a special, I may be able to twist the nursing office's arm into sending somebody." While continuous observation is not a specific treatment, a full-time staff nurse can defuse a frenzied patient. However, it is a major expense for the hospital, and the charge nurse, not the doctor, is in the middle, arguing with the budget-conscious nursing department in the middle of the night. Vuckovic feels like thanking Nancy again.

"Of course, you're saving my behind tonight. And if she does chew the rug, you'll just have to restrain her, gently."

"Thank *you*, Alex." Nancy chuckles dryly. "Hope I don't have to call again."

"Me too, my dear." As Vuckovic replaces the receiver, a bead of sweat rolls from the corner of his forehead.

Two hours later, as Vuckovic and his wife snuggle on their family room sofa, dulled by the regular appearance of Peter, Paul, and Mary on the Boston PBS station, the phone rings again. This time it is the hospital operator. A Mr. Thomas has called, very agitated, insisting on talking to Dr. Vuckovic. The psychiatrist jots down Kiesha's husband's number. He debates first calling the Unit to find out if something has happened. However, if Kiesha has tried to hurt herself, or someone else, Nancy or Terese would have called.

Vuckovic dreads talking to Henry Thomas, anticipating a rerun of their brief conversation the night of his wife's admission. It was clear to Vuckovic on Sunday evening that Mr. Thomas was too distraught to seriously discuss the implications of his wife's psychotic episode. Vuckovic had settled for reassuring the man that no medication would be given to his wife without consulting him and had thus gotten Mr. Thomas to consent to her hospitalization.

Vuckovic assumes his most authoritative tone. "Mr. Thomas, this is Dr. Vuckovic returning your call."

"You lied to me, doctor, and you lied to my wife, and you're in big trouble. I hope you have a lot of malpractice insurance 'cause you're going to pay. Dr. Graybill called me this afternoon. Said Kiesha was taking medication, lithium. Said she needed a 'mood stabilizer.' Well, I looked up lithium in the *Physicians' Desk Reference* because, doctor, although you might think so, we black people are not illiterate. And you know what it says? It uses a fancy word, doctor: 'teratogenic.' Am I pronouncing it right? Dangerous for the fetus. Contraindicated in pregnancy, it says. *You're* the crazy one, man, not her!"

Vuckovic uses the man's brief pause to reflect on his malpractice coverage. Was it $15 million per occurrence or $2 million per occurrence up to a total of $15 million per year? Let's see, that would be seven and a half lawsuits a year. . . . Mr. Thomas's voice intrudes.

"If anything happens to my babies," he hisses, "you'll be busing tables!"

"Mr. Thomas," Vuckovic attempts to soothe. "I'm very

sorry about the lithium. The order was a mistake. But I assure you that your wife never received the medication. The error was corrected before it was dispensed." Although Vuckovic briefly considers placing Mr. Thomas's noose around Graybill's neck, he goes with his second instinct: attend to the patient.

"Your wife is getting the best care possible." What else can he say? He can't guarantee much beyond vigilance and compassion. And he has already lost a large element of the trust of this patient and her family.

"You better not give her *any* drugs. And I'm still calling my lawyer. You're going to pay for this." With that, Henry Thomas slams down the phone.

By 7:30 the next morning, Vuckovic is on the Unit poring over every word in Kiesha's record. Although Nancy has tossed the student's lithium order into the trash bin, Vuckovic is horrified to read Graybill's daily note, written in indelible black ink. It is a masterly, obsessive piece of work, fully four single-spaced progress-note pages long, ending in a flourish:

"While the patient refuses neuroleptic therapy, she agrees, after extensive discussion, to take lithium therapy. This is certainly appropriate and may cause her fewer side effects than would antipsychotic drugs. Will discuss with Dr. Vuckovic. (Signed) John Graybill, HMS IV."

As Vuckovic reads in the conference room, sipping his second of many daily coffees, Jack Springer slides into a chair across from him. Vuckovic doesn't have to look up to know it's Jack. He recognizes the socks. Jack defies what a nurse should look like. A stylish dresser with a weakness for cashmere and silk, only Jack would wear paisley dress socks in a putty color underneath tailored slacks.

"You probably don't need to hear this," Jack asserts, "but Kiesha had a real bad night. Barely slept, singing much of the time, I think it was 'Jesus Is a Way Maker.' She slept for a couple of hours but was up early this morning, sermonizing in the halls. I'd rather not put her in restraints, but she won't stay in her room, and some of the other patients are becoming agitated."

Vuckovic assumes that Jack has heard about the lithium incident. Nancy would have informed the clinical nurse supervisor as soon as she hung up with Vuckovic. Springer doesn't like students writing prescriptions and occasionally reminds Vuckovic of it; the PIC is grateful for his forbearance this morning, though Jack is pressuring in the opposite direction, clearly hinting the patient should receive some neuroleptic medication.

"Jack, my hands are tied. Her husband says *nothing*." Vuckovic shrugs helplessly.

Springer continues. "If she keeps going the way she has been — no sleep, little food — we could argue pretty persuasively that she's not competent and that the child's at risk. What about asking the legal office to file for an emergency guardianship?"

"Who's the guardian? The cooperative Mr. Thomas? Besides, she's still voluntary. I'd rather go for commitment and ask to expedite it." This scenario is a last resort, although McLean keeps a district court judge busy every Tuesday afternoon. If a patient is clearly at risk to himself or others because of a psychiatric condition, the hospital can petition the court to force the patient to stay under lock and key until improved, for up to six months. At the same time, the doctors can request a so-called substituted judgment treatment plan to allow them to administer antipsychotic drugs by mouth or injection. The judge attempts to determine from testimony by doctor and reluctant patient if the patient, in a previous state of competency, would have agreed to antipsychotic drugs in the eventuality of becoming incompetent.

No other class of drugs is governed by judicial decision. Doctors can administer immune-system-destroying anticancer drugs or severely teratogenic retinoic acid to a comatose or incompetent patient without having to go to court. Only antipsychotics require such legal rigmarole. Though the substituted judgment provision is ostensibly a response to the indiscriminate use of antipsychotic drugs in institutionalized retarded patients, Vuckovic is convinced that it offers more evidence of the ghettoization of psychiatry by both the legal and administrative factions of the medical profession.

Mental health aide Frank Wilson bursts into the room. "Kiesha's throwing food at Matt. Nancy got her to stop, but she's not moving out of the dining area."

In the background, Vuckovic detects a change in the usual noises of the Unit. Nursing station conversations, patients asking for cigarettes, phones ringing, pagers beeping, all ebb, leaving only the raised voices erupting from the patients' dining area. Vuckovic looks at Jack as if to say, We have no choice.

"Let's put her in restraints. And let's get internal medicine over here." Though McLean has a fully staffed internal medicine clinic with twenty-four-hour on-call internists, it is not an acute care medical facility. Nurses and mental health workers track every patient's vital signs, blood pressure and temperature, daily. When a medical problem arises, the internist on call sprints from the clinic, and a "code cart" with resuscitation equipment is wheeled over by security personnel. While the nursing and medical staff can stabilize patients, they lack the experience of a general hospital acute care team whose daily work is a series of crises. Once stabilized, a severely ill patient is transferred by ambulance to Massachusetts General. The weak link in the system snaps when an acutely ill patient is so agitated that he needs a psychiatric team. Such "train wrecks" are often shuttled back and forth from general to psychiatric hospital as the severity of the two conditions rises and falls.

But Kiesha is in robust physical health, and has already been seen by an internist the night of her admission. She also allowed her blood to be drawn, and her blood counts and chemistries were completely normal. But if Vuckovic is going to put a manic, pregnant woman with a litigious husband in four-point restraints, he wants a renewed blessing from his colleagues.

Frank returns to the dining room, where Kiesha is holding Nancy and Kelly Reilly at bay. The morning sun floods the room, which is equipped with drink dispenser, sink, and microwave, and has a large eating area. The square room feels almost like a home kitchen — a bowl of fruit sits on the round table that dominates the middle of the room, and potted plants and flowers decorate the windowsill.

Kiesha is backed against the sink, and the staff tries to calm her, as if coaxing her off a ledge. Frank nods at Nancy, and the three close in. Kelly, a thirty-nine-year-old mental health worker who competes in triathlons, is quick and gentle in subduing agitated patients.

"Kiesha, think of your baby. All this excitement can't be good for it." Although a lean five four, Kelly moves confidently within a foot of the larger woman, whose fists are clenched and mouth pursed. Frank plants himself on her other side, aware that his height makes him imposing, even threatening, to a frightened female patient.

"We're not going to hurt you, Kiesha, but you have to come with us." Putting a patient in restraints makes Nancy apprehensive, and her anxiety oozes into the atmosphere.

Kiesha spits at the charge nurse. "You devil! Get away!"

Kelly keeps inching toward her. "Kiesha, you're going to have a healthy baby. That's what God wants, isn't it? Why don't you rest and pray for a while?" Kelly slides her hand up Kiesha's arm and secures a firm grip on her shoulder.

Kiesha's muscles loosen. "Yes, I should pray. I'm scared. I'm really scared." The large black woman in her white dress collapses in tears as a phalanx of nurses and mental health aides rush her, smooth as a conveyor belt, toward the quiet room area.

Twenty minutes later, Vuckovic visits Kiesha, who lies facedown, in the quiet room, her wrists and ankles strapped to a bed frame beneath the blue mattress. From the room next door, he hears Dave, the new admission from MIT, arguing with himself, his absent mother, the world. McLean has a contract with MIT, so the Unit has had numerous students among its patients.

Vuckovic crouches at the head of the bed so that the patient can see his face on a level with hers. "How are you doing?" he asks softly.

"Oh, I'm all right, doctor," Kiesha states flatly. "Although it's not very quiet in here."

"If you feel uncomfortable or want a drink of water or anything, Frank's right outside. Just ask him."

"Frank, can I leave?" Kiesha laughs, softly, tears streaming down her face. Vuckovic shakes his head, smiles. His haunches hurt.

The neurochemical origin of psychotic mania is taken for granted in the field of psychiatry. Vuckovic is as certain of the biological foundation of Kiesha's illness as he is of his own name. But while the potential for the disease is hidden deep in her brain, something has shot it to the surface. Doctors hypothesize that this trigger can be environmentally inspired, even by stress causing sleeplessness and a breakdown in daily or even hourly biological cycles. Drug abuse can trigger a manic episode, either stimulants (from speed to over-the-counter diet aids and cold pills) or prescription antidepressants.

In Kiesha's case, the likely cause is the massive hormonal and metabolic shifts induced by her pregnancy. Postpartum depression and psychosis are classic examples of hormonally mediated disorders, although they seem to result from the body's swing back to a nonpregnant physiology. Though Vuckovic knows of cases of acute psychosis occurring in the middle of pregnancy, he has never treated such a case. Looking at Kiesha, he feels sadness. In the short time she has been in the hospital, her light brown complexion has broken out with splotches of acne and dark circles rim her once-bright eyes. She has aged far more than the few days she has spent in the hospital.

"Kiesha, do your voices ever tell you to do something you

don't want to? Are they ever angry or bossy?" Commanding voices sometimes create great conflicts between the sick and healthy parts of a person — a war of wills with the patient as the battleground.

"Sometimes." She reflects for a moment. "Like when Gabriel told me to watch for a sign, and I waited and waited and stayed up all night. I wanted to sleep, but Gabriel said watch, then yelled at me but I fell asleep. I couldn't help it."

"What does Gabriel say about taking medication?" Vuckovic asks.

"He says it's the Devil's poison, and that you're Satan and I shouldn't trust anyone," she replies calmly.

"Do you ever disagree with the voices? Do you ever *not* do what they ask?" Vuckovic hopes for a brief moment that a sliver of her will is still intact.

"Oh no, I couldn't do that."

Vuckovic worries. Unchecked, Kiesha's delusions and mania dig a deep hole from which only medical treatment can lift her. And time is running out; under her managed care policy, even though she can nominally stay in a private psychiatric facility for up to sixty days, a case manager may determine that her refusal of treatment constitutes grounds to cut off coverage. She would have to move to the state hospital, where the overworked doctors have no time for cajoling, and where, if she is not acutely suicidal, she might be turned away to her overwhelmed family.

Vuckovic never expected doctoring to include so much financial juggling. The diseases psychiatrists treat can be more costly than any coronary bypass, chemotherapy, or other medical protocol. Unlike treatment failures in other specialties, psychiatry's incurable cases live on, for years and decades. They are admitted and readmitted to private and public facilities, where they are stabilized after crises and sent out to families, state facilities, and the streets to begin the cycle again.

Hospital treatment itself is enormously labor-intensive, resulting, in the case of McLean, in a per diem charge of $729 for each bed. For almost every patient, Vuckovic has to design some part of the treatment with insurance coverage and personal finances in mind. The reality of life at McLean, like virtually all private psychiatric hospitals, is that many people cannot afford it. Those who can, whose medical insurance includes payment for "nervous/mental disorders," are covered for between seven and sixty days a year.

McLean also accepts Medicare and Medicaid patients, and like private insurers, the government limits its coverage. Medicare reimburses McLean $18,000 for every patient, regardless of length of stay. The fee covers the costs of two to two and a half weeks of hospitalization, and the government adjusts this amount yearly, depending on the actual average length of stay. A hospital's reward for shortening its average length of stay is a lower reimbursement for the same service the next year. Consequently, the hospital is under pressure to patch people up and discharge them within two and a half weeks.

For doctors, nurses, social workers, and therapists, stingy psychiatric insurance coverage creates a steady crisis atmosphere. The staff is forced to practice mental-health triage, requiring them to diagnose quickly, admit only the most virulent cases, then race to mend and discharge.

Kiesha is rapidly depleting her psychiatric coverage and not being treated. Vuckovic has already lost almost a week, and any treatment needs at least three or four weeks to show results. And the hospital's "patient advocate," who monitors patient treatment for managed-care insurance carriers, is asking about her progress. Vuckovic has to do something. Kiesha's voices provide the impetus.

Two days later, as Vuckovic listens in his office to the chief executive of a software firm describe his panic attacks, Nancy calls from downstairs. Sessions with private patients are interrupted only in emergencies, situations that can't wait fifteen minutes.

"Kiesha's slamming herself around her room, pounding on her stomach. Her voices have told her to destroy the baby. She's determined to hurt herself. You've *got* to do something." Nancy's voice is succinct and cool.

"All right," Vuckovic deadpans, not wanting to alarm the patient in front of him. "I've got to talk to Mauricio. I'll be down later."

Mauricio Tohen, the forty-three-year-old clinical director of the psychotic disorders program, is Vuckovic's most immediate supervisor, and his best friend at the hospital. The two men share many qualities. Both are the sons of successful immigrants — Vuckovic's father is a poet and mathematician from Yugoslavia, and Tohen's is a successful Mexican orthopedist — and both possess Old World discipline and New World ambition. Each harbors an aptitude for the precision of hard science along with a fascination for the human psyche. While studying at Harvard Medical School, Vuckovic also enrolled in a health sciences and technology program at MIT. After earning an M.D. at the National University of Mexico, Tohen enrolled in the Harvard School of Public Health for a master's degree, then a doctorate in epidemiology, the study of illness in large population groups.

When these enterprising doctors were assigned to be psychiatrists-in-charge on the same unit, friendship was inevitable. For three years, they were alter egos on Proctor House, complementing each other. When Tohen was slow and methodical, Vuckovic was quick and intuitive; when Vuckovic was impulsive, Tohen was thoughtful. What Tohen was unfamiliar with, Vuckovic was sure to know, and vice versa.

However, while Vuckovic preferred to devote his days to hand-to-hand combat with mental illness, Tohen parceled his time between patients and research, an activity that put him on the McLean fast track. A tireless researcher, Tohen's name appeared in numerous medical journals every year over studies of psychosis, schizophrenia, diagnostic trends. Tohen's star grew brighter with every byline and research grant. Vuckovic, on the other hand, shoved research behind his teaching and patient care, and measured his nongrant research projects in increments of about one publication per year, enough to stay academically respectable but on a slower track.

As a result of their divergent interests, Tohen and Vuckovic were not destined to be paired forever. They parted ways as day-to-day colleagues when Tohen was tapped, over his friend and eight other psychiatrists, to become their boss, the clinical director for the psychotic disorders units. Most friendships wouldn't survive such a parting, and to outsiders it seemed as if Tohen had publicly bested his friend. But if the appearance was of a fierce competition won and lost, neither man seemed to notice. They continue to be each other's close friend and champion.

Vuckovic knows he will find his friend at the DeMarneffe cafeteria having dinner. Tohen eats there many evenings, then returns to his office in North Belknap for late-night grant writing. Vuckovic usually logs just twelve hours a day; Tohen regularly racks up fifteen.

Vuckovic strides into the modern, airy cafeteria, the central eating facility, which resembles a sushi bar more than an institutional eatery. Food service is dispensed over the usual chrome counters but typically includes Uno pizzas, special wok-cooked meals, and fresh baked goods. Staff and patients (those with cafe privileges) eat at tables of two or four, surrounded by elegant ficus trees and partially lit by skylights. Tohen is at a table by himself overlooking the patio and flipping through *Tennis* magazine as he sips soup. Vuckovic, after grabbing a cup of coffee, sits down.

"Geez, Mauricio, if you insist on making a spectacle of yourself here, at least bring some decent reading matter. Something inspirational. I've got some sexy back issues of *Psychopharmacology Bulletin*." Vuckovic smiles slightly and waits for Tohen's retort.

"Alex, *you* get the *Bulletin?* You mean your students share their copies with you," the clinical director teases.

"Ah, students," Vuckovic admits. "Touchy subject."

"So I heard. Nice screwup." Tohen's voice has both a note of chastisement and sympathy. In truth, he considers Vuckovic to be an exceptional PIC and trusts his judgment implicitly.

"You can bet that Mr. Graybill will never forget Ebstein's anomaly." Both men laugh softly.

"And I'll never forget Kiesha Thomas," Vuckovic adds, then continues. "I'm afraid this crisis isn't over, either. Her mania's totally out of control. She's trying to kill her baby now, throwing herself against walls, doors. She's been in and out of restraints all week. And still she and her husband refuse all medication. I've got to do something, Mauricio."

Tohen doesn't hesitate, talking as he finishes his soup. "Of course you do. No matter what anyone says, you've got to treat her. If her judgment were any good, she wouldn't be here. If you don't treat her, you're not doing your job." His matter-of-fact tone sharply contrasts with Vuckovic's emotional turmoil.

"I know, but I just wanted to warn you. This one could end up with all of us in court."

"Don't let the lawyers scare you off. You're the doctor."

Vuckovic takes a final gulp of his coffee and rises to leave. "Thanks, Mauricio. And really, consider a subscription to *Hospital Supervisor's Bulletin.* Maybe I'll give it to you for your birthday."

Emboldened by his friend, Vuckovic heads straight for the Unit. Early evenings there are quiet; patients eat either at the cafe or unit dining room, then many leave for evening activities. Although the Unit has two television rooms — one for smokers, one for nonsmokers — many patients seek out other ways to pass the time. Heidi, a recreational therapist, has recruited patients for a game of Trivial Pursuit in the poolroom. Kelly, the mental health worker, polls patients on what flavor cake to bake in the kitchen.

Staff thins out in the evening, pared to a small complement of nurses and mental health workers. The consultants, psychologists, and attendings who wear down the carpeting during the day are long gone. Only two psychiatrists and one internist on call patrol the hospital grounds, dashing from crisis to crisis and admission to admission through McLean's spookily lit underground tunnel system. When help is needed on a unit, emergency beepers pull staff from adjacent buildings.

As Vuckovic enters the nurses' station, Kelly and Frank are arguing about when to dim the hall lights. It is an endless debate: the "let's dim them now so the patients quiet down sooner" argument versus "if you dim them too soon, patients will get restless in the middle of the night." A nurse leans against the half door looking out on the floor, eating a submarine sandwich delivered from a nearby Greek restaurant. The Unit smells of tomato sauce and microwave popcorn.

Vuckovic finds the evening charge nurse, forty-seven-year-old Diana MacKenzie, in the conference room writing patient notes.

"Any change in Kiesha?" Vuckovic asks, picking up the medication order book.

"She's pacing around her room, I think. There was a real tussle earlier. She's calmed down a bit, probably getting ready for the next storm." MacKenzie watches him scribble in the order book, a quizzical look on her face.

"Can you fax this to the pharmacy so we have a supply this evening?" Vuckovic hands her a yellow slip of paper, the official order.

"Sure. I can do it right now." She scans his scrawl, which states that if Kiesha Thomas needs a chemical restraint, she is to receive intramuscular injections of haloperidol, five milligrams. Although this does not constitute a directive to give her the medication, staff is now free to ask either the doctor on call or Vuckovic for a chemical restraint along with a physical one the next time she endangers herself or her baby.

"Going to bite the bullet, huh?"

Vuckovic scowls, as if swallowing a bitter pill.

MacKenzie nods in agreement. "Look at the alternative: if she doesn't get any meds, someone's going to get hurt. It could be her baby, or one of us."

Vuckovic appreciates her support, but it doesn't make him feel any better. He hates forcing medication on anyone; he feels boxed in.

"She should be on five-minute checks," he reminds the nurse.

"She is. I'll let you know if there's any change."

Before leaving McLean for the day, Vuckovic has one more onerous task, and so returns to his office. He flicks on the overhead fluorescent light, creating a stark glare. It is after eight o'clock. First, he calls his wife to tell her he will be home after making one more phone call. Then he dials Henry Thomas to tell him what he had done.

Thomas does not yell at Vuckovic; his rage is cold. "You son of a bitch," the husband seethes. "Tomorrow morning, I'm going to be on your doorstep, with my lawyer, and we're taking Kiesha out of there. And then you and that fancy-ass hospital of yours are going to get hit with the biggest lawsuit you ever saw. Your doctoring days are over." Henry Thomas slams down the phone.

Numb, Vuckovic stares at the heap of papers on his desk, wondering if he should call someone, maybe the hospital's legal counsel. He extracts a handful of jelly beans from the dispenser on the corner of his desk, eats a couple, pauses, and thumbs the rest, one by one, into the overflowing wastebasket next to his desk. He picks up the phone one more time.

"Hi, honey, I'm on my way," his voice sags.

"I know, you just called. What's wrong? You sound awful."

"Remember Mr. Thomas, the husband of the pregnant woman? I'm giving her Haldol, and he's coming after me with lawyers. How's Bumby?" His three-year-old son.

"He misses you. Come on home. You can't do anything more."

The next morning, Vuckovic is back on the Unit for rounds and braced for the imminent arrival of Mr. Thomas and retainers. In the nurses' station, he reviews the flow sheet on Kiesha written by one of the night nurses. As expected, she flung herself at the walls of her room and the doctor on call was summoned, and approved both the restraint and the administration of five milligrams of Haldol intramuscularly. Around 3:00 A.M., she declared that the angels were quiet and she wanted to sleep. The restraints had been removed.

Vuckovic decides to stop by her room before rounds. Her door is slightly ajar, and he hears her talking and laughing and assumes she is conversing with her voices. He knocks softly and pushes the door. Kiesha sits on her rumpled bed, dressed in a pale pink sweat suit and holding hands with her husband.

"Dr. Vuckovic!" Kiesha rejoices. "Look who's come to visit! Although I'm a little mad at him," she says in a coquettish voice. "I asked him to bring my favorite sweater, a real pretty blue angora, but he didn't. Says he didn't get the message. Well, I sent it, beamed it at him all day yesterday." She smiles again. "But no matter. Isn't he wonderful?"

A subdued Henry Thomas looks at Vuckovic, grins sheepishly, and turns back to his wife.

"We're going on a walk later," Kiesha continues. "To the gift shop. I need some personal things." She giggles.

"Um, sure, I'll get a staff member to go with you two. Be back for rounds?"

"You betcha, doc. I'll be there with bells on my toes. Or is it 'bows on my toes'?" She roars at her rhyme.

Henry Thomas smiles at his wife, and says nothing.

Henry Thomas probably didn't know that when it comes to psychotropic medication, McLean Hospital is home to some of the most knowledgeable scientists in the world. If he ever walked to the DeMarneffe cafeteria, he might have paid little attention to the dark red brick building beside it, except perhaps to wonder at the purpose of the tall silos framing the entrance. They are elevator shafts for the Mailman Research Center. The 135 or so scientists and technicians at Mailman specialize in the brain, and not an insignificant amount of their labor is dedicated to inventing and testing chemicals that may someday help patients like Kiesha.

Ross Baldessarini, in addition to being the director of the hospital's psychotic disorders program and director of the umbrella research department at the Mailman Research Center, the Laboratories for Psychiatric Research, also heads his own lab, the Neuropharmacology Laboratory. A full professor of psychiatry and neuroscience at Harvard Medical School, Dr. Baldessarini has authored more than seven hundred articles and publications, as well as the textbook *Chemotherapy in Psychiatry,* an authoritative tome on psychopharmacology. His prolific and lucid writing, in a field famous for unpronounceable words and dense descriptions, have made him a common name in medical schools around the country. The source of this notoriety is Baldessarini's research into a special family of psychiatric medications, antipsychotic drugs.

Antipsychotics have been prescribed since the 1950s, when the first compounds were discovered by accident. Before then, general sedatives like barbiturates, narcotics, and bromides were given to the mentally ill, with flawed results. The first antipsychotic medication was reserpine, a derivative of the Indian snakeroot plant used to treat high blood pressure. Doctors noticed that it sedated psychotic patients more efficiently than the other drugs available, but at a high cost: at the doses required to combat psychosis, patients taking it were prone to falls from the low blood pressure it could cause. At about the same time, Dr. Henri Laborit, a French neurosurgeon, was using the new drug chlorpromazine as a pre-anesthesia sedative.

Its power to put agitated patients into a state of profound sedation, an "artificial hibernation," prompted Laborit to suggest to psychiatrists that they try the drug on psychotic patients. The psychiatrists found, to their relief, that patients' delusions and hallucinations faded from consciousness after taking chlorpromazine for several weeks. The powerful antipsychotic they discovered is still used under the trade name Thorazine.

Psychiatrists today have more than twenty antipsychotic compounds available to them, and most of them work the same way. They calm psychosis by sedating or depressing the central nervous system, and they do this, researchers suspect, by altering the way chemicals pass between various brain cells. The chemicals that carry messages in the brain, called neurotransmitters, number about fifty and transmit their signals in different regions of the brain. The neurotransmitter that scientists think is responsible for psychosis is dopamine. While dopamine is present in every human brain, the psychotic brain, scientists suspect, has an excess.

Antipsychotics block the action of dopamine on receptors at the end of nerve cells (neurons). Receptors absorb neurotransmitters that are sent from one neuron to another, so the blockade created by antipsychotics means that less dopamine is absorbed and able to pass through the brain. Dopamine receptors are located in a region of the brain involved in thinking and feeling, and in a region where physical motion originates. The ability of antipsychotics to block dopamine in the thinking-feeling region is what helps erase psychosis. However, the drugs' powerful effect on the other region, an area around the extrapyramidal motor pathway, produces another result: patients on antipsychotics often develop a stiff gait and appear to lose the mobility of their facial muscles. They look as if they have Parkinson's disease. Medicines given to counter these side effects help to some degree, but not in all cases. In the last forty years, scientists have found only one new antipsychotic drug that doesn't impair the extrapyramidal pathway and distort muscle actions. Its name is clozapine, and it was developed in the early 1960s. But, in one to two percent of patients, clozapine can fatally shut down bone marrow production. Despite this danger, it remains a unique drug, and its introduction to the American market, coupled with weekly blood testing, took place in 1990 only after it became clear that no similar, safer compound was on the horizon.

Clozapine notwithstanding, the existing antipsychotics are imperfect in many ways. Their most obvious flaw is that not all people suffering from psychosis improve with the drugs. They also produce a host of physical and cognitive problems. Their routine side effects, besides the Parkinsonian symptoms, include constipation, blurred vision, bloating, weight gain, dry mouth, rapid heartbeat, extreme restlessness or sedation, and a slowing of thinking and movement. Another side effect, which appears in about twenty percent of patients, is tardive dyskinesia, which literally means "delayed, distorted movement."

The signs of TD are unmistakable: tics, facial grimaces, and jerky movements of the arms, legs, or trunk. The syndrome is in many ways opposite to the Parkinson's-like stiffening. It results from a frenetic attempt by the neurons controlling movement to fight against the blockade the drugs impose. The blockade creates an explosion of receptors, which in the extreme results in uncontrolled, continuous movement. Tardive dyskinesia is the brain's equivalent of the body's immune response to foreign invaders — akin to developing a fever — but with disfiguring results.

While TD may take years to develop, it is nevertheless considered the most crushing side effect because it can be irreversible, even if the drug is immediately withdrawn. Ironically, the easiest way to get rid of the symptoms is to *increase* the dosage of the antipsychotic drug, thereby blocking the extra receptors. Unfortunately, this only accelerates the process and the movements come back with a vengeance as the receptors again proliferate wildly in response to the new blockade. A patient's psychotic symptoms are prone to recur if the medication is withdrawn, leaving patients and families with the agonizing choice of staying mentally well yet becoming more and more physically debilitated, or halting the progression of the movement disorder at the cost of becoming institutionalized.

The side effects of antipsychotics, especially tardive dyskinesia, have been the inspiration for researchers exploring new types of medicine. The ideal of a drug that clears up psychosis without simultaneously harming the nerve centers that control a person's muscles and coordination, or suppressing bone marrow production, tantalizes many scientists, including Ross Baldessarini.

Baldessarini and other scientists believe that the secret to finding this elusive drug lies in the neurotransmitter dopamine. Much of Baldessarini's research involves learning how this particular brain chemical works. Every neurotransmitter relays a slightly different message, although the mechanism by which they communicate is the same. As a result of an electrical discharge within the neuron, individual nerve cells release neurotransmitters. The neurotransmitters then travel the synapse, the space between cell endings, and are absorbed, or "caught," by specialized receptors. This triggers an electrical discharge in the receiving cell, which in turn passes along the message, and so on down the line through hundreds of thousands of these individual switching stations, to the organ — muscle, stomach, genital — for which it is bound. Within the brain itself, these messages go back and forth with a speed and efficiency unmatched by the most powerful computer.

Dopamine carries messages along the extrapyramidal motor pathway and through the limbic system, the home of human emotion. From the limbic system, dopamine courses through the prefrontal cortex, which contains nerves in charge of memory and thinking, into the midbrain and the motor centers, and through the hypothalamus, which regulates the flow of many of the body's hormones. Dopamine is continually created and destroyed within the neurons. When that delicate balance is upset, scientists theorize, upheavals follow. For instance, a destruction of dopamine-producing cells in the motor pathway is the cause of idiopathic (nondrug-induced) Parkinson's syndrome. To treat this form of Parkinsonism, doctors give patients a drug that is converted to dopamine in the brain. Thus, to treat naturally occurring thought disorders, psychopharmacologists have devised medications that lower the amount of circulating dopamine or block its action.

Think of dopamine-regulating, antipsychotic drugs as cluster bombs, scattering destruction throughout the brain, knocking out not only the impaired regions but also healthy sections. Baldessarini refers to them as "sledgehammers." The next advance for researchers is manufacturing the equivalent of a neutron bomb, a highly selective weapon that targets one area, the limbic system. In essence, they're seeking a bomb with little fallout. This "clean" drug is Baldessarini's quest.

Ross Baldessarini possesses all the tools and instincts to solve this neurological mystery. While in medical school at Johns Hopkins, he devoted nearly a year to studying the cat brain, exploring its structure and how sounds travel to certain nerves. He became so engrossed in neurobiology that he seriously considered switching from medical school into a Ph.D. program and, as he puts it, "becoming a real scientist." But his mentor advised against it.

"He said one degree was enough. That you have to jump through a lot of hoops to get two degrees and it takes six years after an M.D. 'After your clinical training, you're going to be an old man,' " the Mailman scientist recalls his mentor saying, noting that he would not give the same advice to a promising student today. Despite all his titles, Baldessarini is one of the few senior researchers at Mailman who doesn't own both an M.D. and a Ph.D.

After medical school, Baldessarini ricocheted between biochemical research at the National Institutes of Health, clinical work as an internist, and learning psychiatry. The range of interests not only suggests a scientific prodigy but also highlights an intellect comfortable in disparate disciplines. In the end, Baldessarini melded his talents, taking his medical degree in neuroscience, then doing his residency in psychiatry at Johns Hopkins. School finished and decisions made, the thirty-two-year-old Baldessarini accepted a position as an assistant psychiatrist at Massachusetts General Hospital in Boston and an assistant professorship at Harvard Medical School.

His job at Mass. General was to create a research lab from scratch. The lab director was Seymour Kety, fresh from leading a prestigious research team at NIH and already renowned as a pioneer of biological psychiatry and the father of brain imaging. The facility they were shaping would eventually become the Laboratories for Psychiatric Research.

The early 1970s was an intoxicating time for a young researcher. Scientists believed they had unearthed the biological basis of mental illness and were picking apart the brain, cell by cell. Basic, as opposed to clinical, psychopharmacology was bursting with new discoveries about neurotransmitters and how they are involved in sending and receiving brain messages. Researchers at Johns Hopkins and Yale were making major breakthroughs in the discovery of the brain areas where dopamine-rich neurons are found. Learning the location of dopamine receptors was a huge advance in understanding the neurotransmitter's influence in psychotic behavior.

Psychiatry was also in turmoil. Revolutionary brain imaging techniques, especially computerized tomography, were showing abnormalities in the structure of schizophrenic brains. And, for the first time ever, a task force of doctors under the auspices of the American Psychiatric Association was devising definitive diagnostic criteria for thirteen mental illnesses.

As a junior pioneer, Baldessarini ventured into new territory. He arrived at his fledgling lab early each morning and put in long days crafting every assay, mapping every step, practicing how to inject chemical mixtures into rats, and dissecting rat brains. It was dirty, hands-on work, and he loved it.

The Laboratories for Psychiatric Research crisscrossed scientific and medical boundaries. The investigative teams swapped findings in genetics, molecular biology, psychopharmacology, and psychobiology. While the laboratories treated psychiatry as a hard science, the scientists never lost sight of the patient. Baldessarini split his investigations between pure neurochemical research and chemical studies with patients.

In 1972, McLean Hospital invited Seymour Kety and his team to relocate to Belmont. Enticed by the promise of more resources and an expanded program, the scientists gladly packed their microscopes and beakers. Equally appealing to Baldessarini was the possibility for interaction between his research and clinical work with McLean patients. Ross Baldessarini needs the emotional jolt that comes only from involvement with patients. He sees himself as a healer as well as a researcher: "I'm a clinically trained person who's a psychiatrist deep down inside who happens to have fun working in labs. It's fun to learn how things work and I'm delighted if it's possible to make a minor scientific contribution. But for me, that's not quite socially satisfying or emotionally satisfying enough. What I'd really like to do is find the perfect treatment for psychotic illness."

Baldessarini's search began in earnest about four years ago, and although he never seems to race around, he is in a hurry. At age fifty-five, he's in danger of becoming a gray eminence whose research may be overshadowed by high-tech successors. His research started as a collaboration with medicinal chemists at nearby Northeastern University to create new mixtures of molecules which might someday be turned into drugs. Baldessarini and his team — postdoctoral trainees, a pharmacologist, a biochemist, and an animal behavior specialist — rearrange molecular compounds. This is the heart of Baldessarini's research from which new drugs will emerge. But finding them demands years of painstaking experiments. Molecular experiments are tedious and time-consuming because each step takes weeks to devise. They require screening a formula, mixing it with a solution of rat brain cells, and then, if all goes well, administering it to live rats. In the last step, the scientist collects the results and looks for clues in the interaction between the newly created molecules and the rat brains. Without rats, Baldessarini cannot do drug research. Rats are ideal experimental subjects because, as mammals, their brain structure is similar to that of humans, and few people get upset when they are dissected for research. Most important of all, they reveal things about chemicals and behavior that cannot be discerned from test tubes. The purpose of Baldessarini's rat experiments was to test what a particular molecule — a dopamine stimulant called an aporphine — does to their behavior, and how it might affect mental illness.

The Mailman Research Center lab has about 300 rats — specially bred albino males that cost eight dollars each — housed in wire cages on the second floor and tended by an animal behavior specialist, Alexander Campbell. Campbell, whose touch with the animals Baldessarini calls "surgical, magical," prepared about 180 rats for brain surgery by cutting a small hole in each head and capping it with a plastic plug containing a channel, called a cannula. The cannula is, in essence, a door into the rat's brain which Campbell could open, then close, thus avoiding repeatedly anesthetizing or traumatizing the rodents.

Working in a windowless room filled with vegetable bin–sized wire cages, Campbell delicately injected a solution of synthetic dopamine into two regions of the rats' brains — the nucleus accumbens in the limbic system and the corpus striatum, a layer of nerves in the motor center of the brain. The shot of dopamine produced the expected results: it was like inducing psychosis in a rat. The animals became agitated and hyperactive, and exhibited abnormal motor control with twitchy head movements to one side. Confident that the animals' brains contained an excess of dopamine, Campbell then injected the rats with the new chemical, the aporphine, and a control substance, a commercially available antipsychotic drug. Each group received a different dose of the testing chemical or a dose of the antipsychotic Haldol, whose effects are well documented. Campbell's surgical preparations, measurements, injections, and data collection continued for months.

Alex Campbell knows rat behavior as well as most parents know the habits of their children; while a visitor watching the rats scurry about their cages cannot tell the difference between normal and abnormal behavior, Campbell can. Their usual routine is to mill about the sides of the cage, so when they huddle in the corners or freeze in the middle, something is amiss. Their social behavior is also revealing. Campbell immediately notices when they become aggressive and feisty, or lonely and docile. Campbell even has a handle on the rodents' "emotional" behavior, citing grooming habits and facial twitches as telltale signs.

The particulars of rat behavior are so telling that Baldessarini and Campbell computerized a system for mapping rat activity. They placed a selection of rats, one by one, in a plastic bin on top of a gray metal electronic box that contained a digital counter and a hookup to a computer printer. Sensors inside the metal box logged each rat movement, which was fed into the computer to produce a page of scribbling that showed the actual motion pattern. Each animal's every step and twitch was plotted.

Throughout the months of testing, Campbell wrote up the results, frequently in longhand on yellow legal pads, and passed them to Baldessarini. Both scientists expected the rats given the new chemical to behave more or less the same as those on the standard antipsychotic. But they did not.

"It was a eureka experience," Baldessarini recounts. The rats given the aporphine showed entirely different motor patterns. Although the drug stymied dopamine production, as expected, it did not harm the rats' coordination. Why it did not is explained by what Baldessarini describes as "handedness." When a new drug behaves like other drugs of similar chemical composition, it's referred to as a "right-handed" version. But if it creates an opposite reaction, a mirror image, as it were, it is called a "left-handed" drug. In effect, the new chemical was a left-handed version of an antipsychotic drug; it inhibited dopamine transmission in the emotional seat of the brain, thus presumably quelling psychosis, but did not adversely affect the motor center.

"With our drug, for reasons that are still not quite clear, when we gave it systemically, there was almost no effect on the basal ganglia but a profound effect on the limbic system," the senior scientist explains. "These drugs are exquisitely — like a hundredfold — selective for the limbic system, and that is a very special, never-before-seen phenomenon. It's one of the Holy Grails of neuropharmacology: to find drugs that are regionally selective," he says. The result was that they did not trigger neurological damage in the extrapyramidal system, so they apparently do not cause tardive dyskinesia.

Despite the dramatic significance of this discovery, Baldessarini has downplayed it. While he's always open to revelation, he thinks like an agnostic. "Scientists are extraordinarily conservative people," he confesses. "Any innovation comes with great risk. Unique ideas in science tend to be very disarming. Scientists are skeptics. Go to any seminar and you'll hear it. If someone offers a new idea, the discussion is about ten reasons why they're full of baloney."

He attributes the discovery of aporphines and their dopamine selectivity to luck and serendipity. Around the time Baldessarini and his fellow researchers were going public with their findings, scientists at a pharmaceutical company were mixing combinations of molecules and logging results similar to the McLean group's.

"It's one of those very interesting phenomena in science —

when an idea is ready to pop, it's ready to pop in Switzerland, the U.S., all over. It turned out that they were working on a totally different set of drugs that have very similar properties. We had really independent ideas that grew up in parallel."

The pharmaceutical company's finding reassured rather than threatened Baldessarini. "I was pleased to hear another group of 'crazies' agreed with us!" The McLean legal department had secured patents for the new chemical family — named "S-plus aporphines" — so proprietorship was not contested. But with drug development, ownership and novelty are just a small part of the process. "The patenting process is expensive, but trivial," Baldessarini remarks. "Anybody can get a patent. The trick is the licensing. No neuroinvestigator and no hospital can afford to get into the drug development business. These days, a typical CNS [central nervous system] drug takes one hundred million to go from idea to on-line, minimum."

This does not mean Baldessarini is backing away from his Holy Grail. He has caught a glimpse of it, and is now trying to confirm the sighting by mixing more chemicals, conducting more experiments, asking more questions. The odds are against his S-plus aporphine ever becoming an accepted medication. "I doubt that we'll be able to go much further unless an industrial partner comes forward," he admits.

Nevertheless, Baldessarini continues to delve into the secrets of dopamine and antipsychotic drugs. Along the way, he has become as captivated by the hunt as by the discovery itself. "Researchers are driven by curiosity and have a certain amount of stubbornness. We like being challenged by unsolved problems that may have answers. A lot of us are pretty weird," he admits. "We live in our heads a lot and get very obsessive about what we're really interested in. We have a high tolerance for ambiguity. We're comfortable with uncertainty."

CHAPTER THREE

Moral Treatment and Shock Therapy

DAVID SELTZER: ADMISSION NOTES

- *Chief Complaint:* This is the first psychiatric hospitalization for a 56yo mwm who presents with a suicide plan, asking, "Should I do it?"

- *History of Present Illness:* The pt. is the informant. He seems reliable but is tangential and often contradictory. The pt. has never been in psychiatric treatment. However, several months ago he lost his job, and noted rapid onset of lethargy, hypersomnia, decreased energy, guilty ruminations, decreased appetite and libido. In the last several weeks, he seems to have developed the belief that he is evil and that the TV news confirms this. He has engaged in ritualistic behavior including repetitive washing. He denies auditory hallucinosis except on one occasion while listening to a newscast two weeks ago. He denies visual, gustatory, tactile, and olfactory hallucinations.

     The pt. has felt increasingly despondent and decided to kill himself. He planned to set himself on fire and jump off a bridge, but instead showed up at the admissions office. He denies homicidality; he denies drug or alcohol abuse.

- *Past Psychiatric History:* Probable depressive episode at 20, when had to leave college due to $$ probs; no Rx.
- *Social, Family, and Developmental History:* Wife and two daughters at home, apparently supportive. Father and grandmother suicided. Denies other fam hx.
- *Past Medical History:* Benign; hx prostatitis; recent GI w/u, inconclusive, for probable irritable bowel sx. Cardiac w/u for atypical cp sev mos ago, reported nondiagnostic. Hx hypercholesterolemia, Rxd Mevacor but not taking. Nonsmoker. s/p appy; NKDA.
- *Mental Status Exam:* Disheveled M in NAD. Anxious, agitated, intermittent eye contact. Speech pressured, tangential, but goal-directed. Mood "rotten," anhedonic, no libido, no appetite, sleeps 14h/d, + active suicidality with plan, no homicidality. + one episode of aud halluc, denies in other spheres; + ideas of reference, ?delusional guilt, no other formal delusions. Est int above avg, insight fair, judgment poor. Suicide risk: High.
- *Physical Exam:* WNL; neuro exam nonfocal
- *Provisional Diagnosis:* Axis I: Maj Dep Recurrent, c̄ Psychotic Features r/o Bipolar Disorder Mixed c̄ Psychotic Features

  Axis II: None

  Axis III: None

  Axis IV: 4, loss of job

  Axis V: Current GAF 20, highest GAF past yr 75
- *Treatment Plan:* Admit to the Unit; body/belongings search; sup sh/fl, 5' checks; TFTs, neuro, med eval; consider antidep/antipsych Rx; needs Rxist; contact family.

Nassir Pritsyatwa, M.D.
Resident in Adult Psychiatry

THE FAMILY ISSUES GROUP is in full swing when Vuckovic arrives with an apology for his lateness. He takes the empty chair beside Art Wiggins, who is steering the discussion. Patients are sitting in a loose circle, except for Matt, who lounges across a two-seat sofa next to the window, and David, who sits bolt upright on the piano stool in the corner.

The gray, rainy day matches the patients' subdued mood. Three days of heavy rain have kept everyone indoors, off the terrace and green grounds, confined to walking through the labyrinthine tunnel system that connects almost every building on the campus. A narrow passageway with a concrete floor, pipes, and banks of stark fluorescent lights running overhead, the tunnel reinforces the feeling of confinement. Patients and staff alike are irritable and testy.

"David, why don't you pull up a chair and join the group?" Vuckovic suggests.

David Seltzer is growing increasingly isolated. Although he dutifully attends groups, he sits apart, and when on the Unit, withdraws to his room. The fifty-six-year-old unemployed salesman stiffly shakes his head and unconsciously tugs on the cuffs of his long-sleeved shirt.

"Easter and Passover are coming up," Wiggins remarks. "Holidays can be tough times for families. Why do you think that is?" The social worker glances around the room and decides he needs a strong opinion to wake people up. "Julie?"

"Holidays are wonderful at my house. I cook a huge ham with sweet potatoes and carrots and pies, and everyone gets dressed up. I get my nails done, my hair curled." As she speaks, her eyes glance at Vuckovic. His face remains blank.

"What are you looking at me like that for?" she asks angrily. "I don't know what your problem is. Holidays are great."

Art Wiggins nods agreeably. "For some people, holidays, what they see on TV, with perfect families having a wonderful time, create expectations that can never be met. So if it's not perfect, they feel defective, angry at themselves, family members."

"For some people, holidays create *nothing*," Matt mimics. "For some people, holidays are a pain in the ass."

Vuckovic doesn't like the tone of this session, given the rainy day and the patients' mood, especially David's obvious withdrawal and depression. While he knows Wiggins is trying to be provocative toward a laudable end, today is not the day for it.

"Rituals are one way people get through tough times, like a holiday everyone's dreading," Vuckovic explains in an upbeat way. "David, are there certain rituals you and your wife have to help smooth things along?"

"You mean, like Passover, the Seder?" he replies softly.

"Yes." Vuckovic pauses. "I really wish you'd move in closer, David. It's hard to hear you."

"I can't," David says quietly, then mumbles something unintelligible.

"Why can't you?" Vuckovic seems perplexed.

"I know why: he's a nonbeliever. Jews are like that. They killed Christ. He's not like us," Kiesha volunteers cheerily. Her mania is now reined in by medication and only occasionally breaks loose.

"She's right. I'm not like you, I'm dirty. The smell of garbage follows me." David shrinks farther into the corner.

"David, I smell nothing," Vuckovic asserts firmly. He isn't surprised by David's bizarre belief. Negative delusions are a defining feature of psychotic depression. Vuckovic's reassurance is partly drowned out by Matt laughing, and Julie and Glenda giggling.

"Yes I do. Like dung, manure. I'm a living compost heap. I can almost feel the maggots crawling under my skin. It's nice of you to be polite, but I know how I smell," he insists.

As the other patients titter, Wiggins crosses the room and sits on the piano bench beside David Seltzer, and the two huddle, then slip from the room.

"I want to talk about holidays," Julie announces, as if the bizarre scene had not occurred. "My old man always gets loaded on holidays. Why do you think that is, doctor?"

Vuckovic continues with the group for another fifteen minutes, maneuvering through the land mines of patients' Christmas and Thanksgiving memories, with side trips to various birthday celebrations. In fact, many of the patients' experiences of these times have been happy ones. Kiesha explains that in her family, birthdays were so special that the lucky celebrant was treated to anything he or she wanted for breakfast, producing some very original, very funny morning meals. Ultimately, however, the group is chastened by Julie's unceasing stream of recollections about sexual abuse at the hands of two stepbrothers and an uncle, who would fondle her while wearing a Santa Claus suit. Vuckovic listens to her with a skeptical ear. Her borderline personality overlying an assortment of other illnesses makes her unreliable, if not outright devious.

Before leaving the Unit, Vuckovic detours to David Seltzer's room, which is three doors down from Kiesha Thomas's on the acute wing. David, Kiesha, Julie, Matt: the first-name basis of his relationship with these people, unknown to him two weeks ago, strikes Vuckovic as incongruous, and somewhat inappropriate. David especially, twenty years older, brings out such thoughts.

Vuckovic knocks, and when he doesn't hear a reply, slowly pushes the door open. The room is as tidy as a barracks: bed made and blanket pulled tight, a neat cluster of toiletries on the dresser, shoes squared in front of the closet.

Vuckovic hears water running in the bathroom. He finds Seltzer sitting on the toilet seat, a pan of soapy water on the white tiled floor. He is drying his feet, rubbing them so hard they have blossomed to a rose red.

"My feet were dirty, but I still can't get the stink out," David laments.

Vuckovic sees a helpless-looking middle-aged man, slacks rolled up to his calves, white feet almost bloody from scrubbing. His clean-shaven face is lined by anxiety, and a thin curtain of sweat glazes his upper forehead and receding hairline. His jaw seems rigid, thrust forward, a little out of kilter. Vuckovic feels a rush of urgency to alleviate the man's anguish.

"Mr. Seltzer, I'd like to talk to you about your treatment. Why don't you put on your shoes and come on out?" Vuckovic leaves the bathroom. Seltzer moves stiffly, his head and neck almost locked in one position, to sit on the edge of his bed. Vuckovic leans against a small oak desk.

"I'm wondering how you're feeling about the medication. The antidepressant, clomipramine, should help the anxiety you feel about your feet. Do you find yourself washing any less the last couple of days?"

Seltzer only briefly makes eye contact. "No, they still smell all the time."

Vuckovic nods. "You've got some stiffness in your face and extremities. That's probably a side effect of the Haldol. Plus, I see some spasms of your neck every few seconds, when your head snaps to the side. That's myoclonus."

For the first time, Seltzer perks up. "You're right, spasms. I get them in my tongue and forearms too, so I can't sleep. I think they're an appropriate punishment for me, for what I've done to my family, how I've humiliated them by coming into a crazy house. Also, I hate the constant dry mouth, the sticky smell of it; I can't shit; I can't piss. Do you think you could increase the dose?" There is an intensity in the older man's eyes as he leans toward Vuckovic. The psychiatrist quickly replies.

"Mr. Seltzer, I'd like to take you off this medicine and suggest another kind of treatment."

Vuckovic pauses; this is always the awkward part, presenting a treatment that is a standard procedure accepted by virtually the entire medical community but viewed with horror by the public. Seltzer's response to his comments thus far, however, reinforces his resolve.

"It's called electroconvulsive therapy, ECT. Sometimes it's called shock therapy. It's the most successful treatment for your kind of depression, and it works far more quickly than the medicine."

"I really would like more of that stuff I'm on."

"David," Vuckovic explains, sympathetically lapsing into the familiar, "the ECT is going to make you feel much better. I promise. The feelings you have are part of your illness, and the ECT will help get rid of them." Vuckovic waits for the patient to ask questions about the notorious treatment.

Seltzer gazes out the window at the gray day. Vuckovic studies his eyes; the man is close to tears. On the nightstand beside the bed is propped a flowery get-well card, probably from one of his children. Seltzer refuses to let them visit.

"And what if I don't get better?" the sad man asks.

"You will," Vuckovic insists.

"And if I don't get better," he rambles on as if Vuckovic hasn't spoken, "it's up to me. I've got to take care of them, my wife and my kids. If I die, they get my insurance. I checked, I bought the policy ten years ago. It pays off, no matter how I die. So if I try your shock therapy and it doesn't work, it's my turn." For the first time, Seltzer's voice is firm.

"It will," Vuckovic asserts, but says nothing in response to Seltzer's veiled threat, which the older man seems to accept as a bargain. If Vuckovic's solution doesn't work, then David Seltzer can apply his own solution — unless Vuckovic is there to stop him.

Vuckovic goes to the nursing station to obtain the single-spaced, three-page ECT consent form, a lawyer's dream of horrific outcomes and qualifiers ("no one has guaranteed the treatment will be effective . . . death can occur . . . confusion and memory loss are frequent complications . . . I may withdraw this consent without prejudice at any time . . ."). How *anyone* could sign after reading it is a constant question for Vuckovic — though if anyone would, it is this man who so strongly feels he deserves to suffer.

A flurry of activity follows the signing of the consent form. The unit assistant calls the medical clinic to arrange an internist's physical, EKG, and lab work. Vuckovic calls the hospital's ECT specialist, Paul McLean (coincidence; he always chuckles when incredulous patients ask him if the place is named after him), who will come see Seltzer that evening. The social worker calls Mrs. Seltzer, anticipating a long conversation. Vuckovic writes orders — no food or drink after midnight, atropine by injection in the morning to dry secretions, discontinue present medication. Nurses take the orders, and Mr. Seltzer can spend a sleepless night awaiting his new treatment.

The next morning at 7:40, an orderly tucks a blanket around David Seltzer's legs before pushing his wheelchair from the Unit through the tunnel under the hospital to the ECT clinic.

Although most people outside the world of psychiatric hospitals believe ECT to be primitive, painful, and dangerous, those with firsthand experience know that it combats mental illness as effectively as any of the other sophisticated tools of modern medicine. Both doctors and patients respect it as therapeutic and, unlike most drugs, quickly effective. ECT saves lives, alleviates misery, and, in its present incarnation, is no more barbaric than an injection, and less painful. Although ECT has been controversial since the day it was conceived, experts agree that it improves depression in seventy to eighty percent of treated patients, and is an effective treatment for manic psychosis. Most significant, it is the most effective therapy for treatment-resistant depression (depression that doesn't respond to two months of conventional pill therapy at high doses), and for the deadliest of affective illnesses, psychotic depression. The psychotically depressed patient has lost touch with, and usually any faith in, reality as we know it. Many are at risk of suicide, and some are also homicidal.

ECT was discovered by accident in the 1930s. Doctors, believing that schizophrenia and epilepsy rarely occurred in the same person, theorized that somehow epileptic seizures warded off schizophrenia. To test this idea, researchers injected the blood of schizophrenic patients into epileptics, hoping to reduce their seizures. The experiment failed, so Hungarian neuropsychiatrist Ladislas Meduna reversed the procedure and induced grand mal seizures in schizophrenics. This time the procedure produced the desired results. A patient who had been catatonic for four years was given five separate seizures and miraculously "woke up." After years of being bedridden, he dressed himself, talked to doctors, and started living an apparently normal life again.

Meduna, after experimenting with various chemicals, used injections of camphor to generate the seizures. Electricity was introduced into the process four years after Meduna's experiments. He and his colleagues reasoned that exactly *how* a seizure was triggered, whether by electricity or medication, was not as important as the electrical storm itself within the brain. Meduna was jeered and criticized for his discovery. Ironically, the medical establishment's seemingly contradictory belief that schizophrenia was a hereditary disease but that the disorder was also the product of psychological trauma and not medically treatable, resulted in the belief that Meduna's treatment could not dispel the illness. He was accused of being a charlatan, but the attacks on him were belied by the success of the treatment.

By the early 1940s, ECT was applied to all sorts of mental illnesses, including mania and melancholic depression. It was a preferred treatment until the emergence of various psychiatric drugs in the 1950s. Then the use of ECT began to wane, especially for schizophrenia and mania. Horror stories about mental institutions and publicity over ECT led many hospitals, especially public and government-funded facilities, to abandon it. ECT was seen as revulsive as psychosurgery, as lobotomy is formally known. Yet the use of ECT never completely stopped, and has been used continuously and quietly in many private hospitals. Today, ECT is a common treatment, particularly in private and university hospitals, where its stigma is less likely to interfere. In a financially sensitive atmosphere that values short hospital stays and focused treatment, ECT also has friends in the insurance industry.

In addition to its use in treatment-resistant depression, it is recommended for women with severe psychiatric illness who are in the first stages of pregnancy, in order to minimize fetal drug exposure, and for the elderly or those with heart disease who cannot tolerate the side effects of antidepressants. It is also used in mania, especially in violent and delusional patients, when other treatments have failed, and it is especially forceful in combating an acute manic episode. One special situation for ECT is in treating patients bent on suicide, when doctors can't afford to wait the weeks required for medication to work.

McLean Hospital, famous in its early days for "moral treatment," was initially wary about using shock therapy. Ironically, public pressure, especially from doctors who had applied it successfully elsewhere and from relatives of patients improved by it, persuaded McLean in the late 1930s to try convulsive therapy.

The first McLean patients to receive shock therapy were chronic schizophrenics, and the seizure was not generated by electricity but by a camphorlike drug called Metrazol and insulin. Metrazol was difficult to use. The seizure might follow the application of the drug by minutes or hours; wary staff and anxious patients waited tensely; and when the patient lost consciousness and began convulsing, all hands would rush to hold down flailing extremities, trying to avoid bone fractures. Insulin shock could be even more dangerous. The seizure in these cases was caused by a rapid depletion of the brain's supply of sugar, without which brain cells quickly die. The unpleasant and occasionally horrific side effects created by these treatments compelled McLean to experiment with other ways to induce seizures. It tried and quickly discarded using hypothermia — the painful lowering of a patient's body temperature by ten to twenty degrees. In 1940, in the wake of research by Italian doctors, McLean began using electroshock. The danger of bone fractures from severe muscle contractions, not fully dispelled by the switch to electric seizures, was eliminated by rapid-acting intravenous muscle relaxants and sedatives.

McLean doctors were finally convinced of the usefulness of ECT by the amazing recovery of a severely depressed, seventy-year-old patient. Frank Kimball had lived in mental hospitals for fifteen years before being given ECT. Three months after treatment began, he returned home and to work, leaving McLean and psychiatric hospitals forever.

David Seltzer is wheeled to the ECT clinic through the hospital tunnel, joining a procession of rolling patients from various units also being delivered to the medical clinic in wheelchairs. The clinic, an addition to the back of the hundred-year-old Administration Building, is a cramped cluster of half a dozen small rooms barely large enough for a stretcher and hospital beds. It isn't packed with high-tech electronics since the relatively simple procedure requires only a few pieces of relatively basic equipment, which are neatly stacked on a trolley and Formica counter in a space adjoining the recovery room.

The cost of this equipment is a striking contrast to the big-ticket machines that are standard fixtures in most hospitals. The price tag of McLean's ECT clinic is about $30,000, with the most expensive piece being the $8,900 monitor that delivers the electrical stimulation.

Dr. Paul McLean, the head of the clinic, is a psychiatrist who's been administering ECT for twenty years. He explains to first-timers like Seltzer what will happen. Some patients are scared and nervous, while others seem indifferent. Still others are caught in the grip of their depression or mania. Probably what influences patients' feelings most is gossip from those who have been through ECT.

Patients ask Dr. McLean whether it hurts; no, they're asleep during the procedure. Patients ask if they have to wear anything special; no, street clothes are fine. Patients ask whether they'll lose their memory. This is the toughest question because the answer is a qualified yes. Most patients lose the memory of the entire treatment experience, though not usually of the condition that led them to seek help. And, with successive shocks, some patients develop a syndrome of confusion about where they are and about recognizing friends and family. Fortunately, this fades after the treatments end. A very small minority of patients, however, claim that they develop irreversible defects of both memory and the ability to learn new tasks. Research has failed to document these claims; most of these patients have not received adequate benefit from the treatment itself, and their cognitive difficulties probably stem from their persistent symptoms.

When a patient comes into the tiny treatment room and lies down on a stretcher, he lays his head across a two-inch-wide, perforated rubber strap. Dr. McLean stands at the head of the gurney, with the anesthesiologist on one side and a nurse on the other. An intravenous line is started and the patient is given a fast-acting barbiturate anesthesia and asked to count backward from one hundred. In about forty seconds, the patient is asleep and Dr. McLean finishes his preparations, preferring that the patient not be awake.

The doctor fastens the rubber band around the forehead and attaches the electrodes — two stainless steel disks about the size of a half dollar — carefully positioning one on each temple and sticking them in place with special jelly. The electrical charge will flow from one disk to the other, traveling through the temporal lobes of the brain, located closest to each side of the skull. (A variation of this is unilateral ECT, applying one disk on the right temple and the second in the middle of the forehead. The electrical impulse thus travels through only the right half of the brain, which is usually subordinate to the left half. Memory loss is minimized by this method, but it may be less effective.) The charge does not travel to the rest of the body; it's just strong enough to generate a jolt of electricity through all the brain's cells, or neurons. Thus, patients with heart disease are not at risk for any electrically generated disturbances of heart function.

A clip is attached to the patient's finger to monitor oxygen intake and a Styrofoam bite block is inserted in his mouth. The anesthesia in the IV is replaced by a solution containing a powerful muscle relaxant, succinylcholine. At the same time, a blood pressure cuff on one arm is inflated, thus preventing the muscle relaxant from reaching the lower arm. This way, Dr. McLean can witness a carefully regulated physical seizure in a limited set of muscles, the right forearm; this shows that the electricity has worked.

The succinylcholine adds the most dangerous element to the treatment. Because all the voluntary muscles of the body are paralyzed, the patient will asphyxiate unless the anesthesiologist breathes for him by using a manually compressed breathing bag. At this point, the patient is asleep and, like anyone in major surgery, at the mercy of the physicians. EKG electrodes monitoring heart activity are stuck around the patient's shoulders. An EEG is hooked up to record brain wave action; this device confirms the generalized electrical seizure within the brain and is a more accurate measure of the treatment's success than the old-fashioned arm cuff. Most of this paraphernalia will be removed before the patient awakens.

Dr. McLean adjusts the dial on the metal box that delivers the electrical stimulus to the lowest level needed to cause a grand mal ("great illness" in French, to distinguish it from the "small illness" of petit mal) seizure. The electrical power required depends on the patient's age (more is needed for older people), gender (higher for men), the number of ECT treatments (higher as treatment progresses), and any history of drug abuse (drugs make the brain sensitive to shock, so drug abusers are given a low voltage). The highest possible charge — five hundred joules — is enough voltage to light a hundred-watt bulb. But for the first treatment, there's no way to know the optimal level, so Dr. McLean does a low-level test, which usually doesn't trigger a seizure, then adjusts the charge based on his experience and knowledge of the patient.

It doesn't take Dr. McLean long to prepare the sleeping patient for treatment. He waits a minute or so for the muscle relaxant to circulate, then flips the switch to trigger the electrical charge. On the metal box, a green light goes on. A thin paper tape recording the brain wave seizures — squiggly lines with jagged peaks — spills from the electroencephalograph. The patient's arm stiffens, bends, and shakes. It's the only part of the body that moves; the rest lies as frozen as a mannequin. The seizure lasts about a minute, then the patient's arm is still and the EEG emits a steady, calm line. Dr. McLean removes the electrodes, the rubber band, and the bite block, and the patient slowly wakes up. It's been less than five minutes since the patient fell asleep.

Decades of experience have shown doctors how many treatments are needed to clear a mind. Someone severely depressed like David Seltzer requires between six and twelve ECT sessions, generally administered three times a week, to show results. ECT works faster than many medications, and just one or two seizures can dramatically dissolve a patient's irrationality.

Despite sixty years of practice and refinement, doctors still don't know how ECT combats the symptoms of mental illness so successfully. They know it interrupts the complex web of electrical activity in the brain by brutally disrupting the electrical impulses that constitute the way neurons communicate with each other. It does this by sending a tidal wave of neurochemicals and energy through the brain, then the spinal cord, and finally to all the muscles of the body. Scientists know that besides affecting brain chemicals such as serotonin, acetylcholine, and the hormone prolactin, seizures affect the very permeability of the neurons to the flow of salts, and alter the brain's blood flow, oxygen consumption, and glucose use. But exactly what happens in the brain during a seizure, and why the fog of depression and psychosis lifts, remains a mystery.

When David Seltzer is rolled into the recovery room, his mind is fuzzy and he can't remember his age, the day, or the year. By the time he returns to the Unit from the ECT clinic two hours later, he has regained some memory but still can't name his favorite TV program or recall what he did last New Year's Eve. He feels stiff, his muscles ache, and he has a mind-splitting headache; he spends the rest of the day sleeping in his tidy room.

The next morning in rounds, Alexander Vuckovic sits at the end of the rectangular table in the center of the poolroom, spinning his fountain pen. Notebooks and binders and coffee cups litter the table, cloud-filtered sun is seeping into the room, and everyone is visibly relaxed. The hospital accreditation committee has made its last inspection the day before, and everyone is breathing easier. Although the inspection was routine, it reminds people that psychiatric hospitals are shrinking and closing daily and that they have little control over their future. For now, staff knows that if the Unit is moved to smaller quarters, the impetus won't come from outside authorities.

Donna, a hysterical, psychotic woman with delusions of being poisoned and an eating disorder that has ballooned her five foot five inch frame to around two hundred pounds, has just left the room, and Nancy is remarking on how gamy she has become. Vuckovic dislikes the word "gamy," slang for patients' graceless attempts to manipulate each other and staff. There is nothing fun or playful in their desperate efforts to secure more privileges, win attention, or otherwise attempt to wrest a shred of control over their bodies and minds from the twin robbers of illness and its treaters.

Yet, he has heard the word many times before and it did not bother him. But when he steps back now and hears the jargon with a patient's ears, it's unsettling. The cool clinical attitude reduces a patient's emotional turmoil to business-as-usual, and the professional detachment saddens him. This feeling comes over him when confronted with a patient like David Seltzer, someone Vuckovic can imagine being a friend of the family's or a neighbor he particularly likes.

The fancy name for this phenomenon is "countertransference," psychiatric terminology for any feelings, positive or negative, that a clinician feels for a patient. Its significance lies in the ways treatment can be compromised if such feelings cause a doctor to treat the patient differently from how he might otherwise. Psychiatrists are especially sensitive to (the uncharitable might say "obsessed with") such seeming esoterica, but the phenomenon is real and affects the relationship between all doctors and their patients.

"Let's move on: David Seltzer." Vuckovic speaks quickly. "He started ECT yesterday. He couldn't tolerate the meds, and, honestly, I think he's been getting worse. He's isolative, morose, and still obsessed with washing his feet. They're going to get infected if he keeps this up. Plus, he's very quiet about suicidality — I don't like that."

"He seemed better last night," reports Diana MacKenzie, a night nurse. "Ate dinner in the kitchen. I saw him talking with Rusty, one of the first conversations he's had. He slept most of the night, with some terminal insomnia, but he was asleep again around six o'clock."

"What privs does he have?" Vuckovic asks.

"Not much. Just one-on-one," Nancy answers, indicating he is allowed to leave the Unit to visit other parts of the hospital only with a staff escort, essentially keeping him on the hall except for trips to the clinic. "He says he's desperate to take a walk, get off the Unit. He says we're driving him crazy," she adds ruefully.

"He's been here almost a week," Vuckovic notes, trying to feel for the pulse of other team members on this potential life-and-death issue. "Do we think he's ready for more? I know he's delusional, but does he let people talk to him? How good is our alliance?"

Nancy jumps in. "I don't think we should let him out of our sights, Alex. The attempt that brought him here was so calculated, so purposeful; this is way too early."

The story of David Seltzer's admission six days earlier has traveled through the McLean grapevine like news of a celebrity being admitted. What is so remarkable is not that he is in a psychiatric hospital, for depression runs through his family, but the way he caught himself at the brink of a self-destructive plunge.

This is not David's first encounter with depression. When he was a junior at Boston University, his father's gambling debts forced him to quit school. He moved back home into his boyhood bedroom, feeling numb and aimless. He tried for a time to see the positive in his predicament: he might get a head start in business, develop skills, be a leader. One evening, he heard a rhythmic creaking emanating from the basement of the silent house. Halfway down the stairs in the quarter light, he found its source: hanging from a power cord, like a pendulum, his father's body circled back and forth, in smaller and smaller arcs.

David did not remember much of the next year; when he thought of it, he guessed that he had spent a lot of time in his room, a lot of time sleeping, a lot of time feeling separate from his body. Eventually, he resumed his life, became a salesman, married, fathered two daughters. But the depression never disappeared completely. He could feel its presence threatening to break into his life at each stress point: a raise was smaller than expected, a child got measles, his wife developed arthritis. Serious or trivial, each crisis sank into him with a dull nausea, as he withdrew, tiptoed, counted the hours. When he was fifty-six, after eight years as a sales manager for a chain of mattress discounters, the company went out of business. Unemployment hit him like a sudden death in the family.

David Seltzer liked being in control, his life neatly ordered and predictable. He always rose at 7:00 A.M., always ate dinner in front of "Jeopardy!" and always called his two daughters, both in college, Sunday evenings. His wife, Carol, stayed at home and made stained-glass window hangers that she sold through a church craft shop.

His older daughter, who attended Simmons College in Boston, reacted rather stoically when he told her that he couldn't pay the following semester's tuition. She said she would drop out and get a full-time job driving a taxi. To enable the younger girl to stay in school another semester, David sold his favorite toy, a tired MGB. But that was a stopgap measure, so within months, his nineteen-year-old "Pumpkin" was out of school with no skills and no job.

The worst part was when Carol offered to work as a clerk in a nearby mall; she had seen signs advertising for help while she was shopping. He briefly, weakly argued with her, but one of them had to have a job or they'd slip behind on mortgage payments.

For weeks after losing his job, David marched through his usual rituals: rising early, putting on a tie, and leaving the house to return late in the afternoon. Carol didn't punch in at work until 11:00 A.M., so he wasn't forced to watch her workday ceremony each morning. Ostensibly, David left every morning to job-hunt — prowl office buildings, drop off résumés, have lunch with old friends who might know of openings, visit employment agencies.

But job hunting is a strain even for the most confident worker, and for David Seltzer it was excruciating. He began to slip back home after Carol had left, bury himself on the living room couch under a thick blanket, and fall into a dreamless, though never restful, sleep. When he awakened, he felt worse. The terrible thing was his inability to enjoy anything; he had been a connoisseur of his wife's cooking, would lavishly praise her for it, and twice a week he had improvised in the kitchen with Chinese techniques. Now mealtimes were a chore.

His previously robust sex drive shriveled; Carol at first

blamed herself but soon distanced herself from the lump on the other side of the bed, usually asleep when she got home. The TV was alternately boring and hideous, comedies unfunny, laugh tracks grating, news good for nothing but showing man's vile nature. And he was truly the worst of men; one evening, while half awake in front of the television, he was startled to see Dan Rather turn to him, his lips forming the unmistakable words: "You are scum. You deserve to die." A stench came to his nostrils, and he identified its source in the putrescent lumps of flesh encased in his socks. Sobbing, fearing for his sanity, he rushed into the bathroom shower fully clothed and directed a stream of scalding water onto his thighs, knees, calves, and feet. He winced at the pain. The steam surrounded his soaking extremities, but he could only smell the dead odor, and it didn't go away.

The day Carol came home early, discovering her miserable husband asleep, Seltzer hatched a plan to kill himself. He saw no other way out of the black hole his life had become. The shame he felt at not being able to support his family more than outweighed his religious convictions; he felt God had blessed his intent by the messages from Dan Rather and his aching, smelly feet.

Years earlier, a friend who had bought a king-size Sealy sold David term life insurance. Although the deal had been an agreeable exchange between salesmen at the time, David now realized it was his ticket out, as the policy paid a benefit even in case of suicide after a two-year waiting period. The two years had long passed. His death would reap his wife and daughters $500,000, and this felt like the only good thing he possessed.

He resumed his morning routine, but instead of looking for work, he drove to the Larz Anderson Bridge across the Charles River in front of the Harvard College campus, parked, and devised a foolproof plan. His plan was like his life: methodical and orderly. The heart of it was jumping and drowning, but he was afraid that natural instincts might take over at the crucial moment and either prevent him from jumping in the first place or, once he had done so, force him to the surface. So he added two more elements: coils of heavy-duty towing chain to be wrapped around his waist, and gasoline that he would pour on himself and ignite just before the leap. With the excruciating pain from the fire, the promise of the water would feel like salvation, and the chain would be his friend under the surface. It all made perfect sense to David Seltzer.

The morning David designated as "S-Day," he left at the normal time, with a dutiful peck to his wife's cheek, and drove first to a gas station to fill a ten-gallon can. As he pulled out of the station, the trunk loaded with the gas can and an iron chain, he was trembling and sweating. He felt his forehead and wondered if he had a fever.

Normally his route to the bridge brought him down Trapelo Road and through Waverley Square and Belmont. But as he stopped at the intersection of Trapelo and Mill streets, he read the small green sign, MCLEAN HOSPITAL, and followed the arrow up the incline and turned in to the hospital grounds. He drove around the perimeter, pulled into the circular entrance in front of the Admissions Building, got out, and walked in.

A young blond woman at a computer behind the counter smiled and asked if she could help him.

"I don't know," David replied tentatively. "I don't feel very well. I'd like to talk to a doctor, but I'm sort of in a hurry. I have to be somewhere."

Something about the man, the receptionist later recounted, rang her alarms. The flushed face, the unfocused eyes, the trembling, the hand wringing. Maybe he had swallowed something. More than anything, she was struck by his coming in alone, spontaneously walking into a psychiatric hospital. Walk-ins at McLean, while not rare, always signify trouble. The woman pointed him to a narrow waiting room and hailed an admissions coordinator from the glass-enclosed work area behind her.

Usually, an admissions coordinator fills out an eight-page "Preadmission Intake" form for a new patient, but David Seltzer cut her off.

"I'm not quite sure why I came here. I feel feverish, nauseous, but I have to do something. I'm not sure it's the right thing. Maybe somebody could tell me. I've messed up everything. Everything. My girls had to leave school, Carol had to go to work. But I didn't lose it all, I have my life insurance, and if I drown, if I stay under, stay drowned, they can have the money. And everything will be OK. That's why I have the gasoline. If I'm on fire, I'll have to jump, I won't be thinking about trying to breathe. And I've got a chain to keep me weighted down. What do you think? They should get the money, right?" He solicited her opinion as if he were debating whether to go to the beach or the mountains for the summer.

The stunned admissions coordinator smiled nervously, said she didn't know what was best, and asked David to sit right there while she summoned the admissions associate director. Ten minutes later, David repeated his story to a psychiatrist who, once he determined that David was covered for health insurance by his former employer, suggested that he be admitted to a locked unit.

Suicidal patients suffering from depression are usually quartered in a unit called South Belknap, which is part of McLean's affective disorders program. But the day David Seltzer walked into the admissions office, the beds in South Belknap were full, so he was shunted to the Unit. In hindsight, when the profundity of his thought disorder became more clear, it seemed the better choice.

The staff members attending rounds knew David's provenance well. And while the circumstances of his arrival were novel, his depression was a common tale.

"Let's call him in and see how he seems," Vuckovic suggests.

Rounds on the Unit, with patients being called to the pool-room, sometimes resemble a ritual akin to a job applicant appearing before a board of interviewers. A mental health worker pokes his head from the poolroom and motions to Seltzer, who is waiting in the lounge area.

Wearing rumpled gray slacks and a starched and pressed sport shirt, David Seltzer walks slowly into the poolroom, sits in the empty chair at the head of the table, pushing it away from the group as he does, and waits. Vuckovic reads a lifting of spirits in his gait and groomed appearance. The clean clothes, and a note on his flow sheet, indicate that he is a regular user of the unit washer and dryer.

"Good morning, Mr. Seltzer," Vuckovic begins. "How are you feeling this morning?"

"I'm still here. That shock therapy wasn't much fun. It made me ache," he replies dully.

"You'll feel better as it goes on. Other than that, how do you feel? How are you sleeping?" Vuckovic inquires.

"OK," Seltzer answers without conviction. In truth, he sleeps a lot, escaping into a deep blackness. His sleep is a thick shroud smothering all light, all consciousness. He likes to sleep.

"David," Nancy interjects, "are you still concerned about the way you smell?" She sneaks a look at his feet, wondering if they are healing. The obsessive washing has rubbed them raw, and they glare at the world, sockless, encased in painfully tight-looking brown oxfords.

He nods, and skews his face in distaste.

After two minutes of questions and clipped answers, everyone around the table forms the same conclusion about Seltzer's progress and course of treatment: a barely perceptible lifting of his depression, delusions still alive, continue ECT. But there is still the matter of his privileges.

"Mr. Seltzer, you've asked for MES privileges," Vuckovic reports, "and your staff coordinator tells me you've assured her of your safety. Assure me. And tell me why we shouldn't start with large-group privileges with you, as we usually do." MES, mutual escort system, means a patient can walk the grounds accompanied by only another patient; large groups mean a staff escort.

"I can't take a walk in large groups. I hate the cafeteria; it's the only place I can go without MES. You might as well keep me restricted. I give you my word as a man that I'll be safe." He sits up and looks at the psychiatrist, then the social worker, and finally at Nancy. "Please."

The nurse turns to Vuckovic, her previous steely determination wavering.

Sensing an opening, Seltzer continues. "I gave you my word I'd give the treatment a go; if it doesn't work, that's another story. Please," he repeats.

Vuckovic surveys the treatment team. Nancy shrugs. No one says anything.

"Fine, then." Vuckovic takes one last look around the room. "Anything else? I guess that's it. Thanks, Mr. Seltzer."

The door hasn't swung shut behind Seltzer before the clamor breaks out.

"Alex, I really don't feel comfortable letting David out on MES." Jack Springer voices the entire staff's uneasiness. Nancy mutters, "Me neither," as she slips out for a coffee refill.

"You guys could've said something while he was here," Vuckovic notes defensively. Some staff members stretch their legs as others get out of their chairs.

"I guess we're breaking for fifteen minutes," Vuckovic remarks. "I understand your hesitation, Jack. But you have to bite the bullet on these people sometime. I mean, we'll be discharging him at some point. I think he's reliable. He did come here of his own volition, and I want to keep him a partner in the process of getting better." Vuckovic suspects he is sounding a bit pompous, but he has gone out on a limb, and feels it's important to let others know his reasoning. He very much wants this patient to regain a little bit of the control he has surrendered to the hospital.

Jack shakes his head in disagreement, and makes his way to the nurses' station.

Seltzer's second ECT treatment is the following morning, but by midafternoon, he is awake, puttering around, doing his laundry, and making phone calls. Private phone booths are situated at the end of each wing, and patients can make and receive calls any time. Patients with a history of making abusive calls, however, are allowed to call only their lawyers, doctors, and clergy (the "unholy triad") without a staff member listening on an extension in the nurses' station.

Nina Lehmann, the social worker assigned to the Seltzer case, watches him from the glass-enclosed workroom that looks onto the floor. She thinks he looks more deliberate, more "together," than when she met with him earlier in the week. His eyes are less downcast, his gaze more straight ahead. He slips in and out of the phone booth two or three times, and she suspects that at least one of his calls was to his wife, to whom Nina has spoken that morning.

Every patient on the Unit is assigned a social worker, who acts as the patient's communication pipeline to the outside world. She talks to the family, explaining the patient's illness and treatment, answering questions like, "What do I tell his friends?" and "Can we apply for Social Security disability benefits?" and "When does he get out?" The social worker is also a relentless broker, finding and negotiating services and, if necessary, housing, for a patient after hospitalization.

Nina Lehmann is an exceptional broker. Although relatively green as a social worker, she is the mother of a manic-depressive daughter and has been doing battle with insurance companies and mental health agencies for years. As a result, she has a Rolodex stuffed with the names and numbers of obscure resources which is considered such a treasure that fellow workers have offered to buy its contents. Yet, despite excelling at negotiating with various parts of the health care system, it is the least enjoyable part of her job.

She likes untangling families, dispelling the myths surrounding the patient and his illness which skew family relationships. If patients and families are willing, the social worker acts as a mediator in family meetings, helping the sick and the well to understand their sometimes conflicted feelings and excise the destructive behavior patterns in patient and family alike. Her own experience has shown her that no family escapes the guilt, anger, and confusion that mental illness brings. Her sessions with patients and families rarely include intense psychotherapy. ("Do no harm" was her supervisor's sage advice. "You don't want to open a Pandora's box that you can't close.") She sees little point in exploring years' worth of hurts, misunderstandings, and small betrayals with families in crisis. Usually, they need practical and immediate help, like learning the whats and whys of medication, the quiet room, ECT, or group treatment. And lately, patients come and go so quickly that a social worker barely gets in a couple of phone calls to the family before discharge.

Some families want nothing to do with her; they won't talk to her, return her phone calls, or come to the hospital. For whatever reasons — emotional burnout, hostility, or indifference toward the sick relative, the hospital, doctors, the seeming unfairness of life itself — they distance themselves. Sometimes patients turn the tables, and refuse to let a social worker contact the family. The hospital's strict rules regarding the confidentiality of treatment place staff in terrible binds in such instances because it is usually the patient's illness, as manifested by paranoia or hostility, that is responsible for the lack of cooperation. In emergency cases, when information is vital to a patient's care (a diabetic's insulin dose, the location of a gun), the hospital has to petition for a court order to obtain the information. Often, staffers stand by the letter of the rule and inform those who call to volunteer information about a patient that, while they can't talk, they are happy to listen.

But earlier, David Seltzer was emphatic when Nina asked if

she could call his wife. "Yes, please, please talk to her. I'm doing this for her. She needs help." The social worker made a note of this curious comment and dialed Mrs. Seltzer as soon as she returned to her office. Over the phone, Carol Seltzer had sounded distraught, her voice quivering with fear. Fear of her husband, fear of him dying, fear of the disease, fear of a psychiatric hospital. Nina had persuaded Mrs. Seltzer to come to the Unit for a family conference by scheduling it for the next day, Saturday, so that she wouldn't miss work.

Now, David Seltzer taps on the window of the soundproof workroom, pulling Nina's attention from a file and motioning that he wants to talk. She smiles brightly despite his dour expression. In her two conversations with him, he has been glum and resigned, going through the motions of treatment with little faith that it will dispel the bleakness that envelops him. She hopes he isn't going to cancel the meeting tomorrow. She pokes her head out of the door separating the patient area from the social workers' room.

"I'd like to go for a walk. In rounds yesterday Dr. Vuckovic said that I could go for a walk." His voice is firm, almost insistent. Nina smiles inwardly; a sign of improvement.

"That's right, MES privileges. But you need someone to go with you. Walk around to the nursing station and we'll fix you up." She sounds like a store clerk eager to please a customer.

As Seltzer circles the perimeter of the nurses' station to the other side of the glass enclosure, Nina cuts through it and finds Nancy at one of the centrally situated desks making assignments for the next shift. Staff is going to be stretched this evening; admissions has just called to tell her that the Unit is getting two new patients. Nursing staff has to be pulled off regular duties to interview and settle in the agitated newcomers. Nancy is also mulling over what to do about a patient whose urine toxic screen has come back positive for cocaine. He claims he got the substance on the Unit, but Nancy is fairly certain that his girlfriend smuggled it in. She debates trying to transfer him to Appleton, the substance abuse treatment unit.

Around 3:30 P.M., the time of the afternoon nursing shift change, the atmosphere on the Unit is one of controlled chaos. A clutch of exiting staff mill around the coatroom, putting on raincoats and emptying lockers, while the arriving shift members make a new pot of coffee, check the patient status board, and listen to change-of-shift reports previously dictated on a tape recorder. From the conference room comes a crisp nurse's voice detailing Kiesha's last six hours; at the end of each shift, staff members record observations and medical information regarding each patient, and these are listened to intently by the oncoming shift.

"David wants to go on a walk," Nina informs Nancy. "But he needs someone to go with him."

Nancy scowls. "I really don't think he's ready, and I'm not comfortable with him on MES." She pauses. "I'll go talk to him."

Seltzer waits outside the Dutch door of the nurses' station. On the blackboard listing patients, privileges, and supervision, his name has just one entry: "SSF." The translation, "supervised sharps and flames," meaning he can't use a knife, scissors, or lighter without a staff person nearby.

"David, you sure you feel up to a walk?" Nancy's voice is challenging. She can't countermand the privilege, but maybe she can discourage him from claiming it.

"Uh huh." He nods resolutely.

"All right. Let's get someone to go with you, then." She studies the board, scrolling through the patients, searching for the safest and sanest who isn't signed out.

"Do you want to see if Rusty would like to go?" Rusty, like most patients on the Unit, had been a suicide risk at one time, but recently ventured into the town of Belmont a couple of times without incident. David finds Rusty in her room, stretched out on her unmade bed, going through a stack of magazines from her son. She gladly agrees to a walk; otherwise she has to attend the women's group and talk about her abusive husband, which she doesn't want to do.

The pair signs out for a walk around the grounds, promising to return within an hour and a half. Wrapped in sweaters and windbreakers for the cool spring afternoon, they leave through the terrace door and cut across the lawn toward the road that winds around the campus. Seltzer's stride puts him a couple of paces in front of Rusty, and he doesn't slow for her. While he seems to be headed somewhere, she strolls.

"Let's go down the hill toward Upham House, where I heard there are some nice woods and trees," he suggests.

They walk in silence for a few minutes as Rusty drops farther behind.

"Slow down, will you? What's your rush? We got lots of time."

Seltzer stops, studying a square concrete building that re- minds him of a Pueblo dwelling.

"What's that place?"

"The Hall-Mercer Center. It's where the kids stay," Rusty answers. "See the play yard?"

"Can you imagine that," David remarks philosophically. "Kids. They're probably not even teenagers. So sick they're in a mental hospital. You got to feel pretty awful. It doesn't seem right."

Rusty is curious about her fellow patient's feelings, but an unspoken code prohibits probing personal questions without an invitation. Despite, and perhaps to some degree because of, being locked together in close quarters, many patients don't cultivate friendships or even much camaraderie. Although they might have shared the intense experience of psychosis, they often have little else in common. On the Unit, as with most other McLean wards, patients are a mixed bag of bright college freshmen, middle-class housewives, blue-collar workers, street people, corporate executives, even famous entertainers. However, there is one topic they regularly and freely talk about, suicide.

"Were you really on your way to jump from a bridge when you stopped here?" Rusty asks.

"Yeah, was going to set myself on fire, too."

Rusty reflects for a moment. "Why do that? That's crazy. The water would've put out the fire. Now me, I prefer something instant and painless. I don't want it to hurt. Next time, I think I'd go out a window."

"Different strokes for different folks," Seltzer deadpans, and picks up his pace again. When he gets to the road lined by the trees behind Upham House, he stops, looking around the bowl-shaped expanse of grass which rises toward the Rehabilitation Building, a long, squat structure with rows of windows that make it resemble an elementary school.

"I've got something to do," he announces. "Why don't you go to the Rehab Building and I'll meet you there." Seltzer stands with his hands jammed into his pant pockets and waits for Rusty to leave.

"Like do what?" she asks, although she doesn't expect much of an answer.

He motions toward Upham. "I have to see somebody in there."

Rusty scrutinizes Seltzer's face, thinking that he'd be much better looking if he trimmed his bushy eyebrows. He avoids eye contact, instead staring at the old mansion that is Upham House, as if anticipating his meeting there. Rusty doesn't believe him for a second. But she isn't going to butt in; a stranger did that to her, and she is still angry.

"Sure," she agrees nonchalantly, and starts walking across the grass, not toward the Rehab Building but veering toward the main campus and the Unit.

Down the road from Upham House, away from the main road that loops through the campus, is Hope Cottage, a seventeen-bed quarter-way residence for patients who don't need hospitalization but require close, constant supervision. Thick woods border Hope Cottage, and Seltzer has no trouble finding a secluded oak tree, its lowest branches seven feet from the ground. He sits at the foot of the tree, his back against the trunk, and pulls from his pockets thick cotton strings. They are drawstrings filched from the laundry room dryer and the sweatpants of chubby patients who won't notice their disappearance. Tying several strings end to end, he fashions three separate strands, then weaves these together to create a single, strong rope.

This isn't going to be easy, but if it were, it wouldn't be David Seltzer's way. He planned to stand on a trash can, but ruefully saw while walking that they are bolted onto their stands. He takes off his shoes and socks, and ties the rope around his neck, with the loose end held in his teeth. He shimmies up the tree to the lowest branch and, panting, drapes halfway over it, tying the end of the rope securely. He yanks and tests his knots, then rests on the limb, and looks at the rustling leaves, set in motion by his trembling body. As the sun slips behind the trees and the sky fades to a rich purple, he lets go and slides off the limb.

The first sound David Seltzer hears when he regains consciousness is the crackle of a walkie-talkie and the voice of a McLean security guard calling for medical help. His first sensation is a pain worse than he has ever imagined, strangling his neck, burning him. He lies on the damp grass, security and medical personnel swarming about, waiting for nothing.

Vuckovic is in his office seeing his last patient of the day when Jack Springer knocks on his door. The patient visits Vuckovic once or twice a year to have her antidepressant prescription renewed. Vuckovic escorts her out past a grim-looking Jack and, with a quizzical look, motions him to come in. Vuckovic wonders if he is quitting.

Jack declines to sit down and leans against the computer table.

"Bad news, Alex. David Seltzer went out on MES and tried to hang himself down by Hope Cottage."

"Where was the other patient? Why wasn't I paged?" The color drains from Vuckovic's ruddy cheeks.

"He ditched her. Said he had a meeting at Upham. When she came back here without him, Nancy alerted security."

"How is he? Where is he now?"

"At Mass. General, apparently really out of it. There's a question as to whether he had a heart attack. They think he was hanging at least a couple of minutes."

The clinical nursing supervisor continues in a more official tone: "People are pretty upset downstairs. Of course the other patients are upset, but the staff is, too. People really liked David." Jack pauses at his use of the past tense. "He's so miserable but so kind. Never wants to be a bother, doesn't ask for anything, always offering to help. You know how patients never answer the phone, letting it ring for hours, driving the nurses crazy, because they figure it's not for them? Well, last night he picked up every call and then went and found whoever it was for. He even took messages!"

Jack seems lost in his story, amazed at the unheard-of thoughtfulness. Throughout the units at McLean, phones are answered with a curt hello, and if a patient isn't in the immediate vicinity, callers are given vague responses. At best, they are told to call back.

"Everyone's feeling a little guilty, and very angry. We should really get together and talk about how we do privileges."

Springer stretches and twists a rubber band as he speaks, making an effort to stay cool. In truth, he is furious with Vuckovic. When the unit doctor goes against the grain of his staff's experience, especially when he runs with his own gut instincts, he alienates the very people who are his eyes and ears. When things go well, these strains are glossed over; when they don't, bitterness follows.

"I'm very sorry, Jack." Vuckovic's mea culpas are rare, and he delivers this with the utmost sincerity. His chagrin is genuine. Countertransference has skewed his judgment. A patient's life has been put in jeopardy, and the bureaucratic workload of his already strained nursing staff is about to explode.

"I'll do a report for the patient care assessment committee." By volunteering to explain David Seltzer's treatment plan and the incident to the hospital's watchdogs, Vuckovic takes full responsibility for his error in judgment. If David Seltzer dies, Vuckovic is professionally liable.

The next morning is Saturday, when the staff schedule is less regimented than weekdays. Although occasionally meetings are arranged, the atmosphere is relaxed, free of the pressing schedule of groups shuffling in and out of the poolroom, patients needing escorts for appointments or lab tests elsewhere in the hospital, and attendings and consultants needing to see someone. But while staff appreciates the slower pace, patients don't.

Weekends are dead time for them: nowhere to go, no one to see. They while away the hours with board games, puzzles, or TV. Although the healthier patients leave the grounds for the day, no one spends the night away from McLean, even with family. Insurance companies might disallow coverage on that basis, arguing that if a patient is well enough to sleep elsewhere for a night, he or she doesn't need to be hospitalized.

After a suicide attempt, whether successful or not, any unit clamps down; Vuckovic's is no different. Privileges are parceled out like fragile gifts. Formal routines, like insisting patients be up and dressed by 10:00, which tend to be relaxed at other times, are strictly enforced. Nursing staff feels guilty that someone has managed to slip through all the precautions and is anxious for everyone's safety. Although Vuckovic granted the MES privilege, the nurses feel a degree of responsibility, irrationally believing that they picked the wrong patient to accompany

David. Nancy especially senses this burden, and she seethes with anger at Vuckovic for ignoring her warning, and with guilt that she did not press him on it. A suicide attempt also terrifies patients. It makes all of them sense a certain vulnerability, as if the impulse to kill one's self is a wild animal that might prey on anyone, and once it has gained access to their camp, it can strike repeatedly.

Alexander Vuckovic usually doesn't go to the hospital on Saturdays, except for the occasional weekend he supervises residents as part of a senior call schedule. PICs take turns coming in for breakfast on Saturdays and Sundays, nominally to review the residents' admissions but far more in the spirit of camaraderie with their younger colleagues. Some of the PICs believe the duty is an intrusion, and many skip it. Vuckovic usually enjoys going in; he likes the banter with the residents and feels his presence sends a positive message. They in turn enjoy his pragmatic and occasionally cynical approach as he recalls his days on call. On this Saturday, though, the doctors on call encounter a dour and silent Alexander Vuckovic. He excuses himself quickly and goes directly to the Unit.

He senses a difference as soon as he arrives: although it is a sunny, warm day, only one patient is smoking on the terrace off the poolroom. There is more milling around the door to the nurses' station, with patients demanding cigarettes, complaining about having to give up lighter privileges, and clamoring for news of David Seltzer.

Diana MacKenzie, the weekend charge nurse, is surprised to see Vuckovic but ignores him as she stands at the Dutch door, fending off a patient's flirtatious behavior.

"Here you are, George. But it's the last time today that you can have it." MacKenzie hands the sixty-three-year-old a bottle of after-shave, which is kept in a cubbyhole in the nurses' station.

The distinguished-looking man, who is dressed in khaki trousers and a polo shirt and sports lightly graying, neatly combed hair, crowds close to the nurse. He holds up the after-shave, Mexicali Brut, which has a bright orange label and what looks like a worm in the bottom.

"This is like an aphrodisiac," he declares. "Makes the girls go wild. What do you think? Do you like it?" He leans forward, trying to nuzzle into MacKenzie, backing her into a workbench.

"George," she cautions, gently maneuvering him out of the nurses' station. He steps back, hitches up his pants, and adjusts his belt buckle repeatedly.

"Did you say Kelly was single?" he asks about the mental health worker as he eagerly casts about for her.

"I didn't say, George," MacKenzie replies sternly over her shoulder, as she disappears into the nurses' station. She plops down at the desk in the common area, where Vuckovic is flipping through a patient's record. A bag of bagels and two tubs of cream cheese occupy the space between them.

"I hate it when they get hypersexual," she declares, ripping a bagel in two. "You spend your whole shift dodging them. And with everyone cooped up this weekend," she continues, "George is going to get on a lot of people's nerves."

"We could bump up his Trilafon until the lithium kicks in," Vuckovic offers solicitously. "How long's he been this way?"

"Since this morning. Not long. He'll settle down," MacKenzie says dismissively, and digs into the cream cheese.

She munches in silence as Vuckovic pages through the patient records. In the workroom behind them, the phone on the wall rings incessantly.

"What's the news on David?" Vuckovic broaches. He could call Mass. General on his own, but he wants the subject out in the open.

MacKenzie doesn't look up from the clipboard she is writing on. "He's off critical. Much better. I think he's coming back tomorrow." Her sentence is barely finished when a loud buzzer sounds, and both she and Vuckovic spring from their chairs and hurry down the hall to the quiet room. Staff members assigned to "specials," sitting outside the quiet room and looking in on a patient continuously, carry an alarm in case they need instant assistance.

Three staffers are gathered around the door of a convertible quiet room where a manic Kiesha Thomas is strapped to a bed and fighting the restraints. She has relapsed from her medicated calm and is belting out hymns and lurching against the canvas straps. Vuckovic pushes his way into the room and kneels beside the singing, twisting woman.

"Kiesha, can you hear me? Kiesha, take deep breaths, breathe slowly. Kiesha, you need to calm down or you'll hurt your baby." Vuckovic lays his hand on her shoulder, and his tone is soothing. He repeats his message three or four times before she stops, resting her head as if to take a nap. But her eyes are wide open.

"That's better," Vuckovic reassures the frightened woman. "Keep breathing slowly, you'll feel better. Try to sleep now." Vuckovic rises and motions to the staff watching from the doorway, exits the room, half closing the door behind him. Kelly Reilly resumes her position in the chair outside Kiesha's door.

Vuckovic and staff stride back to the nurses' station, accompanied by a cheery young man in a college sweatshirt marching alongside them, chattering about baseball, grateful for the excitement and the break in the usual dull hum.

Vuckovic retrieves Kiesha's chart from the conference room. He nibbles a bagel as he stands over the desk in the center area, perusing her medication history. MacKenzie gives him a quizzical look.

"What do you think, notch it up to ten milligrams Haldol?" she asks.

Vuckovic shakes his head. "If anything, I'm inclined to cut back. I wonder if it's making her too restless." Akathisia can make a patient feel as if she is crawling out of her skin. "Besides, you know these folks can wax and wane as part of the natural history of the episode. I don't feel like having to tell Mr. Thomas we're upping his baby's drugs."

"Yeah, things have been entirely too tranquil around here, Alex. I don't think we've had a crack-up in at least twelve hours," MacKenzie jests. "With David coming back tomorrow, that'll perk things up. It'll be a challenge to see if we can keep tabs on him long enough for the ECT to work." She smiles, and Vuckovic is grateful for her silent forgiveness.

Vuckovic is early for the family issues group Tuesday morning, first swinging through the nurses' station to grab a cup of coffee and scan the flow sheets on Kiesha Thomas and David Seltzer, who returned Sunday afternoon. A new patient was admitted Monday afternoon, a painfully thin woman in her early twenties. Vuckovic skips through Susan Beekman's admission note, picking out the kernels of her story: binging and purging for three years, panic attacks, arrested once for shoplifting, one prior hospitalization after collapsing in her therapist's office.

It is familiar ground to Vuckovic, a bulimic and anorectic finally pushed by circumstance and necessity to confront her illness. What is unexpected is the attending physician who is shepherding her treatment. Dr. Sean Whelan is the well-known biochemical researcher with only a handful of patients, among them Julie Swoboda. Whelan's high profile, which he cultivates by writing for and giving interviews in the popular press, and developing a dramatic persona that includes a shaved head and a small hoop earring, brings him many consultations. The patients he accepts are the hard-core cases: those whom standard treatment has failed. Vuckovic is bemused to see that Whelan, who has a flair for the grand gesture, has introduced a woman with a primary eating disorder to a psychotic disorders unit.

It is 9:25 when Vuckovic and Art Wiggins take their places in the poolroom. Two patients are waiting: a bright-eyed Kiesha, prayer book in hand, and a tall, young woman in very baggy trousers and an oversized shirt. But there is no hiding the jutting wristbones, the hollow eyes, the bony collar line. She smiles at the men; she has a beautiful face, ascetic in its emaciation, cheekbones overly prominent. But her lips curl back over an uneven landscape of grayish yellow, jagged teeth whose incongruity is shocking. Stomach acid, Vuckovic concludes.

The other patients, in various degrees of wakefulness, amble into the room. Vuckovic studies their gaits, which he has used over the years as a reliable litmus test for how someone is feeling. David doesn't drag his feet, but his steps are small, tentative. Matt has a cocky stride, and Julie sort of minces. Glenda's slippered feet shuffle, advancing in uncertainty and confusion.

"Let's get started." Art turns to the thin woman. "This is Susan. Welcome." He briefly recites the ground rules, emphasizing that this isn't therapy.

"I want to say something," Julie bursts forth dramatically. Her eyes bounce off Vuckovic and Matt, and she waits a number of beats to ensure that she has everyone's attention. "Somebody stole my shampoo. I left it in the bathroom, and a little while later, I went to get it and it was gone. That's very expensive shampoo, has special herbal conditioners in it, and I want it back. Or I'm signing a three-day note."

"Oh, give it a rest. Who'd take your stupid shampoo? You probably left it in your room. If I saw it, I'd throw it away," Matt spits out. "Especially if I knew you'd sign a three-day note and get your fat ass out of here."

"Matt, that's inappropriate," Wiggins interjects. "Have you checked to see if anyone's handed it in?"

Julie shrugs indifferently. Although she hasn't found out what happened to her shampoo, she has managed to focus the group on herself.

"Well, guys," Vuckovic starts, "this kind of brings up the issue of trust, doesn't it?"

Matt rolls his eyes.

"I saw that, Matt. And I'd think about it if I were you," Wiggins cautions sternly. "I have a feeling you wouldn't be here if you had been able to develop trust in someone as you were growing up. Susan, is there trust in your family?"

"It's OK . . ." she replies. "Except."

"Except what?" Vuckovic prods.

"Except . . ." she hesitates. "Except my mother. She doesn't trust me at all. I mean, she locks up things, like food and stuff. That's why I'm here. It was all her idea. Kept calling Dr. Whelan, telling him what I was doing. Putting me in the hospital just because I'm dieting. Really stupid."

Kiesha nods firmly, considerably calmer than on Saturday. "You're right. Your mother should trust you more. Mothers are supposed to love their children." She pats the girl's arm.

"You *diet?* Have you looked at yourself lately, honey? I've got a floor lamp that's fatter than you." Matt's eyes linger over her facial features — hollow cheeks, a sculpted nose, sunken, large eyes.

"Well, yes," Susan says belligerently. "I've got very fat thighs. They run in the family. Fat and cellulite."

Kiesha clicks her tongue. "You don't look very fat to me."

"But you don't *diet,*" Matt says viciously. "You throw up, you barf, you stuff your face, then heave, don't you?"

Susan looks to Vuckovic and Wiggins, who remain silent. "Fat, sure!" Julie chimes in sarcastically. "You want to see fat, get a load of Donna. That's fat!"

"I am, too," Susan asserts. "You just can't see it, the rolls and fat dimples. If I don't watch it, I get really gross."

Vuckovic wonders how long to let this continue.

"Oh, pleeeasse —" Julie stretches out her disgust.

"Enough," Art Wiggins jumps in. "David, welcome back. We're all happy to see you well." The patient stares at the social worker silently. "Would you tell us about trust in your family? How would you describe the trust between yourself and your wife? A lot? A little?"

Vuckovic sits back in his chair; isn't Wiggins putting too much pressure on this fragile man?

"I think we're like most couples," David says thoughtfully. "We're pretty trusting until one of us does something stupid, then we have to earn it back. It's like being a teenager with your mother giving you later and later hours, then you miss your curfew, you're grounded and have to start all over again. Which is what I have to do," he adds.

Vuckovic is encouraged by David's response; perhaps the ECT is beginning to show results. He had a treatment Monday.

"You know what gets me," Matt pipes in, "is all the funny looks, the suspicions, the nosy questions about where I'm going, who I'm seeing. Just because people live together doesn't mean you gotta know everything."

"My mother's always nagging me, like, 'What'd you have for lunch?' and 'Get out of the bathroom.' You'd think I was a drug addict or something," Susan complains.

"Addicted to barfing is more like it," Matt snipes.

The group proceeds in this tone for another half hour. As Wiggins orchestrates the discussion, Vuckovic's mind wanders to the plot of flowers outside by the patio and his recollection of a patient the previous spring who was a gifted gardener. As he remembers this woman, he surveys the patients around him, thinking they look and sound very much like the group sitting here last year at this time. He feels a familiar frustration with the steady parade of patients — different names, different faces, but the same illnesses — who never seem to get well. What is the purpose of this group, this medicine, this hospital, if it doesn't stop the pain? He wonders how long he can keep it up, medicating and hoping for health, until he retreats from being a psychiatrist-in-charge to the less demanding practice of tending to the worried well. He himself worries that the calluses from the Unit are becoming permanent.

As he enters the nurses' station, Vuckovic sees Sean Whelan walk through the stairwell door. Although the nursing staff continues its conversations and note taking, everyone is alert to his presence. His demands are unpredictable: he can be as temperamental as he is charming. He retrieves Susan's chart from a rack, sits at a desk, alternately skims over it and scribbles. Vuckovic lingers by the coffeepot and Whelan, noticing him for the first time, beckons.

"What's this three-day notice all about?" Whelan scowls at Susan's flow sheet.

"She hasn't put it in yet," Vuckovic explains. "But I think she plans to. After she was admitted, the resident sat down with her to go over her menu and told her she'd have to take Sustacal three times a day. She went ballistic, ranting and raving over how she refuses to have her eating monitored, and if we insist on making her take a calorie supplement, then she's bailing out. I'm going to talk with her this morning. See if we can reach an agreement."

Whelan grunts noncommittally. "Well, her antidepressant should be kicking in pretty soon. I'm increasing the Zoloft to two hundred milligrams," he informs Vuckovic. "How long you going to keep her on fifteen-minute checks?"

"Until I've had a chance to talk to her about her menu."

"Good," Whelan concurs. "I don't think she needs that much watching. She's gained two pounds in the last couple of days."

Vuckovic is skeptical, suspecting she is pocketing rolls of pennies for her weigh-ins, but says nothing. He isn't pleased to have a bulimic on the Unit; the staff has twenty other patients to tend to. And bulimarexia in its extreme carries the risk of all sorts of medical complications: low blood pressure and the possibility of faints and falls on a brittle, porous bone structure, bleeding from esophageal tears, and potassium depletion so severe it can lead to cardiac arrest.

Clinicians and researchers don't quite know what to do with bulimia nervosa and its sister illness, anorexia. On the one hand, bulimia and anorexia have a definite biological, genetic predisposition. Men and women suffering from these illnesses also show a high incidence of depression, obsessive-compulsive behavior, panic disorder, and kleptomania. Manic depression also tends to run in their families. As a result, the illnesses are often treated with antidepressants; the compulsive binging and vomiting of bulimia especially improves with such treatment, at least in the short term. Like depression, eating disorders are far more common in women than in men. On the other hand, many experts believe that the origins of these disorders are primarily cultural, and that the sex distribution demonstrates this. For causes, they point to social pressures on women to be thin, resulting in damaged self-images, family conflicts, and the assumption of a victim mentality in vulnerable young women. Some posit that these self-destructive behaviors are reactions to emotional or even sexual abuse. Given the presumed psychological basis of the illnesses, many doctors prefer to treat them with psychotherapy. While many clinicians prefer behavioral therapy, other avenues such as cognitive therapy, interpersonal therapy, and even psychoanalysis are employed.

There is no single treatment plan for bulimia or anorexia at McLean. While Upham House, literally a house converted into a two-story, unlocked, inpatient unit offering behavioral therapy, has a steady flow of eating disorder patients, other units at the hospital also wrestle with these illnesses. How a patient is treated depends on the practices and philosophies of her doctors.

When Vuckovic goes in search for Susan, he finds her in the tiny library, a converted room lined with bookshelves and furnished with lounge chairs and a Ping-Pong table. Located away from the nurses' station and the routine traffic of patients and staff, it is quiet and isolated, a place someone can hide out. She is thumbing through a book, *Food: Your Miracle Medicine.*

Sometimes Vuckovic presents his treatment plan to a patient

in small, gentle doses, reassuring as he goes along. At other times, when he feels control and a firm sense of direction and purpose are needed, he is blunt and forceful.

"Ms. Beekman, Dr. Taylor tells me you don't want to take the Sustacal indicated in your treatment plan. May I ask why?"

The emaciated woman is sitting at the reading table, taking notes from the book in front of her.

"Dr. — what's your name? — Voluminious? Like there's no way I'm going to drink that shit. And if you try to make me, I'll be out of here before sundown. *I'm* in charge of my eating, and I know what I'm doing. An eight-ounce can of Sustacal has two hundred and forty calories; the same amount as two rice cakes each topped with a tablespoon of chunky peanut butter. And that's a much healthier snack."

Vuckovic replies, "I know you can get the equivalent calories in some foods, but Sustacal contains vital nutrients and is less likely to upset your stomach."

"Look, I'm here because my parents freaked out. I don't want to put on a lot of weight, especially fat. Sustacal has a lot of fat in it; my diet has the same calories in protein form and is quickly convertible into energy, not fat cells," she lectures.

Vuckovic resists debating the fat quotient of Sustacal versus peanut butter. She is wrong, but patients with eating disorders usually rely on a library of nutritional shibboleths, some true, some distorted; this woman sounds willful and sophisticated enough about these topics to argue him into exasperation. And the argument is not about calories, but about control. Confrontation is not the way.

"I'll take you off Sustacal if you eat three of your rice cake snacks daily along with a three-meal schedule, and if whenever you feel like binging or purging, you tell someone, a nurse, a mental health worker. Whether it's in the middle of the night or while you're having a regular meal, you go to the nurses' station and talk to someone." Vuckovic locks onto her eyes.

"Sure," she agrees readily. "I did that when I was in the

hospital before. It worked OK. But I gotta warn you, like some-times I feel that way *a lot*. If the nurse gives me the brushoff, then . . ."

Vuckovic hears her carving out a gaping escape hatch but doesn't object. At least she's made a concession, and he'll re-mind the nursing staff to be alert to her approaches. Neverthe-less, he is skeptical. The binging, purging, and starving cycle is notoriously tough to break. Most of the bulimics and anorexics he sees get better relapse once they are beyond the hospital routine or a regular doctor's care.

"That won't happen. The nursing staff is here to help you, but you have to take some of the responsibility." He stops before launching into his "It's Your Life" lecture; this patient won't hear it. He gives her a reassuring smile, reminds her to attend as many groups as possible, and leaves the library.

Vuckovic expects Susan Beekman to resist her purging im-pulses for at least twenty-four hours, but when he stops by the Unit early the next morning to check the doctor's order book, he hears Nancy and Kelly arguing in the conference room. Staff members are lingering by the doorway while still others slip in and out of the cramped room to grab a binder or check the patient-status blackboard. Vuckovic plants himself at the table to get the full flavor of their disagreement. A priority of his job is to keep nursing staff happy; he puts their comfort and contentment almost ahead of patients', or certainly a close sec-ond. But recently his track record has been a little shaky.

Nancy lectures, "We don't have the staff, there's just no way. David and Kiesha are on fifteen-minute checks and Glenda's about to go into the quiet room. We can't baby-sit that wom-an." Although relatively young for a charge nurse at age thirty-three, Nancy is somehow matronly. Maybe it is the sensible Rockport shoes or the below-the-knees skirt. Although she is older, Kelly's animation and tapered-leg chinos make her look younger.

"I'm not saying she should be on fives," Kelly retorts in

exasperation. "I'm saying that she needs to be watched more closely. If someone had kept an eye on her, Rusty couldn't have smuggled her those candy bars from the vending machine, and she couldn't have barfed them up twenty minutes later."

"Kelly, we *can't* keep her under constant surveillance. Her eating disorder *does not* constitute a safety risk!" Nancy states emphatically, then adds, "She shouldn't even be here; she should be in Upham. We're not equipped to handle bulimics and anorectics. I mean, look at our kitchen — wide open and Heidi's always baking cakes or cookies. This is no place for someone with an eating problem."

"Dr. Whelan obviously thinks we can do something for her," Kelly shoots back.

Nancy rolls her eyeballs, as if to say, Get serious. We all know that Sean Whelan has his own agenda. Talk of another doctor's treatment is Vuckovic's cue, and he lifts his gaze to the two women.

"We are stretched thin with the new admission and David's return," he notes. "Rather than argue about this now, let's wait until the staff meeting."

For years, staff meetings on the Unit were pro forma discussions of schedules, pet peeves, smoking on the floor, and, more recently, union negotiations. But the tenor and frequency of meetings changed as McLean painfully contracted. Now, a regular visitor to the meeting is Mauricio Tohen, who, in his role as clinical director for the psychotic disorders units, tries to explain seemingly arbitrary movements of treatment units from building to building, and the more frightening question of which units may close next. The meetings are held at the end of the day shift so evening staff can attend; representatives from the night shift stop by when especially weighty items are up for discussion.

The management of the Unit as a whole, rather than the treatment of a specific patient, is usually the central topic. But

Susan Beekman has stirred up strong feelings. Many believe she doesn't belong on the Unit. The staff specialize in people with scrambled thoughts and radical mood swings; these are the types of patients they prefer, not the character-disordered types who delight in manipulating other patients and staff and don't improve when given the usual psychotropic remedies. Character disorders — at times referred to as personality disorders, borderline personalities, or antisocial personalities — skew a person's behavior much more than his or her thoughts or emotions. One patient with characterologic problems at a time was usually enough for Vuckovic; Julie, Matt, and now Susan threaten to overwhelm the Unit.

Scheduled for 2:30 in the poolroom, the staff meeting doesn't get started until 2:45, when most of the staff and Vuckovic are finally in place. Every chair is taken, and overflow staff lean against the walls. A couple of people hang by the door so they can slip out to check on patients. Staff at the nurses' station is down to a skeleton crew of two; they'll get a report later.

The question "What to do with Susan?" is not a formal item on the agenda but is broached almost casually, toward the end of the meeting, while the ultimate decision makers, Vuckovic and Sean Whelan, specially invited to today's meeting, are still there. It falls to Jack to lay out the problem of Susan. He is a reluctant moderator, although not inexperienced. The situation before him is a common dilemma: patients routinely play one staff member off another, not unlike a troublesome child pitting one parent against the other. Such "splitting" is regular fare on the Unit, and Jack often has to intercede. He starts by addressing Whelan.

"Sean, Susan doesn't seem to be adjusting. She's still binging and purging. We don't have the staff to put her on short checks, and she keeps getting into fights with other patients, usually around mealtime." He chooses his words carefully. "She's not an easy person to coexist with."

"So? What do you want me to do about it?" Whelan snaps back. While at times abrasive and direct, the psychiatrist is also respected for his forthrightness. The room is motionless.

"Have you considered putting her in Upham? You know they're much better equipped to handle such cases."

Whelan waves his hand in dismissal. "Come on, Jack, you know better than that. They treat every bulimic as if she were a sex abuse victim. That's not a tenable position, and even if it were, Susan doesn't fit that profile. She's got an underlying depressive disorder and needs the medical care you provide. She doesn't need a lot of talk therapy."

Kelly Reilly is slowly nodding and looking around the room for fellow travelers. Nancy has her eyes on Vuckovic for signs of what he is thinking. He keeps his eyes cast downward toward his papers and fiddles with his pen.

"That's not fair, Sean," Nancy protests. "They do a very good job over there. You may not like their method of treatment, but for some patients, it's very effective."

Vuckovic admires his charge nurse's backbone; no one intimidates her. He feels himself lately the need to back up his staff.

"She's right. We're not the best place for Susan," Vuckovic declares. "I'm sorry, Sean, she really should be in Upham. We're really too stretched out and she's pushing us to the breaking point. We're going to transfer her."

Whelan sighs in disgust but doesn't argue. The senior PIC has the last word.

When McLean was designed in the 1890s, it was intended to resemble a colony of elegant country residences. Each building was commodiously appointed and constructed with varying materials — the Administration Building with a yellow brick exterior, North Belknap and Proctor House in red brick, trimmed in sandstone. Today, the only building that maintains the nineteenth-century leisurely facade is Upham, and while many of the units at McLean are called houses, Upham truly looks like one. If McLean were a college campus, this would be the president's home. Situated on the edge of a large grass field, down the hill from the yellow Admissions Building, it's a rambling two-story wood frame structure with columned porches on two sides and worn concrete steps where someone's usually having a cigarette.

Upham differs from the Unit in more than its architecture. As the home of McLean's cognitive behavior therapy unit, its treatment methods are vastly different from the Unit's biological therapies. The director, Philip Levendusky, a congenial man who eschews ties and formalities, is not an M.D. but a Ph.D., a clinical psychologist. Patients coming here have personality or character disorders, which mainly affect behavior: bulimia and anorexia, obsessive-compulsive disorders, phobias, chronic pain, and some chronic depression. Treatment at Upham concentrates on symptoms, whether they be abnormal eating habits or foot washing a dozen times a day, rather than speculation on underlying causes.

Not all patients come to Upham from other McLean units. Upham prefers to apply its unique treatment to a mixed group of patients, and so has virtually no exclusion criteria for admission, except that a patient must have a psychiatric disorder. It accepts people not only from its own cadre of referring clinicians, but also from outside doctors, general hospitals, even schools.

Regardless of where they arrive from, every Upham patient joins the therapeutic contract program, the unit's way of teaching self-control and coping skills. For an eating disorder patient like Susan Beekman, treatment largely consists of learning to deflect impulses and fight the anxiety associated with eating. A patient also learns skills for managing particular problems, techniques like meditation, self-hypnosis, or relaxation.

The average length of stay in Upham is nineteen days, and being a patient here is not unlike enrolling in a strict boarding school. One's first day is spent learning the rules and routine. Patients are housed two or three to a room, furnished with twin beds, dressers, and night tables: functional, almost spartan. Bathrooms at the ends of halls are shared, and supervised meals are eaten in a wood-paneled dining hall that frequently smells of fresh-baked cookies.

Upham House, with lots of small rooms, winding hallways, and high ceilings, has a serious, academic atmosphere. There's little noise, except for the never-ending hum of low-toned voices in various meeting rooms. Many of the rooms are trimmed with crowned molding and, in the style of an earlier era, have false fireplaces. Furnishings look like a combination of yard sale collections and office pieces. Although there's a lounge with a television, VCR, and comfortable nooks, there's little hanging out.

On arrival, Susan Beekman's belongings are checked for sharps, which are kept in the nurses' station. For the first twenty-four hours, she is restricted to the hall; although the doors aren't locked, patients can't walk out. This is a privilege that's earned.

Everyone must be up and dressed by 9:00 A.M. Patients have to be on the unit by ten in the evening, and lights, CD players, and TV must be off by one o'clock.

Writing a therapeutic contract is a patient's first task. Susan meets with her treatment team — psychologist, psychiatrist, social worker, nursing coordinator — and drafts a list of goals. The aim of the treatment contract, especially for someone with an eating disorder, is to shed the feeling of helplessness, take control of daily living, and resist destructive impulses.

The contract contains about half a dozen distant goals, such as normalizing lifestyle, building self-esteem, and improving relationships with family members. For each of these, Susan lists things that she can do over the coming week to begin to change the unhealthy behavior, such as eating three normal meals and two snacks a day and keeping records, attending twelve hours of behavioral groups, wearing clothes that fit, asking a staff member for help in dealing with frustration, calling a friend outside the hospital, and writing down two positive experiences per day. The contract is not confidential. It's typed and posted on the unit bulletin board in the first-floor main lobby for all to read and to use as a yardstick in gauging each other's behavior.

For many patients, adhering to the contract is a struggle. The anorectic doesn't want to eat; food may repulse her. With each sip of the high-calorie Sustacal, she envisions instantaneous obesity. Or, if bulimic, and not a "restrictor" who simply limits intake, she can't imagine eating, then letting the food stay in her body. Vomiting or swallowing handfuls of laxatives after eating have become second nature. An obsessive personality may be asked to "be aware of negative thoughts of being dirty" and to "restructure thoughts," feats that require insight and asking for help.

Few patients sail flawlessly through their contracts. Backsliding and outright defiance are not uncommon. Along with the carrot of more freedom is the stick of fewer privileges and the quiet room. Like other quiet rooms at McLean, this one is furnished with only a mattress. Patients, however, aren't put in restraints, and no one sits at the door, which is kept open. Like everything else in Upham, correct behavior, even in the quiet room, is the patient's responsibility. The quiet room can be a mighty stick, especially for anorectics who refuse to put on weight. A standard routine is restricting a patient to the quiet room throughout the day with thirty-minute time-outs earned by eating a meal or snack.

The Upham day is highly structured, with virtually each hour earmarked for a meeting, therapy session, or activity. While part of the reasoning seems to fall under the maxim "Idle hours are the devil's workshop," behavioral psychologists argue that patients need to be instructed, and healthy behavior practiced and repeated before it will take hold. The meetings patients attend cover subjects such as body awareness, social interaction, assertiveness training, cognitive restructuring, relaxation training, jobs, anger management, coping skills, stress management, women's issues, men's issues, and gender identity.

Upham's approach to altering the behavior of its patients is somewhat novel. The traditional approach to behavioral therapy is what's called the "token economy," meaning patients spend hospital time being conditioned by receiving rewards for completing certain activities dictated by their caretakers. And though the Upham method also includes rewards, it adds another layer, teaching the skills and thinking that constitute healthy behavior.

Each week, Susan will meet with her treatment team to hammer out a new therapeutic contract. Some activities will carry over from the previous week and more steps will be added. These sessions can involve complex negotiations. Early in the treatment, suggestions for activities come from the professionals. While the nurses and doctors try to mold her behavior, the patient wants goals that can be met, something manageable, obtainable. So they wrangle over details: the exact number of hours of therapy or staff talks daily, or the precise meaning of the phrase "I will restructure my feelings of guilt."

At the end of every week, the patient's contract is dissected during Upham's most anticipated assembly, the contract evaluation meeting. At 10:30 every Friday morning, all patients, staff, and doctors gather in the downstairs meeting room to appraise contracts. This is raw guerrilla theater, with no scripted roles, no set order of speaking, only the imperative that patients be active participants. A patient reads aloud his or her contract, with the more accomplished, more confident players leading off. They present their list of short-term and long-term goals, tell the group how they've done, and give themselves a "mood monitoring" score. In mood monitoring, patients rate themselves on a one-to-ten scale according to how well they feel they're controlling unhealthy thoughts and impulses.

Other patients offer their assessments of the presenter's behavior. This can be a brutally frank exchange, with patients hashing over each other's actions and conversations. Some typical comments: "You're supposed to be working on being more mature, but you whined all day Tuesday 'cause you had kitchen duty." Or, "You must have asked me five times whether you looked like you'd gained weight." Or, on the positive side, "We had a nice talk Wednesday night. You asked interesting questions and made steady eye contact."

Doctors and staff interject their impressions, too, but it is the patients' voices that resonate loudest. Adept in the games and machinations of avoiding painful personal changes, they can easily spot such maneuvering in others, and, given the right encouragement, readily point it out. In Upham, patients become sounding boards for each other, and the airing of peer reactions becomes the central theme running through the contract evaluation drama.

Before a patient is finished with her presentation, the group suggests changes in her contract — like being aware of nonverbals, such as handwringing, or being more assertive in the stress management group. Changes in privileges are also aired, although the charge nurse has the final word.

Upham reports a high success rate despite the fact that forty percent of its patients have been here before. The unit doesn't claim to cure people but to teach them to control the impulses that have been ruining their lives. Almost all Upham patients complete their contracts. They put on weight, stop vomiting, halt compulsive habits, whether hair pulling or hand washing, learn to control depressive feelings, and conquer phobias. And by and large, patients feel much better when they leave. But for some, the lessons fade. Newly acquired knowledge, whether it be chemistry formulas or behavior, dissipates without constant reinforcement.

A week and a half after David Seltzer returns to the Unit from his emergency stay at Mass. General, he has become Mr. Congeniality. He organizes Monopoly games, cajoles staff members to make popcorn for everybody, and acts as nature lover and tour guide on group walks. The staff marvels at his ability to draw out the most sullen patient with funny stories about his inept suicide attempts.

Yet, while his depression and psychosis have burned off with the help of ECT, one symptom lingers. David still believes his feet smell and has taken to wearing white socks (changed four times a day) with sandals so his feet can get fresh air and "breathe." Part of David knows his obsession is irrational, and occasionally, gesturing to his oriental-style footwear, he jokes about his Japanese ancestors. Virtually every morning, he makes a promise to himself to ignore his feet, to refuse to smell the odor that creeps into his consciousness. By noon, though, he is overcome by the stench and slips into a bathroom for a thorough scrubbing.

At rounds, the discussion of David Seltzer's discharge is remarkably harmonious. David has become the Unit success story, and the staff has a special affection for the man who came to them suicidal and depressed, and is now alert, funny, and ready to take up his life again.

"He's still got this thing about his feet," Nancy reminds the people gathered in the poolroom. "He just can't let go of it."

"Don't you think it'll pass?" Frank wonders.

"Hard to tell," Vuckovic replies. "We've started him on Prozac, but it's too early to know if that'll break it. At least now he admits only he can smell them. Actually, I think I'm beginning to." Other members of the team chuckle politely. He goes on, "I think a stretch in Upham could help him immensely. A jolt to break that quirk, which is almost like a nervous tic." The group nods in unison.

"And knowing David, he'll make sure his contract has lots of loopholes." He smiles at the image of the supersalesman maneuvering for treatment goals he can meet. "He'll give everyone at Upham an education in negotiating!"

CHAPTER FOUR

The Demanding Houseguest

GLENDA BELLINI: ADMISSION NOTES

- *Chief Complaint:* This 42yo swf carrying a dx of Chr Par Sz presents for one of multiple McLean and psych admissions following an assault on her roommate.
- *History of Present Illness:* Pt. is well known to McLean Outpt Clinic, followed by Dr. Jeffries in psychopharm. Her last admission was on one of the inpatient units, Nov 11–22 of 1992, when she presented with similar delusions and was stabilized on Haldol po and decanoate. She was discharged on Haldol Decanoate 50 mg q 4 wks, Haldol 5 mg bid, Cogentin 2 mg q hs, Inderal LA 80 mg q hs, and Ativan 1 mg tid prn. She apparently saw Dr. Jeffries in one follow-up visit but did not return for her next appointment. According to roommate, who also carries a dx of Sz and sees Dr. Whelan, her self-care has been deteriorating for the last several weeks. Roommate says she had not left the house for fourteen days and had begun to eat her feces. To-night, she entered the other woman's room and berated her for planting insects and other animals in her mattress, and then began beating her. The roommate called 911 and police brought the patient to the

Choate Hospital emergency room, where she was given 5 mg of IM Haldol and briefly restrained. At present she's calm but unable to give a coherent history, repeating, "You would've hit the bitch if it was you" and denying any emotional problems. She shows orobuccal movements consistent with TD. She did sign in voluntarily.

■ *Past Psychiatric History:* This is adequately documented in previous McLean discharge summaries. She had the insidious onset of psychotic symptoms in her teens and was apparently subjected to physical abuse by alcoholic father. First psych admission was to Met State Hospital at age 18. She has never had remission of her psychotic symptomatology and is on disability. She has responded poorly to multiple neuroleptics and mood stabilizers, and has been recurrently noncompliant with treatment. There was a remote hx of hallucinogen abuse, and she has been prone to binge drinking, but not recently.

■ *Social, Family, and Developmental History:* Pt. has never married or held down a job. Mother has been institutionalized for two decades with a dx of Chr Sz. Father was alcoholic, and died in an MVA 15 yrs ago. No sibs or other family are known. She has lived in shelters, and more recently in a rooming house in Arlington.

■ *Past Medical History:* Edentulous, looks malnourished, no known medical problems. Did have syphilis age 32, recent RPR negative in Nov 92. No IV drug hx, never tested for HIV. S/P appy, NKDA. Smokes 3 ppd. No hx head trauma, paralysis, or seizures.

■ *Mental Status Exam:* Disheveled malodorous wf looking older than stated age. +orobuccal TD as above. Paces, poor eye contact, spontaneous speech rapid and pressured. Affect agitated, mood "fine." Denies SI/HI but assaulted roommate tonight. Prominent delusions about insects in mattress, unable to elicit other delusions. Denies hallucinosis but seems to respond to internal stimuli. Oriented times three, refuses formal memory testing but cognitively grossly unimpaired. Estimated intelligence below avg. Insight and judgment nil.

■ *Physical Exam:* Refuses.

■ *Diagnosis:* Axis I: Schizophrenia, Paranoid Type, Chronic with Acute Exacerbation

  Axis II: None

Axis III: Tardive Dyskinesia, mild

Axis IV: Acute stressors 2, mild

Axis V: Current Global Assessment of Functioning: 15. Highest GAF in past yr: 45

■ *Formulation and Treatment Plan:* This unfortunate woman has chronic unremitting psychotic illness with poor compliance and poor prognosis. At present, she requires hospital HLOC due to assaultiveness, florid delusions, and inability to care for self. Will admit, obtain baseline labs, unit restrict, begin Haldol 5mg po bid, Haldol Decanoate 50 mg IM, Cogentin 2mg qd, Inderal LA 80 mg q hs, Ativan 1–2 mg q3h po prn agitation. Have left message for Dr. Jeffries at OPC. She may benefit from a day rx.

> *Anita Velasquez, M.D.*
> *Resident in Adult Psychiatry*

"WHAT ARE THE USUAL BOUNDARIES in a family?" Art Wiggins prods the family issues group. The social worker is eager to challenge people today because the group seemed to sleep through its last session. He wants to see insights, hear revelations.

"You mean like dos and don'ts?" Kiesha asks timidly.

"Yeah, but not like 'do take out the trash.' It has more to do with psychological privacy and sensitivities," Art explains.

"Like 'don't ask about sex,' " Julie declares. The group twitters.

"And especially don't call your foster father a faggot!" Matt snorts, smiling at his outrageousness. His comment momentarily silences the group; sex is a touchy subject. Patients with characterologic problems or post-traumatic stress disorder often report histories of sexual trauma; while sometimes distorted, these stories reflect a personal experience. Paranoid patients, for unclear reasons, fear being labeled homosexual, and frequently are uncomfortable when a conversation touches on sexual orientation. Manic patients, on the other hand, are casual and usually grossly inappropriate about sex. The mix is potent, rendering any uncharged discussion of sexual issues rare.

"Elvis kissed me," Glenda exclaims to no one in particular.

As usual, the group ignores the squat woman whose nonsensical logic knows no boundaries of time or space. Her constant scowl, although only a reaction to the voices clamoring in her head, pushes people away. When they do interact with her, it is difficult to ignore her nearly continuous lip smacking and tongue protrusion, a side effect from years of antipsychotic medication.

Patients are respectful of other sufferers' illnesses and treatment-induced deformities, for the most part, except for the obnoxious likes of Matt Mullany. Curiously enough, many patients with severe tardive dyskinesia seem unaware of their movements or their effects on those attempting to communicate with them. When aware, they tend to be matter-of-fact about their presence. After a while, others react to the patient with the movement disorder as if it is not there.

Alex Vuckovic shifts in his chair to cross his legs and thinks about Glenda. Elvis and JFK are her male fantasies, and she tears their rumpled pictures from magazines and plasters them on the wall beside her bed. Although a thin thread connects her declaration to the current conversation, her thoughts are largely severed from life on the Unit. Patients like Glenda, whose mental illness has moved in on their minds like a demanding houseguest who never leaves, sometimes blend too easily into the landscape. They become part of the furniture — silent, vacant fixtures occupying quiet corners.

She sits in her chair, legs extended, feet raised off the ground. An uncomfortable position, but typical for some patients with schizophrenia. Usually, she is oblivious to physical discomforts; her mind, like a scratched, repeating record, fixes on something else. Once or twice, a foot suddenly jerks. She has been like this since the group started.

"When was that, Glenda?" Vuckovic asks, hoping to bring her into the room.

Glenda gazes at him for a few seconds and pulls her blue nylon windbreaker tight. "It's the truth!" she insists angrily, stomping her feet.

"I didn't say it wasn't," Vuckovic protests.

"Stop picking on her!" Matt leaps in, to Vuckovic's surprise.

"No one's picking on anyone," Art Wiggins says, noticing that the group is growing restless. Kiesha has started to hum, and Julie is staring at a pair of patients smoking on the terrace. "Let's get back to boundaries," he suggests. "How do you know when you've crossed over them?"

As if alone in the room, Glenda rises from her chair and wanders to a corner of the poolroom dominated by a stack of board games and puzzles. While Rusty ticks off all the things she can't mention to her husband ("He's got more boundaries than those Arabs in Israel"), Vuckovic surreptitiously watches Glenda. A restlessness has seized her; she shifts her weight back and forth as she rummages through the game boxes until a puzzle picture of a seascape catches her attention. She examines the box.

Vuckovic counts up the days since she was admitted in a frenzy of paranoia aimed at her roommate. Treatment started a week ago, the day she arrived and attended the first group, and the psychiatrist detects only the faintest improvement in her attention span. He recalls her medication history, a virtual survey course in psychotropic drugs: lithium, Thorazine, Mellaril, Trilafon, Navane, Loxapine, Taractan, Serentil, Prolixin, a smattering of anticonvulsants and antidepressants, and now, long-acting Haldol injections. She has had brief encounters with psychotherapy, but it never accomplishes much. Her mind is so muddled, her insight so fractured, that she can barely pay attention to someone for much longer than a few minutes, let alone learn to understand what has happened to her head and body.

And with the passing of the years, her limbs have become gnarled like dying vines, bent by tardive dyskinesia and ravaged by her inability to care for herself. Her wrinkled face is toothless, and she has burn marks on her hands and arms, not from suicide attempts but from simple inattention at stoves and with lighters and cigarettes. Her fingertips are a bright yellow, matching her dentures when she wears them. When not dragged into a group, she sits in the smoking room, puffing at cadged butts, seeming to disappear behind the thick haze.

"Glenda, please come sit down." Vuckovic aims his request over the discussion of family taboos. She doesn't seem to hear him, so he slips from his chair and sidles up to her at the game table.

She looks up at the psychiatrist, her thinning, dark, frizzled hair framing an angry face. Then for a moment, the lines jutting across her forehead and away from her mouth melt away, and her eyes widen.

"I'm so tired," she says softly. "My head hurts. Help me, or let me go."

Her gaze is steady, and Vuckovic is certain she is speaking her mind. He has seen this in other chronic schizophrenics. Despite their cage of insanity, they slip out at odd moments to articulate their agony and plight, before the dark force within pulls them back.

"I'll do the best I can, Glenda," Vuckovic promises, as he guides her back to her chair. The senior psychiatrist is quiet for the remainder of the session, as he spins through the options and odds for Glenda.

Following group, Vuckovic retreats to the nurses' conference room to write new orders. Also scribbling in a blue binder is John Graybill, looking very much like a medical student in corduroy jeans, knit tie, wrinkled white oxford shirt, and a prominent McLean ID. He laughs to himself as he writes.

"I finally solved Mr. Enderly's medication worries," the fourth-year student announces.

"Oh yeah?" Vuckovic asks, feeling as if he is on the end of a knock-knock joke. "And how's that?"

"You know how he's been bugging everybody about his meds, asking about their chemical composition and unusual side effects, saying his aren't working and he needs something else? Well, I took him aside and explained that for his medication to work, he had to refrain from certain activities. Like patients who take MAO inhibitors can't eat certain foods. I told him, 'The efficacy of this particular medication depends on voice rest.' That was yesterday, and he's barely complained since!"

Vuckovic smiles, pleased that his apprentice is learning to match wits with a seasoned patient.

As Graybill chats, Nancy squeezes behind him into a chair next to the wall and flops open a fat red binder. Her abrupt page flipping and stony silence tell Vuckovic that he may have run afoul of his favorite nurse again. He turns to her with his best "we're all in this together" look and tilts his head quizzically. "What's cooking?"

"Mark Tannenbaum was being discharged today, and I thought we had everything lined up, with him going to Hope Cottage. But it seems someone forgot to mention to his father that his insurance doesn't cover residential aftercare and that the monthly charge on that place is over five thousand dollars." She snaps the binder rings open.

"I just talked with him," she relates. "He assumed that since Hope was on the grounds, it fell under coverage for hospital care. Now he says, 'No way, can't afford it.' And, of course, he's heard about David Seltzer's episode down there and wonders if anyone was paying attention. Who can blame him? So, unless Nina works some kind of magic and finds a place for Mark this morning, he's not being discharged. And I've got to shuffle beds for the new admissions."

"Sucks, doesn't it?" Vuckovic responds sympathetically, relieved that for once he is not the object of Nancy's wrath.

The phone on the wall behind the psychiatrist rings. Frank, who has been leaning against the bookcase to hear what was happening to Mark, picks it up, listens, then hands it to Vuckovic, mouthing the letters "QA."

Quality Assurance is the office in the hospital administration that keeps an eye on patient care and acts as the communication link between units and private insurance carriers, Medicare insurers who pick up the costs in excess of the federal program's allowance, or Medicaid. Nurses assigned to the QA office monitor patients' length of stay and level of care, and raise pointed questions to PICs about keeping a patient in the hospital beyond a certain point of improvement. The Quality Assurance nurse keeps a close eye on all patients, but especially on those covered by Medicare and Medicaid.

The hospital receives $535 a day for a Medicaid patient, far short of the $729 a day it charges adults with private coverage (the latter rate, of course, is higher still than the actual cost of caring for the patients, in order to make up for the shortfall in the government rate). The Massachusetts body that administers Medicaid funds to hospitals, Mental Health Management Associates, has a fixed yearly budget and puts unrelenting pressure on hospitals to shorten the lengths of stay for these patients, usually the sickest of patients with the fewest resources. This pressure is passed on to the PICs by the QA nurses, a group whose natural sympathy for the patient and the care team is superseded by their job description.

While Vuckovic is sympathetic to the hospital's plight in balancing a shrinking revenue pool with the escalating costs of caring for sicker and sicker patients, he has a natural antipathy for any bureaucracy, be it the government's or his own hospital's administration. He doesn't look forward to the vexatious QA conversation.

John Graybill and Frank leave the conference room, but Vuckovic motions Nancy to remain as he listens on the phone.

"I know she's already been here a week and getting Haldol injections, and that the clozapine's going to take at least a couple of weeks. But with the Medicaid and Medicare, she's got the coverage, and, really, she is exactly the type of patient who can benefit from it."

Vuckovic frowns at the phone, and scribbles a word for Nancy: "Glenda."

"Fine," Vuckovic says flatly, indicating everything is not. "I'd be happy to review the case with the adviser. Dr. Elliott can call me anytime. But I'm starting the medication as soon as Ms. Bellini signs the consent forms."

Vuckovic sighs in exasperation as he hangs up. Arguing with Quality Assurance about a patient's treatment rarely bears much fruit. A half hour of torture at the hands of that entity usually results in an allotment of, say, four more hospital days for the patient before the exercise begins again.

"You're going to have compliance problems, you know." Nancy interrupts his reverie. "She's like all the chronics who come through here — does just fine for a month or so, then goes off and crashes. Remember Dana Singer? When she was admitted last time, her family was sending her more than four hundred dollars a month for medication. Know what she was doing with it? Flowers. Fresh flowers."

Vuckovic sneaks a glance at his watch. Ten minutes until an outpatient is due in his office upstairs.

"So she received some aesthetic benefit. Come on, Nancy, you know we can't let these people's disorganization dictate treatment. If we did that, no one would get clozapine. Glenda's an ideal candidate; she has TD and the standard drugs don't do squat for her."

Vuckovic ambles over to the large silver urn sitting on a counter beside the window separating the nursing station from the patient area. He leans against the counter, giving him a full view of the patient lounge, and Glenda Bellini. She sits beside a window by herself, not smoking for once, her face impassive but her lips moving, her body slowly rocking.

Nancy's voice again cuts through his coffee-glazed reflections. "I guess I'm afraid it'll work, and she'll look at herself and her life, and she won't have Elvis to protect her anymore." Nancy straightens her scarf, glances at the wall clock, and brusquely declares, "I'm due at a meeting."

The story behind the "miracle" drug clozapine highlights the most contentious issues in psychiatry today: How much are we willing to pay, in money and medical risk, to treat mental illness? Developed by the Swiss pharmaceutical giant Sandoz, clozapine was first used in Europe in the 1970s, but not approved for use in this country until 1990. Its prolonged path to FDA approval hints at its controversy.

Clozapine, whose trade name in the United States is Clozaril, is the first truly new medication for the treatment of schizophrenia and other psychoses in twenty years. It possesses three unique properties, two being the reasons it's hailed as a wonder drug, and one being the reason it's cited as a cautionary tale.

Its most heralded property is the absence of neurologic side effects, both the immediate symptoms, such as Parkinsonian stiffness and tremor, and, much more importantly, the insidious movement disorder known as tardive dyskinesia. Patients who take clozapine simply do not develop TD as they do with other widely prescribed antipsychotic medications, such as Thorazine and Haldol. The prospect of being able to treat a patient's psychosis, without risking this dreaded consequence, has raised many hopes; remarkably, the drug may also reverse a pre-existing case of TD in some patients.

The drug's second wonderful characteristic lies in how it attacks schizophrenia. When examining a schizophrenic patient, doctors see what they call "positive" and "negative" symptoms. The positive symptoms are hallucinations and delusions; the negative are emotional flatness, passivity, and social isolation. Clozapine's predecessors vanquished the positive symptoms but often missed, and in many cases exacerbated, the negative ones. Clozapine is especially powerful in combating both types of symptoms; it not only dispels the voices and bizarre delusions but also lifts patients from their crippling lethargy, giving them a new outlook and new energy.

But there is a dark side to clozapine, although psychiatrists disagree on just how dark. It produces a number of side effects, some tolerable and some less so. Drooling and weight gain are common with the drug. It also can damage a patient's bone marrow and interfere with its ability to manufacture white blood cells, a condition called agranulocytosis, which can be fatal if not caught in time. This rather scary prospect, and the high price of preventing its occurrence, are the source of clozapine's controversial reputation.

To meet government safety guidelines, Sandoz Pharmaceuticals requires every patient who uses the patented drug to obtain a weekly test of white blood cell count. Each patient is given a seven-day supply of the drug, which is refilled only after the blood test returns with normal results. The upshot of this constant (some psychiatrists say unnecessary) monitoring is a very expensive medication. A year's worth of clozapine, including the regular blood screens, can cost from $3,000 to $9,000, depending on the dosage. By comparison, a year's worth of a generically available equivalent of a standard antipsychotic drug such as Haldol can cost as little as $500.

The cost of clozapine puts it out of reach for many sick people. Only those with the means, with private insurance, or whose state Medicaid programs cover it, can receive the treatment. Ironically, the added cost of the blood test, designed to ensure personal safety, renders the drug too expensive for hundreds of thousands of schizophrenics, who are also at a very high risk for suicide. So far, about 48,000 people are taking the antipsychotic, but mental health experts say up to a million or more mentally ill could benefit from it.

The risk of developing agranulocytosis is small — less than two percent. Furthermore, psychiatrists say, it is readily detected even in the absence of white blood cell monitoring and easily halted in most cases simply by discontinuing the medication. Doctors point out that drugs like AZT and chemotherapy agents are far more dangerous than clozapine but are not subjected to such strict monitoring. The risk of clozapine is felt to be so minimal in Europe and South America that blood testing is not mandatory in any of the countries on those two continents. Consequently, the cost of the drug overseas is about one sixth of what it is here.

Perhaps surprisingly, once chronically psychotic patients are started on clozapine, many stay with it. The inconvenience of weekly visits to a laboratory or clinic become a social event for some, a chance to meet and chat with others who share the routine. As group psychotherapy, the clozapine monitoring system can be effective, but it is expensive psychotherapy indeed.

Not all schizophrenics get better on clozapine. While it's especially successful with patients who've responded relatively well to standard treatment, only a little less than half of the truly treatment-resistant population benefit from it. Yet often it is the last and only resort for the hard-to-treat. And when it does work, it can be a minor miracle. Schizophrenics who for decades have shuffled between mental hospitals and doctors' offices feel reborn. The hallucinations and delusions vanish, their thinking becomes ordered, and they become motivated to live normal lives. They leave halfway houses, return to families, and in some cases hold a job or go back to school. To a significant extent, these lucky few rejoin the human race.

To secure the weeks required to put someone on clozapine and see results, Vuckovic needs the approval of the Quality Assurance office and the cooperation of the patient. Unlike with other medications, the hospital's legal department requires clozapine patients to sign a formal disclosure statement warning them of all possible dangers. While some psychotropic medications are toxic at very high doses, none carries a significant risk of death, except for clozapine. The disclosure statement makes this frighteningly clear, warning patients of the grave consequences of agranulocytosis. But Vuckovic can be just as passionate about its constructive properties. He always finds that persuading a patient to try a new medication, especially someone who knows the insides of more psychiatric units than he, is like selling a high-flying investment. Clozapine has a reputation for working magic, but it can also bomb. He doesn't promise a stellar performance but broadly hints at a possible jackpot. But patients, like investors, are often skeptical.

Glenda is in the lounge area when Vuckovic approaches her, form and pen in hand. She's wearing two sweaters underneath a nylon windbreaker, to which is pinned a magazine picture of Elvis, and he wonders if she is waiting to be escorted somewhere. But she doesn't seem to be looking for anyone, and except for occasional glances at her pink fingernails, her expression is vacant. Vuckovic sits on the square oak coffee table.

"Glenda, I want to talk to you about your medication." He positions himself so he is in her direct line of vision, and he uses her name often. She is stony silent, her only movement an occasional flick of her tongue.

"Glenda, I'd like you to try a new medication, something I think will make you feel better and have fewer side effects than what you're taking now." He waits for a sign of recognition.

"Do you like my hairdo?" she asks with a girlish giggle. "Kelly helped me. And my nails, too." She holds up her hands for Vuckovic.

"Very nice." He never ceases to be touched by the nursing staff's care. On weekends especially, when the Unit is slow and quiet, staff helps patients with all sorts of personal tasks, from writing letters to trimming mustaches. Normally, he is more vocal with his compliments, but he doesn't want to divert Glenda's attention.

"You might have heard about this drug, Glenda. It's called clozapine. It's similar to the Haldol decanoate you're taking now, being an antipsychotic medication, but you won't be getting it in injections." He pauses. She squirms in her chair, still not making eye contact.

"This drug will help with your restlessness," Vuckovic tells her, trying to keep his message simple, yet professional. Sometimes it is a struggle not to address helpless, confused patients as children.

"I painted a picture," she declares flatly.

"Glenda, remember that we decided to give you the Haldol by shot because you had stopped taking it, and with shots, we could make sure you got your medication? But clozapine can't be given in shots." He emphasizes each word: "It's up to you to make sure you take the medication."

Despite his efforts, his stern tone sounds vaguely parental, and a look of fear passes over Glenda.

"We'll help you, Glenda. We'll remind you, and after you leave, someone will help you get to the clinic every week. Before you start this medication, though, I need your permission."

Vuckovic slides the consent form in front of Glenda's uncomprehending visage. He knows she can no more understand the legalese than she can read Arabic. In theory, consent forms for risky medications are right and proper. But, in Vuckovic's mind, the lawyers and regulators have taken a reasonable premise to a ridiculous end; asking someone who is floridly psychotic to agree rationally to a particular course of treatment is like taking a deaf person to a symphony.

He flattens the two pages on the table. "This says that I've told you about clozapine, and its side effects, and that if it causes a dangerous condition, then it will be discontinued. And that you agree to take it regularly and have your blood tested every week so that we can make sure it's safe."

Vuckovic holds out a pen, which Glenda ignores as she aimlessly scans the lounge. "Gloria put beetles and ants in my bed, and she laughed at me," she says, referring to her roommate in a three-quarter-way boarding house, and the incident that led to this admittance at McLean. Glenda stands up, seemingly signaling the end of their conversation, but Vuckovic knows it is the akathisia that keeps her constantly shifting or moving.

"The clozapine will help get rid of the insects," Vuckovic gently explains. "Sit down for just a minute more." He holds out the pen. If pleading would help, he would do that. Anything for a chance to help this woman. For a few seconds, neither moves, and Vuckovic, thinking she might refuse, weighs alternative tactics. He does not want to complicate this woman's or his life with a guardianship proceeding. With a drug that can be administered only orally, even that drastic step is often insufficient.

"Will it hurt?" Glenda asks plaintively, gripping the ballpoint.

"No, Glenda. The needle sticks hurt less than the shots you're getting now, and the pills are easy to take," Vuckovic replies softly. The small woman painstakingly writes her name while standing, with Vuckovic holding his pocket-sized appointment book as a hard surface underneath the papers. When Vuckovic leaves Glenda, she is standing in the lounge area, admiring her manicure.

Before leaving the Unit, Vuckovic initiates the process of entering the patient in the clozapine monitoring program with a phone call to an 800 number. He writes an order for twenty-five milligrams of the drug to be administered nightly and gives the consent form to the unit assistant for faxing to the pharmacy and the monitoring agency.

Groups meet every weekday on the Unit: there are "working" groups that deal with vital patient issues, like substance abuse or the medication group, which discusses side effects and compliance problems. Other groups help patients cope with daily living: the education group talks about health and fitness, and the transition group is for patients with a discharge date who are anxious about life outside. And some groups, like current issues, help pass the time, for patients and staff alike.

Frank Wilson runs the Wednesday night current issues group, a task that requires only a passing familiarity with recent news events and a copy of the *Boston Globe*. The thirty-eight-year-old mental health worker enjoys leading this group. Before McLean and a brief stretch working in a state psychiatric hospital, he was a newspaper reporter for almost ten years. He likes stirring up arguments, taking contrary positions, and poking fun at politicians, qualities that make for lively evenings.

The patients and mental health workers gather in the poolroom, push together two square tables, and spread out the newspaper. Matt plops down next to Armando Rodriguez, but then won't let Mark Tannenbaum sit on the other side, keeping the chair empty. Mark is in a foul mood because his plans to leave the Unit and go to Hope Cottage have been scuttled. He is in limbo about when, and where, he is going next.

"Armando, my man, did you see the Celtics last night? I don't care what you say, without Larry Bird they look like a bunch of high school kids. No, make that junior high." Frank shoots an air ball toward the wastepaper basket.

Armando follows the imaginary trajectory, his head bobbing to suggest that it falls short. "He shoulda retired years ago. You too!" He guffaws.

"Very funny," Frank replies in a good-natured tone. "But it'll never happen. I *love* my work too much! All right, sports fans, enough of this drivel. On to important stuff, like politics and civil wars and 'man bites dog.' " He smooths out the *Globe*'s front page.

"I see President Clinton is having trouble finding an attorney general," Frank observes. "I guess one reason is that he's trying to find a woman for the job. Why do you think he's having such a hard time, Kiesha?"

Kiesha sits up straight and crosses her legs. She is bright and perky, like an eager schoolgirl. The Haldol has brought her mania largely under control and she's due to be discharged tomorrow. "Well, maybe because there aren't many women lawyers around. Like, I know a lot of women have been going to law school, but maybe they're still too young, not experienced enough." Her tone is serious, as she weighs and chooses her words.

Frank nods approvingly and turns to Matt. "What do you think about that? About experience? President Clinton has no experience being president."

Matt leans back, slightly tipping the chrome-framed chair, and passes his fingers through his long, gel-cemented hair. "Well, some things come naturally, and you don't need any experience for them." He smirks. "But, like running the country, he doesn't have it. The man's inept. He's just a dumb state governor."

"Yeah," Armando chimes in. "A tax-and-spend Democrat. Paying all that welfare. He wants to tax the rich people. Hell, he should make those welfare mothers get a job!" Armando surveys the table, and seems pleased to see the others shaking their heads in agreement.

"But if he did that," Frank tosses out, "then he'd have to cut back on Medicaid and Medicare and some of you guys couldn't get in here."

Just then, Glenda ventures into the room, bearing her usual frown, accentuated by her pock-marked nose and distinct mustache. She makes a slurping noise. Matt motions to the seat beside him, which she dutifully takes.

"What's she doing here?" Mark asks angrily. "She doesn't know anything about what's going on." With his patient status due to be changed any day, Mark Tannenbaum seems to hoard his sanity, perhaps fearing contamination by delusional patients.

"What's it to you?" Matt growls, leaning into the table. "And you try to steal her cigs again, and I'll break your fucking face!"

"Gentlemen, gentlemen," Frank interjects. "Let's not fight. Glenda's welcome. Mark, what's your opinion of President Clinton?"

"He's OK, but he keeps breaking his promises. And I don't think Hillary's got any business running the country."

Frank scans the room. "Is she running the country? Kiesha?"

"She may be running this place pretty soon! Her new health care project is gonna change how doctors and hospitals work," she summarizes.

Glenda is rocking in her chair, and her mouthing noises are distinctly audible. She draws nasty looks from Kiesha, who glares at her. Before Frank can react, Glenda stands up and spits at Kiesha. The pregnant woman comes out of her chair and is lunging across the table when Frank grabs her arm.

"Stop it! Both of you!" He hesitates calling for help. Glenda has become feisty before, but she usually settles down with gentle prodding. He has half expected another outburst from her. Since she is about to start on clozapine, her Haldol has been discontinued, and the injection of medicine she received when she first arrived has not yet settled into her system.

Glenda sits but doesn't relax. "She put maggots in my bed!" The small, weathered woman is on the verge of tears.

"Glenda, maybe you'd feel better if you lay down for a while." Frank wordlessly appeals to Matt to escort her out.

Frank silently marvels at Matt's unpredictable behavior — vicious sociopath one minute, gentle guardian the next. That's what he loves about life on the Unit — the patients are constantly surprising him, exhibiting new facets of their illness. It forces him to be always alert, always in tune; dull routine never rules. While he would not have predicted an affinity between

Matt and Glenda, in hindsight it is not improbable. Both have a history of disrupted families. But whereas Matt has rejected and broken away from natural and foster parents, Glenda doesn't have his will or intellectual resources. Nevertheless, the result has been equally disastrous.

Glenda's father was a bricklayer from Manchester, New Hampshire, who married Catherine Mancuso at the end of a mutual friend's drunken wedding weekend. Despite the haste and impetuousness of their union, they seemed well suited. Tom Bellini's drinking and erratic employment meshed with Catherine's flighty, sometimes bizarre behavior. She frequently took long walks — treks that lasted four or five hours — then became disoriented and lost, to be returned home by the local police. Both Tom and Catherine had been born angry. Two beers were enough to set him off on a tirade against employers and landlords; she was even more easily ignited, screaming constantly at neighbors and squirrels in the yard.

Glenda's difficult birth — labor that lasted for over sixty hours until emergency surgery ended it — guaranteed that she would be their only child. She grew up in a household where yelling and arguing were a ubiquitous white noise. The cacophony was so constant that Glenda's oddities were barely noticed. A child with few friends, she had two imaginary companions and by the time she was ten, her incessant chattering with Dolly and Moo precipitated repeated separation from her fifth-grade classmates. She never really outgrew her make-believe companions; instead they became tormenting voices. By sixteen, Glenda was unmanageable, more like a boarder than a daughter. She drifted in and out for a meal or night's sleep and then would disappear for days. She attended school more often than she bathed, both infrequently, and had a brief yet intense affair with drugs, especially LSD.

Glenda's introduction to psychiatric wards took place at age eighteen, soon after the family's move to the working-class Boston suburb of Arlington. She ran into the street naked one moonlit night, screaming at passing cars. She was discharged from the Metropolitan State Hospital in Waltham to her parents' home with a prescription for antipsychotic medication. Neither the living arrangements nor the drug treatment lasted long. Her father, drinking heavily and rarely working, slugged her with a frequency and thoughtlessness akin to swatting flies. Her mother had retreated into a delusional haze, holing up in the attic above their third-story brownstone apartment, mesmerized by a small radio that she never turned off. After a fire in the attic brought the fire department but caused no serious damage, Tom Bellini admitted his wife to the chronic ward at Met. State, a place she never left.

Tom Bellini died in a car accident while drunk when Glenda was twenty-four and still, more or less, living at home. With her mother's institutionalization and her father's death, she became a disturbed and lonely orphan.

A few weeks after her father died, Glenda visited her mother at Met. State. Having traded her attic asylum for a room in the state psychiatric hospital, Mrs. Bellini was virtually unchanged from the day she was admitted. Diagnosed with catatonic schizophrenia, the older woman rarely moved or spoke. Occasionally, a mental health worker heard a burst of fast, angry words shoot from Mrs. Bellini's room, then silence.

The day Glenda visited, her mother had been given a fast-acting barbiturate, and woke up from her introspective daze for a short spell. The women didn't say much to each other as they sat side by side, each in her own cocoon, on the edge of the bed. Glenda gave her mother a disjointed account of her father's death and sharply quizzed her about a mythical grandmother she never knew. The visit lasted less than thirty minutes. The women bickered over the name of a kitten Glenda had brought home when she was eight, and which had died of exposure. Crying and rambling, Glenda stormed from her mother's room and never saw her again.

By the time Glenda was admitted to the Unit, constant bouts of paranoia were disrupting any possibly stable living situation. Insect infestation, satanic voices emanating from televisions and radios, and the evil eyes of various kinds of animals produced a frenzy of fear, and she'd disappear into the streets. Hospitalizations, initially to the acute ward at Met. State, and then to McLean after budget cuts closed the state facility, were followed by brief periods of compliance with prescribed drugs followed by relapses. The revolving door had again deposited her at the entranceway of her occasional home on Mill Street in Belmont.

A teary Glenda, recalling her bug-infested bedding, gazes imploringly at Matt, as if he can make the image go away. Announcing that he is bored with current events, he shepherds Glenda from the poolroom as she complains she's hungry and wants ice cream.

At bedtime Wednesday, Glenda receives from the med nurse a paper cup containing, instead of her usual complement of Ativan, Haldol, Cogentin, and Inderal, a single yellow tablet. She at first refuses the unfamiliar pill but relents after some cajoling. Over the next several days, Frank notices changes. While Glenda continues to inhabit a corner of the lounge, her restless feet remain motionless for as long as fifteen minutes. The morning she appears for the cafeteria group to be escorted to breakfast free of layers of sweaters and windbreaker, and with her blouse tucked in and tennis shoes on, Frank almost applauds.

Vuckovic feels a twinge of sentimental pride when Glenda attends rounds the following week. She makes eye contact with staff at the table and requests a "towns privilege" to buy a lipstick and walk along the shops. Even more remarkable is what she doesn't do: her mouth doesn't twitch and she doesn't blurt out disjointed thoughts. Her rate of improvement is striking to Vuckovic. With most patients, progress is measured painstakingly, over weeks and months of subtle behavioral changes. But every so often, the transformation of a patient taking a new treatment is stunning. This is the satisfying part of psychiatry for Vuckovic. Although his profession never offers miracle cures or procedures that mend fractured bodies, it does, sometimes, patch a broken brain.

Despite her striking cameo appearance at rounds, Glenda's condition stirs up debate. As soon as she leaves the poolroom, her social worker describes the behind-the-scenes developments.

"The Quality Assurance people have been calling daily," Nina reports with exasperation. "They want her discharged." She speaks nasally, mimicking a bureaucratic drone: " 'We're paying for this patient; maybe one of you would like to contribute your paycheck for her care.' "

There is a groan around the table. The backwash from the hospital's shrinking financial base is lapping at the Unit and its staff. This spring, for the first time anyone can remember, McLean Hospital is running on an operating deficit.

Most staff understands the economics of the situation. Psychiatric hospitals are highly labor-intensive. They're full of people, not rooms or wings of costly equipment. About seventy-five cents of every dollar spent on the Unit is spent on staff, and a year's worth of unit salaries tops $1.5 million. Other expenses — supplies, medications, food, professional consults — reach about $500,000.

These are direct costs but not the end of the Unit's expenses, because it's part of a large, expensive enclave. For a hospital, McLean's design is completely impractical and inefficient. Its quaint, well-intended, elegant architecture carries an enormous price tag. The hospital's 240 acres of trees and lawn need landscaping and its 45 buildings need heat, electricity, and maintenance. Another unavoidable expense for McLean, and indirectly the Unit, is the cost of administration — billing, receiving, managing. The Unit's share of these indirect costs is $2.6 million, making its bill at the end of the year total $4.6 million.

At the same time, the Unit's twenty-one beds generate billable income of about $5.7 million. Most of that money is due from patients and third-party payers, like Blue Cross and Medicare. But compulsory discounts imposed by payers, invoices patients or carriers refuse to pay, and bad debts take a big bite from that. Actual income is closer to $4.5 million.

So the Unit is losing about $100,000 a year. In many hospitals, this shortfall might barely raise an eyebrow, but McLean is not only a place for patient care but also for teaching and research. Its role as the flagship institution for the training of students from Harvard Medical School and its own resident physicians, and home of the Mailman Research Center, enhances its clinical units. This triumvirate structure is one reason behind McLean's stellar reputation. Although vital, teaching and research are not moneymakers, so McLean's patient units support these ancillary activities. When patient units lose money, everyone on campus suffers, including individual patients like Glenda Bellini.

"I know, I know," Vuckovic says impatiently. He hates the financial pressures on his unit. "But she's not ready. You people know the score. If Glenda's going to stick with the clozapine, she needs to really feel the effects, get a glimpse of life without voices and beds without maggots for more than a few days. She's still disorganized in subtle ways. Until we get some sense that she'll stick to her treatment, we run the risk of throwing all this progress down the toilet when she leaves."

Rounds adjourn with staff tacitly agreeing to help Vuckovic avoid the Quality Assurance watchdogs and extend Glenda's treatment for as long as possible. But the PIC happens to be going through the doctor's order book that afternoon when he unthinkingly answers the phone. Dr. James Elliott of the Quality Assurance office is on the other end, and Vuckovic listens and nods as if he knows the words before they are out. Jim Elliott is a particularly sticky character, an administrator who has not treated inpatients for a decade, not since the hospital's leisurely, sixty-day average stays. Now, he regularly expresses surprise to exasperated clinicians that a psychosis might take longer than a week to clear.

"I know she's better, Jim, but not *that* much better. Her sleep still stinks, I think she has residual akathisia from her Haldol shot, and she's still too addled to know to take the meds at home." Vuckovic purses his lips. "No, she's been on it seven days, not ten." He listens some more.

"Look, she's at seventy-five milligrams. That may not be enough, and she may get more side effects that need monitoring." He pauses again. "For Christ's sake, Jim, the lady could be a save. Give us some time to make sure."

Vuckovic holds the phone slightly away from his ear as he scribbles in the red binder, then hangs up. He scrutinizes the patient status board, picks up a piece of red chalk, and in the box at the bottom, labeled "Discharges," he writes Glenda's name and a date three days away.

Frank looks up from the assessment flow sheet he is filling out.

"That's it, huh? Well, easy come, easy go." Like most of the staff, Frank has acquired a fatalism about the limits of its influence.

"Who knows." Vuckovic shrugs. "If we set her up with the clozapine clinic, maybe get someone to take her there once a week, she might hang in."

Nancy comes in, sits next to Vuckovic, and flops open a new patient binder. Each page has already been stamped with the patient's name and accounting number, creating a scrapbook ready to be filled. She talks as she jots.

"Frank, you remember Melissa Stanwyck? In here last fall? I'm sure you remember — the talking sneakers?"

Frank lets out a howl of delight, then catches himself. "How could I forget the Nattering Nikes! She was really sweet. Giggled a lot."

"Talking sneakers?" Vuckovic interrupts.

"You don't remember? She must have been in while you were on vacation," Nancy explains. "Nicest woman. Chronic schizo. Was convinced transmitters had been embedded in her tennis shoes and that they were sending her messages. She'd sit in the lounge, staring at her feet."

Vuckovic tilts his head, wondering what the point is.

"She's back," Nancy says helplessly, indicating the binder. "Pulled a steak knife on a postman. She was living in a boarding house but went off her meds and couldn't hold it together. She's in Proctor House until we have a room."

The charge nurse studies the patient status board, reads Vuckovic's latest addition, and notes with a crisp finality, "We'll give her Glenda's room."

Every Thursday, up the hill from the Unit in an office on the third floor of the North Belknap building and just across the path from the Mailman Research building, a man named Bill meets with Francine Benes. Although Bill has probably never met Glenda Bellini, he has much in common with her. Just possibly, he holds some answers to the illness they share.

Benes is both a psychiatrist and a neuroanatomist. Although she and Ross Baldessarini have offices just a few steps from each other, the two scientists represent opposite ends of the spectrum of psychiatric research. While Baldessarini unravels the chemical secrets of the brain, Benes explores its structure.

Most of Benes's long days are spent in the Mailman lab consulting with technicians and assistants, scrutinizing data, and writing scientific articles. She sees patients like Bill, who has schizophrenia, to keep her honest as a scientist. Every two weeks she meets with Bill, asking about his work as an electrician and his significant other, a parakeet. Benes listens and watches carefully. She remembers fifteen years ago when she first met Bill and was doing her residency in psychiatry. Thirty-two-year-old Bill was brought into the hospital after almost successfully diving off the roof of an apartment building.

"He'd gone berserk," Benes remembers. "Feeling very paranoid, hearing voices."

Treating patients consumed only part of her workday; she was also assembling the pieces for a research lab at Mailman. As a research scientist and physician, Francine Benes specializes in prying apart the secrets and treating the symptoms of the most severe form of mental illness. Striking one percent of the population — almost three million people — schizophrenia, doctors suspect, has many causes and initially can resemble a number of other mental illnesses. It can emerge from apparently milder illnesses, such as schizoaffective disorder and severe personality disorders, or from medical conditions such as Huntington's disease and tertiary syphilis.

Schizophrenia has distinct characteristics — hallucinations, delusions, illogical, bizarre thinking, and apparent lack of emotion or inappropriate emotional responses. The disease often appears in the late teens or early twenties, and comes in a variety of forms, namely catatonic, hebephrenic, or disorganized type, and paranoid, depending on which symptoms predominate. Its most awful symptom, which is present in all varieties, is what it does to a person's sense of identity.

"Bill and people like him — schizophrenics, the acutely psychotic — have no sense of self, no sense of existence," Benes interprets. "It's hard to explain to someone who hasn't felt this loss because identity is so fundamental to who we are. It's at the core of the personality disintegration that happens with severe mental illness. But ask a schizophrenic about it, and he'll understand immediately."

Bill's absence of identity was clear to Benes from his first visits and his apparent lack of emotion. This so-called "flat affect" is typical of schizophrenics, and obvious in conversations and responses to people and social situations. The speech of the schizophrenic patient tends to be monosyllabic, with no give and take of smiles or nods, no eye contact, no effort to share ideas. When emotion does burst through the schizophrenic facade, it's usually isolated and incongruous. Upon hearing that someone has died, the patient with schizophrenia might giggle; when asked to pass the salt and pepper, he or she might erupt in anger. Like a spark from flint passing over steel, emotion flares, then dies.

Bill's robotic demeanor vividly illustrated to Benes the fragmenting of his emotions and thoughts, and constantly reminds her of the schizophrenic's disintegrated personality. "The ability to experience emotion, and to integrate emotion into the thought process, is the core of human existence," Benes asserts. "Imagine feeling an emotion and not having an accompanying thought. For the normal person, it's virtually impossible. But this is what happens to the schizophrenic all the time."

Bill inadvertently revealed another classic symptom after three years of treatment. In the middle of one of their regular talks, he remarked out of the blue, "So that's what you look like."

When Benes asked what he meant, he admitted that until that day, he had never truly seen her face. "For years, I was no more distinct than a piece of furniture," Benes explains. "Gradually he focused down and saw my desk, then the chair, then all of me, and finally looked at my face."

Bill's lack of attention, his inability to focus on anything in particular, is common among schizophrenics. It's what Benes calls "over-inclusiveness," which is caused by Bill's "loss of a central filtering mechanism." Instead of individuals or objects, he sees a flat, monochromatic landscape. His brain seems to have no way of organizing the bombardment of lights and sounds that everyone experiences. While a healthy central nervous system regulates sensory impressions, adjusting and arranging what is sensed, the diseased brain does not. It absorbs and magnifies all sounds, sights, even smells, flooding the senses and making normal thought and speech virtually impossible.

Getting to know Bill so she could treat his symptoms was an arduous, tentative process. He was often suspicious and hostile, sitting silently in Benes's office, barely responding to her questions. When he was especially noncommunicative, Benes noticed his head tilted slightly to the right, as if he were listening to something. She assumed he was hearing voices and worried about what they might be saying. Command hallucinations are very dangerous to schizophrenics because voices may instruct someone to hurt himself, or others. Benes decided to confront Bill about his voices, acknowledging their reality and power and hoping to learn their content.

"Are your voices talking to you now? About me?" she asked. Bill admitted that she was being talked about.

"That frightens me," she confessed. "I'm afraid of what they may tell you to do and that you may do it."

This admission surprised her patient; he had never considered that his therapist was anything other than omnipotent and fearless. Benes offered a suggestion to make both patient and therapist feel safer, and to show him that he was not completely powerless, that he had some control over the situation.

"If you don't mind, I'd like to open the door," she told him. "That way, if I'm feeling unsafe, I can leave, and if you're feeling threatened or uncomfortable, you can leave."

Benes also made a deal with Bill: in exchange for his trusting her with the existence of the voices, she gave him her home phone number and told him that whenever the voices directed him to hurt himself or anyone else, to call her first. The bond stuck, for one night when the voices were insisting that he jump off a roof, true to his promise, he called her first. A brief hospitalization resulted, and the crisis was defused.

Bill continues to show Benes hidden corners of schizophrenia. She has started him on clozapine, and it has evaporated some of the fog of unreality and lack of identity he feels. "For the first time, he's feeling more like a person," she reports, then adds with a touch of sadness, "but he's not used to feeling normal. He doesn't always know how to act, or what's expected of him. Some of my patients have become miserable as their psychosis dissolves. They lose the comfort of their illness, and some have stopped treatment."

As a shy, lanky student at St. John's University in New York in the sixties, Francine Benes logged B's and C's, dabbled in student government, and dreamt about going to graduate school. Her teachers assumed she would "do something with people" and become either a nun or a teacher. But she had an aptitude for science. At age six, she pried apart the family piano and flawlessly reassembled it, just to see how the instrument made music. Although engineering might have suited her as well as biology or chemistry, she was drawn to science and medicine partly to assuage a family frustration over her father's career. Though his ambition was to be a doctor, the Depression had scuttled his plans, and he settled for becoming a pharmacist.

For the first three years of college, Benes drifted, and her lackluster grades showed it. Getting into graduate school required a minor miracle, but she convinced the biology department at Adelphi University that she could do the work by agreeing to probation and promising to leave if her grades faltered. Her confidence never wavered, and she reaped straight A's and a doctoral degree in molecular neurochemistry.

She first met schizophrenia while studying at Adelphi, when she spent an evening visiting with a friend who worked at a mental hospital. She still recalls the experience vividly, remembering patients' faces so ravaged by pain that they reminded her of sketches by Goya. Before this chance encounter with mental illness, her neurochemistry had been limited to chick and frog brains. But lower forms of life no longer satisfied her curiosity; she was ready to graduate to the human brain.

When she finished at Adelphi, Benes headed to California and the City of Hope Medical Center for a postdoctoral fellowship in molecular neurochemistry. It was at a conference in Vail, Colorado, however, that she first became intrigued by schizophrenia. Dr. Janice Stevens gave a lecture raising the provocative possibility that schizophrenia might be like epilepsy, which originates in specific regions of the brain. The next day, Benes was riding the ski lift with a researcher from Italy and swapping reactions to Dr. Stevens's presentation, "Anatomy of Schizophrenia?" To Benes's surprise, the Italian scientist dismissed the lecture as irrelevant, declaring, "There's no point in studying the schizophrenic brain because this was done earlier in the century and nothing was found."

The modern history of schizophrenia dates from the early 1900s and a German psychiatrist named Emil Kraepelin. Although virtually unknown in America outside the medical profession, Kraepelin is considered the father of modern psychiatry. His textbook *Dementia Praecox and Paraphrenia* offered the first formal description of schizophrenia. It was Kraepelin who identified specific symptoms like hallucinations, delusions, and scrambled thinking, and gave order to what had been a random use of terms. He coined and popularized the name "dementia praecox," which means a breakdown in mental functions in early life. Naming and describing a disease is the first step to understanding and successfully treating a disorder.

Kraepelin cemented his place in history with landmark studies linking mental illness with anatomical deformities in the brain. He examined slices of postmortem schizophrenic brains and saw evidence of degenerated nerve cells. Although controversial, Kraepelin's belief that nerve cell death contributed to schizophrenia helped revolutionize the field, moving theories of the origins of mental illness away from psychology toward medical anatomy and physiology.

The next major breakthrough in brain research came in 1927 when two scientists, Walter Jacoby and Helmut Winkler, used a new type of x-ray machine to photograph the brains of schizophrenic patients. What they found — evidence of volume loss in the schizophrenic brain — reinforced what Kraepelin and other researchers had suspected: the schizophrenic brain was anatomically defective.

Despite the findings of active brain researchers, research into mental illnesses stalled during the 1920s and later largely because of Sigmund Freud, who galvanized America with a very personal, human perspective on mental illness. Freud first aired his ideas on this continent in 1910 in a series of lectures about a new science of the mind, psychoanalysis, and over the next thirty years, his ideas came to dominate American psychiatric thinking. His theories of repression, resistance, dreams, and sexuality, coupled with the radical idea that mental illness was the result of abnormal thought processes, not structural defects in the brain, captured the American imagination. Ironically, Freud was trained in neuroscience.

As psychoanalysis flourished in Boston, New York, and other places, institutes for learning and applying Freudian psychoanalysis popped up across the map. It wasn't until after World War II that psychiatrists switched their focus from individual psychology back to brain mechanics. The discovery in 1952 of Thorazine helped push the psychiatric pendulum back toward a biological, medical approach to mental illness.

The advent of antipsychotic drugs launched a new era in brain research, as scientists eagerly searched for reasons why they were so effective. The discovery that galvanized researchers, and continues to be the cornerstone of any foray into the psychotic mind, came from the Swedish pharmacologist Arvid Carlsson. His "dopamine hypothesis" explained that antipsychotics were effective because they reduced brain activity sparked by the neurotransmitter dopamine. The corollary to his discovery was that schizophrenics suffer from too much dopamine flowing through their brains. The dopamine hypothesis confirmed what many researchers had suspected all along, that the causes of schizophrenia were in part, if not largely, organic. For some reason, the neurotransmitters that spark the nerve cell connections regulating thoughts and emotions are out of balance.

But the dopamine hypothesis was just that — a theory. So

as some scientists picked apart the brain, probing into its structures and systems, looking for telltale signs of schizophrenia, others followed trails marked by genes.

The most successful gene hunters were a team led by Seymour Kety when he was at the National Institute of Mental Health. His landmark study of schizophrenic twins concentrated on adopted persons who became schizophrenic and examined both biological and adoptive relatives to determine the incidence of mental illness among them. Kety found that the biological siblings of a person who became schizophrenic had a ten percent chance of also being mentally ill, as opposed to adoptive siblings, whose risk was close to the general population's one percent risk. The identical twin of a child who was adopted and became schizophrenic had up to a forty to fifty percent chance of becoming ill. A clear conclusion of Kety's study was that schizophrenia had a familial, genetic, rather than environmental, source. Kety's discoveries about schizophrenia went beyond gene pools. His studies into cerebral blood flow and the brain metabolism of schizophrenic patients laid the groundwork for brain imaging techniques.

Francine Benes was just finishing graduate school as psychiatric research was expanding its reach. What really intrigued her about schizophrenia was the way it affected thinking and the possibility that the schizophrenic's abnormal thought processes came from flawed circuitry. She knew enough about neuroanatomy to speculate that a defect in the firing of neurons in a particular part of the brain might skew a person's reasoning ability, sensory perception, and even emotional responses.

Years later, she would pinpoint the fascination that launched her career. "The last frontier of our science is how the brain gives rise to cognition," she asserts. "The best scientists are always trying to get to the frontier, and if you're thinking in those terms, you have to think of schizophrenia. Because it is the illness that really takes thinking and disturbs it in very discrete ways. I really believe that ultimately, when we understand schizophrenia, we'll have learned more about the human mind and how it generates information and integrates affect with thought, which is so intrinsic to what we are as humans."

For Benes to learn her way around the schizophrenic brain, she had to go to medical school and train in psychiatry. Undeterred by the prospect of seven years of schooling, plus residency, she enrolled in Yale Medical School while also teaching neuroanatomy to undergraduates.

Ironically, Benes learned more as a teacher than as a student. Teaching brought her together with two men who eventually steered her to Mailman. The first was a colleague who wrote the book that Benes still remembers as a turning point in her life. *The Synaptic Organization of the Brain* by Gordon Shepherd stirred Benes's imagination, pointing to an area of the brain, the cortex, as the possible source of schizophrenic patients' inability to filter out irrelevant stimuli and their emotional flatness. Even more intriguing was the book's suggestion that this behavior could be the result of a defect in a particular system of nerve cells, the pyramidal neurons.

While absorbed by the idea of a link between an area of the brain and a singular schizophrenic trait, Benes knew that locating exactly where this faulty wiring lay among the approximately ten billion cortex cells was not only a daunting task, but perhaps an impossible one. Nevertheless, Benes was drawn to the possibility of pinpointing the precise damaged nerve cells that so disfigured a personality.

Just as Francine Benes was grappling with the human cortex as a potential abyss, she was introduced to a visiting professor at Yale, Ewald Weibel. Weibel owns a footnote in the annals of research as the architect of an arcane branch of mathematics that uses quantitative analysis in the study of brain cells. He called his science — in practice, it's more like a technique — stereology. The formal definition of stereology describes it as a way to assign a three-dimensional quality to something viewed in two dimensions, for instance, nerve cells underneath a microscope.

Until then, Benes had devoted countless hours to examining slides of brain tissue under a light microscope, depending on her naked eye to count mutating cells. Nevertheless, she was confident that she witnessed all changes; to her steady eyes, it was like watching a young stream subtly change course, slowly but unmistakably.

Then she applied Weibel's mathematical formulas to a cell count and arrived at a very different number from her own. Although her eyes told her that a cluster of cells was not responding to certain chemicals, the stereographic method convinced her they had. The young scientist acquired two invaluable lessons from Weibel's method: one, never trust your eyes, and two, damaged brain cells can be accurately identified and counted. This second lesson would form the foundation of the next ten years of her research.

From one of her students, Benes heard of a newly established "brain bank," a lab that was methodically collecting samples of normal and schizophrenic brain tissue. Acquiring brain tissue from schizophrenic patients is an ongoing headache for researchers. Many of the brains come from suicides or accidents befalling older schizophrenic patients, who often have a complicated history of medication and substance abuse, which affects the quality of their brain tissue. Adolescent brains, which are preferable, are difficult to locate. Hospitals and doctors don't immediately think of researchers when confronted with a young suicide or accident victim, and families are reluctant to release their children's brains to researchers.

One of only two such facilities in the country, the brain bank (officially, the Brain Tissue Resource Center) at McLean was amassing tissue samples from more than 450 diseased brains, and a similar number of healthy specimens. As if the extraordinary brain bank wasn't enough attraction for Benes, it was based at the Mailman Research Center, which was connected to a teaching hospital where she could finish her psychiatric education. The week she heard about the brain bank, Francine Benes applied for a spot as a psychiatric resident and researcher at McLean Hospital.

In the late 1970s, neuroscience was hot. Studying the brain was considered a sexy yet serious pursuit, the ultimate combination of philosophical musings on the nature of the mind combined with the hard science of exploring the biology and chemistry of mental processes. When Francine Benes arrived at McLean in 1979, the cutting edge for neuroscientists was immunocytochemistry, the use of immune responses to label cells. Scientists were developing antibodies to locate specific proteins in the central nervous system. Its researchers attracted attention from the press and were showered with federal grants. One of the busier scientists was Ross Baldessarini, who was toiling on studies of schizophrenic brain chemistry. But Benes doesn't pay much attention to fads. In fact, she took a decidedly contrary view, what she calls "kamikaze" research. The path Benes chose was unglamorous and precarious, the back room as opposed to Mailman's showcase. "My career was fragile," she says. "If I didn't deliver answers, didn't show anything, if the data wasn't strong . . ." Her voice tapers off, visions of professional ostracism, a teaching position at a community hospital in the hinterland, flashing before her.

Adding to her anxiety and the feeling that she was walking a tightrope was the recognition that among her neuroscience colleagues, schizophrenia was an unpopular battlefield. "It's not like Alzheimer's, where once the plaques and tangles were identified, you had the key. In schizophrenia, there's just a lot of tissue that looks healthy but with something fundamentally wrong at a subtle wiring level." While the field's lack of cachet suited Benes just fine — she prefers to labor out of the limelight — its back-burner status meant that funding and professional support were never automatic.

"I knew that I would have to deal with the likelihood that

my work would initially not only be disregarded, but even worse, the possibility that it might cast a negative shadow over me as an investigator," Benes recalls. "This problem was compounded by the fact that, in deciding to become a physician, my research career was interrupted at a rather early stage, and," she adds, "being a psychiatrist would constitute a negative credential for a relatively young scientist with only a small track record."

Regardless of the risks, Benes had made up her mind. "For more than a century, it had repeatedly been suggested that schizophrenia was a neurodegenerative disease, but there had been no well-controlled studies that addressed this problem," she declares, in explaining why she staked out her research territory.

Benes went in search of the "why" of schizophrenia neuroscience: Why do the brains of schizophrenic patients have fewer nerve cells? Are they born that way or does something happen during infancy or adolescence to kill them off?

In asking why, Benes juggled competing theories. Number one: the schizophrenic brain is damaged early in life, possibly during fetal development, then evinces symptoms of the brain damage around adolescence, and progressively gets worse. Researchers call this theory "neurodevelopmental." They suggest that early brain injury, what they call "perinatal insult," is the culprit. Records from families and mothers of schizophrenics indicate that a notable portion of the births of schizophrenics were difficult deliveries. The high incidence of complications at birth which may have reduced the oxygen to the infant (prolonged labor, maternal illness) made researchers think that children destined to develop schizophrenia might have suffered a trauma at birth. They explained that the effects of the birth trauma might not appear in a person until the late teens or early twenties, prime time for the onset of schizophrenia, when abnormal brain development may begin to show symptoms.

Number two: a genetic fault in the schizophrenic brain predisposes it to deteriorate gradually and reach a breakpoint during late adolescence. This pattern, in the language of brain researchers, is "neurodegenerative," and the model for it is Alzheimer's disease, which scientists understand much better than mental illness. Researchers are fairly certain now that Alzheimer's springs largely from a genetic mutation. However, a person's faulty genetic construction doesn't become obvious until later in life, when certain proteins speed up the production of fibrous plaques and tangles in the brain. As the years pass, these blotches of fiber disconnect and kill healthy nerves, destroying the brain's ability to process thoughts and feelings. Perhaps schizophrenia is like Alzheimer's and arises from a genetic defect which slowly, surely kills.

The debate over a neurodevelopmental origin versus neurodegeneration reaches back to the 1920s and remains unresolved even now, when powerful imaging machines can peer into live brains. Magnetic resonance imagers and computerized tomography scanners can picture a brain in remarkable detail, but they cannot pry apart individual cells. The search has to take place on a much smaller scale, at the microscopic, individual cell level. Benes's approach to this clamorous, contentious issue has been stereology, cell counting.

It is 9:20 A.M. on the third floor of the Mailman Research Center, and Benes, having swapped her tweed suit jacket for a white lab coat, heads for her laboratory. Down the hall from her office, the lab is a group of rooms equipped with cabinets for tissue storage, Formica workbenches, computers, and monitors. Two lab assistants — college graduates spending a year away from school before deciding what to do next — are hunched over Leitz Diaplans microscopes equipped with epifluorescence, which shines a light of a certain wavelength to pinpoint an image produced by a particular spectrum of light. What they are focused on is magnified on the monitor 3,800 times. Tucked under the workbench is an Image Analysis System, a computer that digitizes what's picked up on the monitor and translates it into reams of data.

Benes hovers behind an assistant who is staring at a computer monitor and what looks like random black dots on a gray field — spilled pepper on a bumpy tablecloth. Using a mouse, the assistant circles an area, clicks, then slides to another bunch of specks. The young woman, who's off to nursing school next year, has been glued to the screen for over two hours.

"How's it going? Is the thionine staining still weak?" Benes asks solicitously, squinting at the screen.

"It comes and goes," her assistant answers agreeably, "but mostly goes. I really am beginning to feel blind!"

The assistant is examining tissue sliced from either a schizophrenic or normal brain — she doesn't know which, rendering her scientifically "blind." Only after all the data are collected does Benes break the code to find out which samples come from which brains.

Benes chuckles sympathetically. "Why don't you take a break? I think we've got some new tissue in downstairs. Go have a look. See how the sectioning and slide mounting is going."

Benes empathizes with her assistant's weariness. In the early days of her lab she did everything from pickling new brain tissue in formalin solution (carefully labeling each vial "SB" or "NB") to cleaning the lab benches to analyzing columns and columns of numbers.

The nitty-gritty of research — hunching over a microscope and masses of data, wrestling with thorny mathematical and chemical puzzles, and constantly driving for something publishable — is physically demanding. It takes its toll. At forty-seven years old, with twelve years of graduate school and ten years of research behind her, Benes nurses her energies. Grueling years in the lab and the pressures to produce have forced her into the role of a CEO instead of a hands-on programmer, selecting the projects, directing the activity, and dealing with all the peripherals. The concentration of energies has paid off. Her one-woman operation has grown into the Laboratory for Structural Neuroscience, with a staff that at various times includes postdoctoral fellows, Ph.D. candidates, students, and technicians. In addition to managing people, she is also responsible for managing money: securing the funding to keep her lab supplied with high-powered microscopes and stacks of gelatin-coated glass slides. An essential role is to boost morale and keep people motivated.

"The stuff we do is very tedious, very labor-intensive," she admits. "It takes someone able to stick with it. You need brightness, enthusiasm, but also the ability to think critically. It's not rote work. You need to analyze what the computers are saying. You can't take on face value everything it tells you. You have to sit there and think about what the computer's saying versus what you can see."

The tissue the assistant was examining is carved from a potentially rich area of the brain that Benes has identified as a possible gold mine. While the spot has been searched before, Benes is applying a new process to extract its secrets. Benes is optimistic; otherwise she wouldn't be searching here. But her profession is littered with careers spent exploring tantalizing but worthless holes. Benes's excavation may yield only fool's gold, or it may be a bonanza.

Although composed of one hundred billion cells, the human brain weighs only about three pounds. The region Benes has fixed on, the cortex, the folded surface of the brain, is about two to four millimeters thick and has an area, if straightened out, about the size of a card table. The cortex (from the Latin for "bark") is made of gray matter and is arranged in six layers of nerve fibers, blood vessels, and cells. Its surface is much larger than it appears because of the many folds, called gyri, and fissures, called sulci.

Different areas of the cortex are divided into lobes according to skull bones around them or as a result of their distinctive function. The lobe or cortex area abutting the frontal bone is the frontal lobe. The other lobes are the parietal, toward the back; occipital, at the back and in charge of vision; and temporal, underneath on the sides. Together, these lobes form the cerebral hemisphere. The other major parts of the brain — the cerebellum, a walnut-sized knot of dense tissue and nerves at the back; the brain stem, which includes the midbrain, medulla oblongata, and pons; and bunches of buried tissue, basal ganglia, thalamus, and hypothalamus — control the so-called "lower functions," like muscles, heart, respiratory system, and hormones.

Neuroscientists investigating mental illness tend to concentrate on the cerebral hemisphere, where "higher functions," like memory, attention, thinking, feeling, and reasoning originate. Psychiatric researchers, however, don't confine their investigations to higher-function regions because most of the drugs used to treat mental illness affect not only the thinking-feeling parts of the brain, but also the centers for movement and involuntary muscles.

The regions of the brain are not separate spheres, each functioning independently. The brain is best compared to a city composed of individual structures, all linked by underground cables and fibers, continuously swapping information and instructions. The main power station for this city is the frontal lobe, which includes a cluster of areas, namely the prefrontal cortex, the anterior cingulate cortex, and the hippocampus.

These patches of the brain constitute the main components of the limbic system, the network of nerve cells and fibers which is home to our emotions. "Limbic" means border or margin, and it operates in the region between the cerebral cortex and deeper hypothalamus. This formation governs our emotions, attention, ability to establish and sustain relationships, ability to think about concepts, and logical thinking.

Brain researchers have suspected for a long time that mental illness arises not from a single flaw in the limbic system, but from a battery of defects. Brain scans show that patients with schizophrenic illness have enlarged ventricles (meaning the volume of the brain matter itself has shrunk) and nerve loss in the hippocampus. Additionally, a thinning of nerve cells has been noticed in a part of the prefrontal lobe and limbic system called Brodmann Area 24, so called because Korbinian Brodmann, a German neurologist, divided the cortex into forty-seven segments.

The mapping of the damaged areas of the frontal lobe and the limbic system has helped neuroscientists like Francine Benes fix on microscopic portions of the brain for clues to abnormal behavior. The region Benes has claimed for her cell-counting studies is a part of the anterior cingulate cortex called the cingulate gyrus. This fold on the cortex lies near the bottom of the longitudinal fissure, the front-to-back crevice that divides the brain.

Patients like Bill and Glenda are the reason Benes has concentrated on this region. These patients, who very possibly have severe damage to the anterior cingulate cortex, sometimes exhibit a condition called "akinetic mutism" — that is, an inability to speak or move, and an overwhelming negativism, behavior very similar to a psychotic symptom known as catatonia. The cingulate cortex, researchers believe, is where thought and emotion become either entwined or separated. The theory that the cingulate cortex is the seat of the integration of thought and emotion is bolstered by animal studies. Cats with lesions on the cingulate region show personality changes by growling without reason or purring at odd times.

Benes's initial cell-counting experiments reinforced her suspicion that nerve cells in the brain of the schizophrenic patient were flawed because of either a trauma at birth or a genetic defect. But a single experiment does not constitute proof, so over the years, Benes has been quietly toiling away in her lab, conducting an assortment of experiments, each building on the previous one, chipping away at the circuitry of these diseased brains.

The Laboratory for Structural Neuroscience is currently delving into the activities of a neurotransmitter that just happens to be the center of attention. Much to Benes's surprise, she now finds that basic scientists, not only psychiatric researchers, and prestigious universities want to hear about her findings. What has pushed her to the forefront is the faint possibility that she has located the neurochemical mechanism in a thin layer of the cingulate cortex which prevents Bill, Glenda, and other schizophrenics from meshing thought and emotion.

In organizing a rat brain study, Benes attempts to confirm what human brain tissues tell her. It may sound odd to use rat brains when trying to unravel a distinctly human disorder, but scientists have ways of replicating, albeit in a simpler form, mental illness in an animal. First, the rat is "insulted," or injured, at birth. Benes explains: "What we do is give the mother rat a stress hormone during the prenatal period. Usually we inject corticosteroids. Increased steroid secretion is really common to all forms of stress, for animals and humans. If you break an ankle or someone calls you a name, your steroid level goes up. And even rats have constitutional differences, with some very susceptible to stress and others not. When the pups are born, we sacrifice them at various ages, from day one to day forty, and collect the tissue and fix it in formalin. In this experiment, we actually counted cells in the rats' prefrontal cortex — the number of cells per hundred thousand square microns — to see if there was a difference among rats."

Three earlier studies all indicated that the anterior cingulate cortex of the brains of schizophrenic patients had less dense nerve cells, more nerve fibers, and, apparently, more neurotransmission, or impulse-sending activity away from the nerves. As Benes continued to count cells, hoping to pinpoint exactly which neurons were missing, she was astonished to discover that they were a type associated with the second layer of the cingulate cortex and with a particular neurotransmitter. It's this neurotransmitter — gamma-amino-butyric acid, GABA for short — that is propelling Benes out of quiet obscurity to address international conferences and editorial boards of influential scientific journals.

GABA is an "inhibitory" neurotransmitter, meaning it slows down the electrical impulses that pass from one nerve ending to another. GABA, in a way, quiets the brain and lowers a person's anxiety. External stimulants like alcohol, barbiturates, and anti-anxiety medication enhance its effect.

GABA is virtually everywhere in the brain, present in about one third of all messages passed between nerve cells. Benes started paying special attention to GABA activity when she learned that schizophrenic nerve cells showing marked thinning were a variety of cell, called "basket" cells, with a special affinity for GABA. With fewer basket cells around to absorb the neurotransmitter, more of the GABA was floating free. With more loose GABA, the nerve endings that "catch" neurotransmitters, called receptors or attachment sites, go into high gear. More GABA locking onto receptors and disrupting the normal flow of information processing could be the beginning of a theory for what causes a schizophrenic's thinking and emotional disruption.

Benes wanted more evidence to verify the neurodevelopmental theory of brain cell deterioration. If the insulted rat's brain showed the same thinning of cortex nerve cells and increased receptor activity, that would bolster what she was finding in the human tissue. So, for six months, two lab assistants counted cells and receptor sites in human and rat brain tissue. Their computers spewed out tens of thousands of pieces of raw data. To the untrained eye, the columns of figures — size of cells, number of grains per cell, number of grains per layer — looked like a nightmarish bank statement.

To Benes, massaging this raw data into something that makes sense is the fun part of her research. For people who relish fitting together distant, seemingly unrelated clues, it's the ultimate jigsaw puzzle. Surrounding herself with binders and computer printouts, Benes does her own calculations, figuring means and standard deviations. This part of her experiment — living with raw numbers and squeezing out meaning — is the heart of scientific investigation. Ironically, Benes must be dispassionate and analytical in order to solve the mysteries of human emotion. The process consumes days, weeks, and it's not until she has carved out two new sets of figures — one for the schizophrenic tissue and one for the normal tissue — that she knows she is on to something.

Benes had an inkling of the inordinate amount of binding at GABA receptor sites months before she could sketch her conclusions in a coherent report. She needed that time to massage the data and carefully describe her findings in an article that she hoped would break new ground for her lab. She wanted a bigger audience for her findings, not only neuroanatomists or readers of the *Archives of General Psychiatry*, but scientists who understood that her results were not just about schizophrenia but, really, about how the brain processes information.

When Benes's article "Increased GABA Receptor Binding in Superficial Layers of Cingulate Cortex in Schizophrenia" appeared in the *Journal of Neuroscience*, it was a milestone, a step out of the wings of neuroscience onto center stage. She joined the ranks of basic scientists whose discoveries cross boundaries and inspire more quests.

Benes's success is slowly altering her research life. She is now sought out to speak at prestigious symposiums, to serve on review boards of distinguished medical journals, and to write chapters for important textbooks. But the accolades and attention haven't turned her head. She is still counting cells, and talking with Bill every other Thursday.

"There's no Holy Grail in this business," she reflects. "I'm just chipping away at the circuits, and if by the time I retire, I can say that I've given this field scientific credibility, given it validation, then I'll be satisfied."

CHAPTER FIVE

Homemade Tattoos

MATT MULLANY: ADMISSION NOTES

- *Chief Complaint:* This 24yo separated WM presents for his 2nd McLean, 2nd psych admission for a court-ordered evaluation following an assault.
- *History of Present Illness:* Information was obtained from Mr. Mullany and previous McLean chart. His reliability is suspect. The pt. has an extensive history including an early diagnosis of ADHD and conduct disorder (see Past Psych Hx). Recently, he has been living by himself since being kicked out of his home by his wife, apparently in the context of physical abuse and intoxication. He denies legal troubles from this, and states that he and wife have reconciled. However, four days ago he was fired from a job as a meat cutter at a local supermarket which he had held for only a week. The pt. states that he had playfully brandished a meat cleaver at a fellow worker, and his boss, misunderstanding, had made him leave immediately. He returned the next day, and he was immediately arrested; as he puts it, "they ambushed me." The court psychiatrist's note states that he appeared intoxicated to coworkers and smelled of alcohol on both

days. Pt. states he had had only "one taste of JD" the first day and denies drinking that night or the day he came back. He states that he's been "wicked depressed" since being kicked out of the house, but he denies neurovegetative symptoms except "I can't get up in the morning." However, he acknowledges having drunk up to a six-pack of beer nightly, sometimes with a "couple of tastes." He states, "I can take it or leave it" tho, and denies history of blackouts, withdrawal sx, or DTs. He acknowledges he lost his driver's license several years ago due to DWI, but states he has one now. He denies other active drug use but acknowledges an extensive history of marijuana and cocaine abuse, the latter intranasally only, tho he states, "I got real paranoid on crystal meth once." He states he has never been able to sit still for extended periods of time and has chronic trouble concentrating on tasks. He remembers a brief period of Ritalin therapy in the past as being somewhat effective: "I could do my homework, but I still didn't want to." He does not identify a problem he needs help with, stating, "Get me off and get me a job, and I'll be your wicked dude."

■ *Past Psychiatric History, Social, Family, and Developmental History:* Pt. was the second of four sibs, product of a premature labor at 32 wks. Apgar scores were low but developmental milestones were on time except for slow speech and motoric hyperactivity noted as early as age 2. Oppositionality was noted at age 3 and persisted; psychiatric consultation was obtained at age 4 around an incident of physical abuse toward a younger sibling. At age 5, he assaulted his mother with a baseball bat and was referred for inpatient evaluation at Hall-Mercer Center. Apparently, biological parents insisted he be placed in foster care at that point, and treatment team concurred. No family history of psychiatric illness was documented in biological family. He was seen at Hall-Mercer outpatient clinic for four years, and had a one-year trial of Ritalin; treaters report some improvement, but truancy and acting out in class persisted. Pt. nearly set foster home on fire at age 9 and was placed with a family on the South Shore. No records are available since then, but patient reports having had contact with multiple social workers and at least three further foster home placements. He spent a year in a DYS lockup at age 15 after an attempted robbery of a 7–11 store using a water gun. He states he was introduced to marijuana and cocaine while there, and began drinking heavily when he left. He married at 17, has two sons ages 4 and 6, said to be doing well. There have been multiple separations and reconciliations; he states DSS "looks in on" the kids, tho it's unclear if a 51A was ever filed. He denies physical discipline of the children, who "are angels, just a little rambunctious sometimes, like me." He acknowledges multiple physical fights with wife, tho denies ever injuring her. There has been no legal involvement since his DYS stay; he states his lawyer suggested this evaluation when he informed her of his treatment history.

- *Past Medical History:* Benign. He acknowledges drug abuse as above, denies opiate, sedative, or hallucinogen use. He has a 14–pack year cigarette history, says he's "in great shape, working out daily," and denies surgeries or drug allergies. He suffers from seasonal allergies to dust and pollen.

- *Mental Status Exam:* A powerful-looking young man who paces almost continuously through the interview, making intermittent eye contact. His speech is rapid and clipped, often interrupted by laughter. He has a broad range of affect, states he's depressed, but denies anhedonia, tears, guilt, hopelessness, or disturbances of sleep, appetite, or libido. He denies homicidality or suicidality, specifically denying he meant to harm his coworker. He denies delusions or hallucinosis, and is free of gross cognitive deficits tho he often has to have a question asked twice. He seems very inattentive tho not at all confused. He recalls only four numbers forward and four backward, and remembers two out of three items at five minutes with prompting. He has a fair fund of knowledge, including presidents to Reagan. Proverb interpretation is bizarre: to the "glass houses" proverb, he says, "You gotta watch where you aim." When asked what he'd do if he found an envelope filled with money addressed to someone else, he says, "Hasta la vista, baby," and laughs. Judgment and insight are felt to be markedly impaired.

- *Physical Exam:* WNL
- *Provisional Diagnosis:* Axis I: Attention Deficit Hyperactivity Disorder, Residual Type. EtOH and Polysubstance Abuse

    Axis II: Antisocial Personality Disorder

    Axis III: None

    Axis IV: Recent stressors: 4; wife leaving, arrest

    Axis V: Present GAF 30; Highest GAF in past yr 30

- *Treatment Plan:* Admit to the Unit, 5' checks, sup sh/fl, urine toxic screen. Neuro and forensic consult. Doubt withdrawal given time since EtOH, but will watch VS. Suggest Ritalin trial. Would be happy to follow this case.

John Graybill, HMS IV
Arnold Schawbe, M.D.
Resident in Adult Psychiatry

"I KNOW THIS STUFF, I was a Harvard professor. Before that, a dean at MIT. That was until the space program called, wanting me to be an astronaut. 'Cause I've mapped the dark side of the moon. But I got too dizzy. All that gravitational pull." The large man with a beach ball belly, dressed in jeans and a T-shirt, paces the poolroom as he loudly lectures the group.

Armando Rodriguez has been on the Unit just three days and is already renowned for his grandiose tales. Charmed at his far-fetched stories, the staff is amused by Armando's manic renditions of his life. His delusions are farfetched, yet harmless. Now, Art Wiggins surmises, he's trying to appoint himself leader of the group.

"Armando, if you can't sit still, at least keep your voice down. You're shouting," Art says.

The social worker is directing the Tuesday morning family issues group solo this morning; Vuckovic is in court at a commitment hearing. All the chairs are filled and everyone is clamoring for attention.

"Shut up, Armando. I'm tired of your loony tunes. We need to talk about our feelings," Julie declares.

"No, we're talking about mental illness running in families, and parents or siblings or spouses who may also be ill," Wiggins interjects. "More than one problem can run in families: it's not uncommon for someone suffering from manic depression to also have a problem with alcohol. Relatives can have one, both, or neither problem."

"I've lived with, let's see, I think the last count was seven families," Matt says, "and not one of them was what you'd call normal. But then again," he pontificates, "more than sixty-five percent of American families are dysfunctional. Abuse, drinking, drugs, have split homes like a big, fat meat cleaver." Matt stands up and walks to the windows looking onto the terrace and continues. "That's what's happened to lots of us here. Our sense of family, our need for comfort and understanding and love, has been ripped apart by sick parents."

"Fucking A," Armando offers.

"That's the truth," Julie chimes in, as the other patients nod.

Wiggins is torn about whether to cut Matt off. While much of his tirade is self-serving, it brings up topics important to the whole group.

"In some of my foster homes, it was hard to tell who was the kid and who were the parents," Matt relates bitterly. "It was my money, the money they were getting for keeping me, that bought their groceries and cigarettes and booze. And half the time, I was doing the cooking. If it wasn't for me, most of my foster moms would've spent their days staring at soap operas."

Matt pauses to scan the rapt patients and pulls a cigarette from his pocket. "Anybody got a light?"

"Stop that, Matt!" Wiggins commands in a voice that startles the group. Matt puts the cigarette in his mouth and bounces it up and down.

"If you want to smoke, you've got to go outside or into the smoking room."

"Look, Art, I don't see the problem here," Matt responds reasonably. "I'm not violating my privs. The smoke won't bother anyone. I'll blow it out the window. What's the big deal?" He aims his question to the people sitting around the room. If one closes one's eyes to the tattoos running down his arm and his leather wrist straps, and hears only his measured, reasoned voice, he could be mistaken for a staff member.

"This is a nonsmoking area," Wiggins insists. "This is not negotiable. Leave!" The social worker rises from his chair.

"Don't yell at him like that!" Rusty objects. "He's not hurting anyone, and he's saying some good stuff."

"Yeah, that rule doesn't make sense anyhow. I've seen people smoke in here before," Julie adds.

"Not during a meeting, and not when I'm in charge," Wiggins declares.

"OK, OK, I'll put it away. No one's got a light, anyhow. But don't you think you're overreacting a bit?" Matt's voice exudes concern.

Wiggins slumps into his chair, fuming at being maneuvered into the role of enforcer.

"So let's talk about family situations when you feel like the parent," the social worker announces, composing himself.

Matt Mullany and his troubles are not unknown to McLean Hospital; as a youth, he was both a patient and an outpatient of the Hall-Mercer Center for Children. It was a good place for him, given the expertise of Dr. Martin Teicher with anyone suspected of suffering from ADHD, or attention deficit hyperactivity disorder.

Martin Teicher is an M.D., a Ph.D., an associate professor at Harvard Medical School, director of the Clinical Chronobiology Laboratory, director of the Hall-Mercer Snider Program in

Developmental Biopsychiatry, and chief of the Developmental Psychopharmacology Laboratory at Mailman Laboratories for Psychiatric Research.

The string of titles reflects not only Teicher's accomplishments but also his flexibility. While at heart a researcher, with an occasional foray into traditional doctoring, he's most happy zigzagging between research projects. Since graduate school, he's been following tantalizing clues to the same puzzle, the biology and treatment of childhood psychiatric disorders.

Psychiatric illness is not limited to adults. Serious behavioral and emotional disorders among children seem to occur in the same proportion as in the adult population: one fifth to one fourth of children might qualify for a diagnosis, but only about a fourth of that group end up in treatment. Mental illness among children and teens encompasses a vast spectrum of developmental and behavioral ailments. Psychiatrists count at least ten major groupings of childhood and adolescent illnesses, with the "developmental illnesses" affecting the most children.

Although schizophrenia, depression, and other forms of "adult" mental illness aren't unheard of among children and teens, they're less frequent than illnesses that appear unique to the nature of being a growing and learning human being. Some developmental disorders are obviously related to wiring problems in the brain — infantile autism, mental retardation, and childhood psychosis, for example. The bulk of childhood psychiatric illnesses, however, are complex mixtures of biological vulnerability and behavioral consequences. Children don't have an adult's vocabulary with which to register complicated discomforts, and the clinician must be guided by observation and a family's perception in making a diagnosis. The illnesses can include conduct disorders, anxiety disorders, eating disorders, and attention deficit hyperactivity disorder.

It's this last category with all its variations — with hyperactivity, without hyperactivity, and residual type (meaning it persists into adulthood) — that snared Martin Teicher's curiosity. Attention deficit hyperactivity disorder (ADHD) and its sibling, attention deficit disorder (ADD), are fairly common among childhood psychiatric illnesses. Estimates of their incidence range from around five percent of schoolchildren to an improbable twenty percent. In some schools, ADHD is blamed for every twitch of inattention and fidgeting, and it has been routinely overdiagnosed. Knowledgeable clinicians peg the occurrence of the illness, found much more in boys than girls, at the low end of the range.

An expert on ADHD children, Teicher has also been tracing the residual version of the illness — its appearance in adults. For years, psychiatrists believed that ADHD was strictly a childhood disorder that youngsters outgrew. And, in many children and teenagers, the illness does disappear. But for some, ADHD persists through adolescence and into early adulthood, sometimes even longer. ADHD, in itself, is not usually cause for hospitalization. But one of the intriguing characteristics of the illness is that it may accompany or herald more serious psychiatric disorders, such as substance abuse, depressive disorders, and sociopathy. These are the cases that end up at McLean.

Martin Teicher's office is just up the hill from the Unit on the fourth floor of the Oaks building, a square, red-brick structure that also houses a children's outpatient clinic. At the end of a narrow hall lined by a threadbare carpet and single side chairs for waiting patients, Teicher's workspace reflects his crowded project list. Although dominated by a massive leather couch, the office is crammed with other furniture, the walls are papered with degrees and citations, and the bookshelves are stuffed with texts, journals, and computer manuals. From here, Teicher orchestrates a multitude of projects that include pure and clinical research, consultations, and treatment with a select group of patients.

He speaks slowly, softly, almost in a whisper, choosing his words carefully. The professional lecturer in him, the ability to enrapture the merely curious, emerges in metaphors and references to well-known events and phenomena pulled from other branches of medicine. He's a master of the quotable quote, an understandable skill given the attention that some of his research, especially the study of the antidepressant Prozac, linking it to suicide attempts among a small group of patients, has attracted from the media.

Personal history and a touch of serendipity first led Martin Teicher to children and psychiatry. While a graduate student at Johns Hopkins University in Baltimore, Teicher had more on his mind than just medicine. The son of overweight parents, he was always dieting. As his medical knowledge expanded, he set out to develop the "ultimate diet pill." He began his search by studying how the body regulates eating and drinking, leading him to the field of developmental research. Knowing that childhood development patterns lay the foundations for adult traits, he observed and measured how young bodies consume food and process calories.

Teicher never invented his perfect diet medication and to this day watches his weight, but he did acquire a fascination for how psychiatric illness develops. (In the category of remarkable coincidences, the treatment for ADHD that Teicher and other doctors use today is psychostimulant medication also taken as an appetite suppressant.) His introduction to ADHD happened by accident. Following a string of educational and research exploits, Teicher was tapped to serve as director of a new research unit, the Hall-Mercer Snider Program in Developmental Biopsychiatry, and to operate McLean's children's unit, the Hall-Mercer Center.

As the new director attending staff meetings at the center, he was struck by the fact that few of the children being admitted were given a firm diagnosis. Teicher was well aware from his training of the difficulties in questioning children about their symptoms or counting on often unreliable and sometimes unavailable family members for clinical data. But he noted that pediatric medicine did not have a problem with the issues of diagnosis, given the same constraints; he surmised that pediatric psychiatrists were uncomfortable with labeling, and presumably scapegoating, innocent children.

Teicher felt the best way to fight this ingrained tendency was to create objective criteria for diagnosis. He wanted a diagnostic tool that was noninvasive, easy to use, would not be influenced by bias in the observer, and could give a ready answer to the question, "Does this child have ADHD, depression, or 'merely' a conduct disorder?" For the most reliable clue to illness, he zeroed in on the youngsters' level of activity and its variation over the course of a day — factors related to their biorhythms.

Why daily activity patterns open a window into psychiatric illness is one of the more intriguing though lesser-known questions of this specialty. The answer lies in the phenomenon of circadian rhythms, the twenty-four-hour cycle of sleep, wakefulness, and biology which affects everyone. Researchers have discovered that abnormal circadian cycles can signal psychiatric disturbances, and that the precise pattern of an abnormal cycle points to a specific illness.

For instance, Teicher recalls a twelve-year-old boy he met in family therapy. Although the youngster was doing well at school, he was hostile and combative at home, and experts assumed the source was his relationship with his parents. Teicher measured the boy's alternating periods of high and low energy for three days and found that instead of exhibiting a series of peaks and valleys for each twenty-four-hour period, the boy's activity profile showed a low-intensity flatness. Furthermore, his activity cycle repeated over twelve hours, half the normal time. The youngster was waking up tired and irritable, and then perking up around bedtime, a pattern that sparked repeated arguments with his parents. Teicher explains the ultimate diagnosis: "A detailed mathematical analysis of that activity profile strongly suggested depression. We treated the boy with low doses of an antidepressant and he quickly went from being a monster to a happy, loving, friendly kid."

With attention deficit hyperactivity disorder, a person's activity level is especially telling. The activity profile of both a child or an adult with ADHD reveals a twenty-four-hour cycle, but most of the activity is high-energy with little quiet or low-intensity activity.

To measure activity, Teicher devised a computerized monitor a little smaller than a deck of cards which attaches to the waist or wrist. In designing this monitor, Teicher found that the computerized technology was readily available; the tricky part was persuading children to wear it. He brought them around by adding a flashy pouch in pastel colors, plus small incentives, like make-up for the girls and milkshakes for the boys. Adults usually don't need persuasion to wear the device, but Teicher still doesn't strap it on all patients. Some of his more disorganized patients don't return the expensive gadget.

Since creating the pocket-sized activity monitor, Teicher has invented a more sophisticated device. Dubbed the Infrared Motion Analysis System, it's a computer that measures body motion. A patient's clothes are studded with reflective markers, small light pieces of metal, and the patient is asked to sit at a computer and perform an attention test. Fifty times a second, the computer measures the horizontal and vertical position of every marker. In essence, it monitors how much a test taker fidgets.

The results, say Teicher, have been "incredibly accurate. It's absolutely black and white" for distinguishing ADHD children from their normal counterparts. Normal children, Teicher has found, move ten millimeters per second, on average; the ADHD child moves forty millimeters per second.

Teicher's motion analysis system is fairly new, and he's still collecting results and measuring the daily activity of his young patients. But if the results hold up over time and under professional scrutiny, Teicher will have developed what may be the *only* definitive and wholly objective diagnostic tool for a psychiatric illness.

The symptoms of ADHD in children are clear. The *Diagnostic and Statistical Manual* says a child has to show symptoms before age seven and they have to persist for at least six months. Its trademark is the "attention deficit," which appears in a child's easy distractibility, impatience, inability to pay attention or concentrate on a single activity. Impulsiveness is another symptom and usually obvious in a tendency to blurt out answers, talk excessively, and in countless thoughtless acts, like running into the street or grabbing dangerous tools. Sometimes the child is socially impulsive, creating behavior problems that lead to further emotional difficulties. The ADHD child is often domineering or bossy with playmates, irritable, temperamental, and moody, displays low self-esteem, and is generally immature for his age. Children with the hyperactive variety of the disorder are constantly physically restless, fidgeting, squirming, always into things, full of energy, and never quiet.

For children with severe ADHD, usually complicated by serious behavioral disorders, McLean's Hall-Mercer Center is a last resort. Youngsters arrive at the unit, a square gray concrete multilevel building in the middle of the McLean campus, having exhausted all outpatient treatment possibilities. They're often brought here in an emergency, referred from therapists, schools, or social service agencies. The children are rarely delivered by parents; many have already run the gamut of foster homes and residential treatment centers.

Virtually all of the children Teicher meets in the Hall-Mercer Center suffer a serious, frequently life-threatening illness in addition to ADHD. In today's climate of managed care, children, like adults, aren't allowed into psychiatric units unless they are in dire straits, usually defined as an imminent risk to themselves or a danger to someone else. Nevertheless, more than two hundred children — ages three to seventeen, the average age being around eleven or twelve — come through the center every year.

Teicher recalls a four-year-old ADHD patient admitted into the Hall-Mercer Center with a referral from a social service agency; he and his mother were homeless after being ejected from his grandparents' house because he had repeatedly set fire to it. At the center, the boy was housed in the Green unit, which is for the youngest children. Children in what are called the midlatency years, around ten years old, stay in the Orange unit, and adolescents in the Yellow unit.

Though appearing cold and hard from the outside, Hall-Mercer has clusters of small rooms whose skylights and low ceilings create the safe, secure feeling of a cave. The children sleep four to a room; the rooms are furnished with single beds and simple oak dressers. The walls are splattered with kids' drawings; cutouts of music and sports stars from magazines; and charts with each child's name, a list of behavioral goals ("listen and follow directions better"), and gold stars for success. Scattered shoes, clothes spilling from half-closed drawers, and rumpled beds confirm that the rooms are inhabited by kids required to make at least some effort toward tidiness.

Most of the children in the center are boys. While boys seem to develop ADHD more than girls, their other mental illnesses are more obvious. Teicher explains, "Boys tend to act out more, be discipline problems. Girls with depression, for instance, may keep it to themselves and continue going to school, living at home. But boys get in fights and create big discipline problems."

When Teicher first met his four-year-old patient, the boy wouldn't talk to him. It wasn't as a doctor or authority figure that Teicher frightened him. The boy was terrified of men. The boy was also "hyperactive beyond description" and bit and kicked anyone who came near. Teicher tried talking to the boy in the playroom, but the youngster pounded and threw toys, and said little. However, by just watching the youngster Teicher detected two other ADHD symptoms: impulsiveness and dis-tractibility. Teicher's suspicions about abuse were later con-firmed: he had been neglected by his mother, and his father had regularly burned him and lifted him bodily by his genitals.

The little boy was so hostile and aggressive that containing this became the number-one priority for Teicher and the cen-ter's staff. Teicher quickly prescribed the standard medication for ADHD, Ritalin. But instead of calming down and becoming more attentive, as expected, the boy grew even more unruly. Within just a day of taking the medication, he was cursing the staff and developing motor and vocal tics. Teicher immediately wondered whether the boy had Tourette's syndrome, a disorder that causes uncontrollable verbal tics and outbursts.

Teicher discontinued the Ritalin and attacked the boy's symptoms from another direction, prescribing a low dose of Haldol, a powerful antipsychotic drug that specifically combats the tics and vocalizations of Tourette's. Although the boy did not have Tourette's, the drug began to show results within weeks. Teicher visited him almost daily, taking him for walks and playing games. Slowly, the four-year-old's personality be-gan to emerge, and he opened up to Teicher, revealing his fasci-nation with fire and his fear of his father.

Teicher became attached to the sweet, loving child who grew healthier every week. Because he was under five, the legal age for placement in a foster home, the boy stayed at McLean for almost three months as Teicher learned more about him and his illness. The psychiatrist asked the child to wear an activity monitor; the readings were the most active Teicher had ever seen.

Teicher's young patient was eventually sent to the New En-gland Home for Little Wanderers, although he still returns to McLean each month to visit with the psychiatrist, who watches his activity level and monitors his medication. Teicher marvels at what he has learned from this young boy. The activity moni-tor soundly confirmed Teicher's theory of circadian rhythms and hyperactivity, but his experience with the child opened the researcher's eyes to the consequences of early child abuse. A frequent accompaniment to ADHD, according to Teicher, is the disorder that arises from abuse, post-traumatic stress syndrome. The link, explains Teicher, makes sense: "Certain kids are likely to be abused because they're hard to manage, they're colicky babies. ADHD children tend to upset and annoy parents because they're always into things and don't listen."

Teicher was surprised, not by the horrific abuse or psychological damage, but by how quickly the boy mended. "What was so interesting was how well he was able to recover from severe early trauma, once the symptoms were brought under control. He's now stable, not pathologically fragile, and can deal with his mother abandoning him." The prognosis is good for one of the Hall-Mercer Center's most extreme cases of ADHD. "He'll do well," Teicher concludes with a mixture of professional coolness and admiration for his patient's resiliency. "He's remarkably intelligent, very good-looking, charming, affectionate. He's still somewhat hyperactive and impulsive, and doesn't have good family support. But he brings out good responses in people."

Like the children Marty Teicher sees, his adult ADHD patients suffer from more than attention deficit and hyperactivity. It wasn't until 1980 that doctors recognized that some people never outgrow their childhood impatience, restlessness, and inability to concentrate or stick to a task.

"One of the most remarkable things about adult ADHD patients' activity profiles is that they're the same as ADHD children. They have the same fundamental defect, lacking periods of quiet restfulness or sitting still. It's just less obtrusive with an adult," Teicher reports.

The week Matt Mullany entered the Unit, Teicher was treating a man whose ADD had turned his life upside down, even though he didn't show signs of the hyperactive variety of the illness. He was rash and impulsive, even during the most innocuous tasks, such as driving, and his frantic lane-changing had become dangerous. The impulsivity spilled over to his work, and he often argued with coworkers. If even mildly criticized, he was likely to erupt into a tirade, turn over desks, and abruptly quit.

Adult ADD, or ADD, residual type, is still a novel disorder that has not yet made it into the official psychiatric guidebook. So psychiatrists like Teicher are fashioning their own catalogue of telltale signs. The leading expert in the field, Dr. Paul Wender, has sketched out a list of symptoms that Teicher and others reach for when first meeting a patient. The essential requirement is having shown signs of the illness before age seven; Teicher asks his grown-up patients to dig out school records and report cards to look for revealing notes about fidgeting or being easily distracted. In fact, the symptoms — inattention, distractibility, hyperactivity, and impulsiveness — are remarkably similar to those found in children. Adults with the illness are also prone to mood swings and temper tantrums, and show a low tolerance for stress; they're typically thin-skinned and become easily flustered. For a grown-up, one of the most disruptive signs is disorganization, whether it's an obvious inability to organize a schedule or paperwork, or a more subtle inability to keep up with work tasks expected at a given educational level. One of Teicher's patients, a lawyer, repeatedly lost client files.

In the same backward way that a clearer recognition of manic depression is based on a patient's response to lithium, the success of certain drugs in controlling ADD has helped to confirm the presence and nature of the illness. One of the paradoxes of psychiatry is the effectiveness of amphetamines, drugs designed to stimulate the central nervous system, in quieting hyperactivity and helping a child or adult settle down and concentrate. Normally, these drugs can be very addictive. But in an ADD patient, the medications — either d-amphetamine or methylphenidate, known by its trade name, Ritalin — aren't habit-forming. Adult patients, however, seem to be more likely to encounter the downside of the drug, its addictive quality.

Most adult ADD patients, says Teicher, are motivated and anxious to quell their illness and so aren't tempted to abuse their medication. If substance abuse is a possibility, a psychiatrist prescribes a low dose of some other medication, such as a powerful and nonaddictive class of antidepressants called monoamine oxidase inhibitors. Interestingly, antidepressants like imipramine or newer ones such as fluoxetine (Prozac) appear to be almost as effective for the treatment of primary ADD as the stimulants are, even in children.

Matt Mullany's behavior epitomizes what most experts consider adult attention deficit disorder. But he poses a special problem for the Unit because psychosis is not his primary illness. His attention deficit disorder has flourished and mutated, or perhaps joined hands, with a pre-existing tendency to sociopathy, one of the most untreatable psychiatric illnesses. From the Unit's point of view, he is the worst kind of patient: an angry, potentially violent sociopath who cannot be readily patched up with medication and released. Not only is the Unit's standard treatment, medication, largely ineffective with his illness, but many of his treaters feel a great antipathy toward him; there is a strong possibility that countertransference could affect his treatment. A nurse reflects the Unit's attitude: "I don't work well with personality disorders, substance abuse problems," she declares. "I don't like their manipulation, the little mind games, the deliberate lying and defying of authority."

Following the Tuesday morning family issues group, the occupational therapist takes Matt into a small interview room to give him a special test. The ACL, for Allen Cognitive Levels, tests a patient's thinking — logic, organization, ability to plan and solve problems, self-control, and reasoning ability. Jean Shaeffer, the twenty-nine-year-old OT from rural New Hampshire, administers the ACL to every new person on the Unit. In less time than it might take to perform a magic trick, the ACL produces a rough diagnosis distinguishing among brain trauma, personality disorders, schizophrenic disorders, and affective disorders and an indication of how well a patient manages on the outside.

Known as the "crafts lady," Jean leads the groups that string beads, paint pictures, bake cakes, and play board games. To outsiders, her job seems frivolous, even childishly demeaning to patients. But among doctors and staff, Jean's activities, like the ACL, offer fresh insights into a patient.

At first glance, the ACL resembles an activity reminiscent of summer camp. Its tools are two square leather swatches with holes around the perimeter, a sewing needle, and a plastic thread. The therapist begins by demonstrating how to sew three basic running stitches, then asks the patient to repeat the action. This accomplished, they move to the next step. Jean describes and completes a whipstitch and hands the patch to the patient to duplicate her actions. And so it goes to the most complicated stitch, a single cordovan. With each type of stitch, Jean notices how the patient moves his hands, seems to understand and follows directions, plans his movements, maintains concentration, paces his actions, and fixes mistakes. A patient may breeze through all the stitches, but more often he falters, unable to mimic a particular stitch, or quits in frustration.

The ACL consists of six kinds of stitches, each corresponding to a level of cognitive functioning. The possible diagnoses for a patient who stitches only to level two include advanced dementia, recent traumatic brain injury, cardiovascular accidents, or severe psychotic disorders. A patient who reaches level five may well suffer from a remitting affective disorder, a schizophrenic disorder with a good prognosis, a personality disorder, or early-onset dementia.

The higher the level, the clearer the thinking and the better the prospect for living outside a hospital. The higher levels also are a stepping-off point for the occupational therapist to suggest social and work activities. Although there are no recommended activities for the level-two patient, who probably has a difficult time dressing and bathing, the level-five patient is likely to be well enough to follow instructions for using work or kitchen equipment, even though he may have trouble cooking for himself or making sense out of a new recipe.

Every level gives Jean not only a broad diagnosis, but offers detailed explanations of the personal, social, and work activities and communication skills a patient can handle. And with every level comes a recommendation for how much "social support" a patient needs — that is, how much supervision, whether it be twenty-four-hour nursing care or only occasional monitoring of relatively independent living. All this from a piece of leather, needle, and thread.

Jean watches Matt nonchalantly sew running stitches, advance through level three, then become more careful as he repeats a whipstitch and notices, as well as fixes, Jean's deliberate mistake. But he twists the level-five cordovan stitch, which requires looping back, and pulls the thread so tight that undoing it requires fine-fingered attention. He refuses to continue, flipping the patch across the table and declaring, "This is stupid, basket weaving for the brain dead. Get someone else to make your Christmas presents." Matt stomps from the room and Jean jots a note about his impatience and belligerence.

Despite Matt's manipulations in group, Vuckovic believes he will not run away or hurt himself. So he gives him a group privilege later that morning to join three other patients, under Frank's watchful eye, at the DeMarneffe cafeteria for lunch. Matt is in high spirits as the group strolls up the hill, joking about the "funny farm field trip" and getting the group to mimic his steps as he announces, "Walk this way." Their silliness is infectious, and Frank finds himself imitating Matt's heel clicking along with everyone else.

When they enter the cafeteria, Frank is grateful that it is just around noon and not packed yet. Snagging a table for the group is easy. The mental health worker instructs the four patients to collect their food and then sit with him at a table on the lower level of the cafeteria near the windowed wall overlooking the patio.

Matt follows Julie to the grill line and waits to order hamburgers and fries. They blend into the crowd of doctors, staff, patients, and visitors milling around the food counters. Except for their not having an official ID tag, they might be mistaken for staff, casually dressed, comfortable and both alert. Once they load their trays with burgers and plastic eating utensils, they head for the checkout line. As they do, Matt sticks a banana in his pant pocket and pulls his shirt over it. He makes sure Julie witnesses his pilfering, and winks at her. They sail past the cashier, informing her they are from the Unit. As patients, they don't pay out of pocket for their meals.

"That was stupid," Julie comments with a withering look toward Matt. "Like did you save some money just now?" He smiles at her and wiggles the banana into the front of his pants.

Frank waves to the pair from the far corner as they stand at the carpeted steps scanning the tables. The bright sunlight pours in from all directions and off the Formica tabletops, making it hard to see. Rusty and another patient are already seated. As he sits down, Matt pulls out the banana and drops it on his tray. He looks around the table; the others are intent on eating.

"I just wanted to see if they'd notice. You know, like a pop quiz, a test." Faced with silence, he wolfs down his burger.

The tables around them fill up with chattering staff, women in tailored suits and Laura Ashley dresses, men in coats and ties. Except for a snack bar in the Rehabilitation Building, the cafeteria is the one place where maintenance staff mingles with researchers, and where administrators bump into patients. At one time, the McLean cafeteria service was china and cloth napkins, but economics forced it into Styrofoam and paper. Each table has a small sign propped on it, a reminder of the hospital's private nature: PLEASE BE CONSIDERATE. RE-SPECT THE CONFIDENTIALITY OF THOSE AROUND YOU.

"I don't know why I bother," Rusty remarks as she spears a cucumber slice. "This is the worst excuse for a salad. Look at this — specks of pasta, globs of mayonnaise. I should have had a burger. This is no place to diet."

"It isn't much for eating either," Matt chimes in. "This tastes like dog food, and I've tasted dog food." He turns to Julie. "It's true. Alpo. There was this guy in school who dared me. Bet me ten bucks. So I smothered it in ketchup and chowed down!"

Frank gives Matt a long look. "Yeah, sure. You always do things on a dare?"

"Why not? I mean, nothing scares me off. Why should it? Especially if there's money in it."

"Anything?" Julie asks. "Like, I've got five bucks that says you wouldn't throw my pie at Armando over there." Two tables over sits the unit patient who had entertained them with his manic harangues at group earlier, with a visitor who looks like his mother.

"Stop it, Julie," Frank intercedes. "Matt's not going to throw anything." He stares at each of them, and at Matt the longest, until they resume eating. For a minute or so, they nibble their fries, and Frank's attention wanders. In a moment, Matt catches Julie's eye, flashes her a toothy smile, and lofts the custard dessert over the table beside them. It splatters on Armando's shoulder.

The patient sits bolt upright, swiveling about to find the source of the missile. He spots Matt, who waves. The woman in a Chanel suit and full make-up across the table from Armando twists around too. Armando acknowledges his fellow patient with a jerk of his head, and from his tray selects a plastic cup of vegetable soup, and flips it in Matt's direction. Peas, potatoes, and watery tomato broth splash over two tables. Frank is on his feet, lunging at Matt, as Julie forks a heap of pickle relish toward Armando.

"A little high and to the left!" Rusty shouts.

People scramble from the tables ringing the warring patients. Everyone scoots off to the side, except for an older woman with a nurse's ID who grabs Armando. Halfway across the room, a man in a tweed sport coat is yelling for security. Chairs tip over and drinks slop as Frank wrestles Matt's arm behind his back. Matt is screaming bloody murder, and Julie is yelling at Frank to let him go.

Frank sees that the nurse has Armando sitting down. Two security guards in blue uniforms and utility belts are weaving through the tables toward the lunchers. Matt goes limp, and Frank steers him toward a chair.

"Take it easy," he says soothingly. "I'll let go of your arm as soon as you're calm." The security guards hover expectantly. Julie has lowered her voice but continues to berate Frank for arm-locking Matt.

"I think lunch is over," Frank declares, and with the two security guards bringing up the rear, leads the entourage back to the Unit. Armando, his mother, and the nurse from Proctor House follow along.

When they get back, Frank sends Matt and Armando to their rooms and finds Nancy, who is with the clinical nurse supervisor in his office. The only staff member to have a private office, CNS Jack Springer relishes his retreat at the end of the hall next to the medication room. It is a good location for private talks; loud voices don't leak into the general area.

Frank shuts the door and blurts out, "That little criminal has done it again! A food fight in the middle of the cafe! And our favorite borderline was in the thick of it, egging him on!" He catches his breath, and enunciates each word. "I think a small adjustment of Mr. Mullany's privileges is in order."

Jack motions the mental health worker to a straight-backed chair. "Feeling a little stressed out today?" he asks gently.

Frank shakes his head in exasperation. "It shows, huh? Things were going so well, the group was getting along, making light chitchat, eating their lunch, enjoying the meal. I should have known better. Seriously, we need to isolate Matt as much as possible. He's like a fire starter: he ignites small blazes everywhere he goes."

"We can certainly keep him from off-unit activities, but he should still attend groups." Nancy is pointing out the obvious. "I don't think he should be confined to the quiet room. That's too punitive."

Frank crosses his arms, and stretches out his legs. "Nancy, maybe, just maybe, we need a strong arm with this patient. Nothing's getting to him so far. It's not as if he's psychotic and doesn't know full well what he's doing."

Nancy scowls, "Look, he's in here with a legitimate diagnosis, he's in here for a reason. This isn't a jail, we're supposed to treat him. Regardless of his sneaky, conniving personality, ADD is a real disorder."

She drops the lecturing tone. "The Ritalin's bound to show some effect soon. Let's keep a close eye on him and give it a couple of days. If he's still causing trouble, maybe we can see about transferring him to AB-II. OK?"

Frank shrugs in agreement, and Jack is glad harmony is restored. As Frank and Nancy are leaving the office, Jack declares, "I suppose I'm writing the incident report? Next time, it's all yours."

"If there is a next time," she retorts.

At 8:00 the next morning, the Unit is sleepy and groggy, and only Armando is fully awake. Still wired, he has been up and down all night, and is in the smoking room puffing on his second cigarette of the day. The loudest noises are the sound of running water and an occasional buzz from the outside door. In the nurses' station, the night shift is milling around, putting on jackets and eyeing a bakery box of brownies sent by Armando's mother.

Most of the day nursing staff is in the conference room,

hunched over the tape recorder, listening to patient reports. Frank, assigned to checks for the morning, sits at the counter behind the glass overlooking the Unit, waiting to make his first circuit of rooms, glancing in and accounting for every patient. As he sits, he sprinkles fish food into the murky goldfish tank. The faint sound of country music tells him that Julie is awake. The smell of bacon from the breakfast cart, which delivers meals to the kitchen, is rousing patients.

Frank watches Matt exit the pay phone booth at the end of the hall. Barefoot and wearing a black leather vest instead of a shirt, revealing serpents and daggers etched up his arms, he looks menacing. He marches up to the glass and pounds on it.

"I'm not an animal, you can't keep me caged up, your drugs are killing my brain! I demand to be released!" The glass rattles.

Frank, with two other staff members on his heels, whips around the corner to quell the angry patient. They stand around him, outside arm's length.

"Matt, stop this!" Frank's voice is firm but not raised.

The young man's face is flushed. "Get away from me, you fuckers. I'm getting out of here!" He feints toward the outside door, then stands still, as if waiting for the mental health workers to move aside. Drowsy patients are frozen around the periphery of the lounge area.

"You know you can't leave, Matt. If you keep yelling and threatening, you're going to have go into seclusion," Frank says in a friendly voice.

"Oh yeah, and who's going to do it? You touch me and I'll knock your fucking head off!" Matt shifts toward the door, and nursing staff members encircle him. They don't want to have to overwhelm him and they can't help thinking of the coworker whose nose was broken two weeks earlier.

"This is going to get you nowhere, Matt. Please go to your room," Frank instructs, his voice firm and calm.

Matt lunges at him, swinging wildly. Instead of backing

away, Frank ducks and grabs Matt by the waist as the other two MHAs grapple to pin his arms. Twisting and straining, Matt shouts obscenities. A patient on the sidelines screams, "Stop it!" As the four rock and reel in a giant bear hug, Frank yells out: "We need help here, need a chemical!"

Inside the nursing station, the day shift members rush toward the Dutch door to aid their colleague. Nancy calmly calls, in succession, security, the nursing office, and Vuckovic on his private line, uttering a silent prayer when he immediately lifts the receiver. She won't have to page him and waste time.

"Alex, we need a chemical and four-points for Mullany," she says in clipped tones. Vuckovic knows the drill and doesn't ask questions.

"Two of Ativan, a hundred of Vistaril; tie him up. I'll be right down to sign off." He hangs up and the charge nurse goes to the medication room and measures out two hypodermic vials of clear liquid. Equally deliberate, she makes her way to the hallway. Staff members have scattered the other patients into their rooms; all that stands before her is a tangle of three staff surrounding a prone Matt Mullany, red-faced and straining against Frank's chokehold. A staffer holds each extremity as Matt tries to kick his lower legs free.

"Do it!" Frank urges raspily. "We'll take him to the QR when security gets here!" Her hand darts to the serpent's head on Matt's bicep, presses, and releases one syringe, then the other. Enraged further, Matt swivels toward her, but Frank tightens his hold as Nancy jumps backward.

Over the next few minutes, Matt's movements grow less purposeful; he has ceased yelling, and the only sounds coming from the floor are the panting of four sweaty, anxious, and exhausted people. Soon a stream of mental health workers from other units begins arriving, as do two muscled security men clutching nightsticks. Nancy sends off the workers but asks security to stay. Vuckovic is next on the scene; he takes a quick, clinical look at the jumble of bodies on the floor and asks ingen-uously, "Well, shall we move the gentleman along?" Nancy and Frank shoot him dirty looks.

The mental health workers carefully load the still-straining patient onto a red gurney, never letting go of his head, arms, or legs. They deftly commandeer their slightly struggling, prone burden onto a plain mattress on an iron frame in the quiet room around the corner. Working with the practiced touch of those who have done this too many times to count, they lash individ-ual canvas thongs around each wrist and ankle, waiting to strap each onto a corner of the bed frame before moving to the next one.

Finally, almost in one motion, all step back and disappear through the quiet room doorway. Nancy quickly kneels for-ward to wind a blood pressure cuff around Matt's upper right arm, and he offers no resistance. A whimper escapes his lips as she works, a keening cry like a newborn baby's.

"Hush, Matt," she answers softly. "Get some rest." Then she too backs out of the suddenly chilly room.

Five minutes later, the Unit is back to normal. Patients wait at the meds window and Kelly stands at the nurses' station door, Bic lighter in hand, igniting the outstretched cigarettes. Deep inside the nurses' station, Nancy and Frank speculate on how long Matt will be in points and log the incident in the patient record book. Vuckovic has left after signing various restraint forms and taking one last look in on his patient.

It is around 9:30 A.M. when the receptionist from the Ad-ministration Building who issues visitor passes telephones say-ing that Matt Mullany's lawyer wants to see him. The unit assistant hands the phone to Nancy.

"His *lawyer?*" the charge nurse repeats incredulously. "Let me speak to him, please." She purses her lips in suspicion, wait-ing to talk to the mystery visitor.

"Hello, this is Nancy Nicholson. I'm the charge nurse on Mr. Mullany's unit." She pauses to listen. "Of course you have a right to see him. However, Ms. Foote, he's here under a court order for an evaluation. I'll have to check with the psychiatrist-in-charge for the appropriate authority before I can let you see him. It's Dr. Alexander Vuckovic. No, it shouldn't take long. If you wait at the Administration Building, I'll get back to you as soon as I can. Yes, yes, I understand." A mixture of professional pleasantness, authority, and a trace of anger emanate from the charge nurse's tone.

"One more thing. Can you tell me when Mr. Mullany arranged for you to see him? I see. Early this morning. Of course, I'll call you as soon as I can, Ms. Foote." Overhearing the conversation while at the coffeepot, Frank stands across the desk from Nancy and mouths to her, "You're kidding." She nods to confirm it.

Nancy clicks the receiver and punches in Vuckovic's outside extension. "Hi, Joyce, it's Nancy downstairs. Is Alex free? I need to talk to him even if he isn't. Thanks."

Put on hold, the nurse asks the unit assistant to hand her Matt's chart. She flips through it as she waits, looking for an answer to her dilemma. Frank remains across the desk, ready for details. But the unspoken hierarchy dissuades the charge nurse from soliciting the mental health worker for a professional opinion. Nancy avoids eye contact as she studies the chart. She feels besieged, not collegial or chatty.

She snaps her professional voice in place. "Alex, I've just received a call from a Ms. Foote, an attorney who's been engaged by Matt Mullany. She's at the Administration Building waiting for a visitor pass. However, as you know, he's in restraints. I have severe reservations about allowing her to see Mr. Mullany in his current condition."

Although the nurses go about their duties, two people linger by the coffeepot, someone studies the shift schedule on the bulletin board, and a mental health worker has moved from the conference room to write notes in the main area. People speak in a half whisper.

"I know it's his legal right to see his lawyer, Alex. But as you know, seeing someone in points can be disturbing. A lawyer might misinterpret the situation, think we're trying to punish him."

For the first time, Nancy looks around the room, making eye contact with her anxious staff. Everyone feels the same about this: outsiders view some psychiatric practices as barbaric. Explanations about a patient hurting himself or others, and all the safeguards taken by staff members to minimize confrontation and protect a patient even as he might be trying to injure them, fall on deaf ears at the sight of the bare bed with canvas straps and a patient spread-eagle across it, facedown.

"I know, Alex, I wish as much as you that he weren't in points. You know we had no choice. In fact, Ms. Foote told me that Matt called her this morning, asking her to represent him and come see him. This was *before* the outburst, which was a deliberate provocation. He *wants* his lawyer to see him in points."

She scowls as she listens. "All right. But do this for me. She's going to be here in a couple of minutes. Can you come down and talk to her, explain the situation, before we take her to see him?"

The nurses' station erupts in a clamor of incredulous voices. Everyone feels defensive, as if forced to justify a heinous crime. Staff is accustomed to a steady stream of visitors, not only medical people but also family members. McLean's long visiting hours, 10:00 A.M. to 10:00 P.M., make it easy for friends and relatives to see patients. But the visit almost always takes place in the lounge area, a patient's room, or elsewhere around the hospital. For the staff, the idea of escorting a visitor, a lawyer no less, into the quiet room, feels like being caught abusing a child.

Nancy notifies the Administration Building receptionist that Ms. Foote can visit the Unit, and prays that Vuckovic will appear before she hears the buzzer at the outside door. When the buzzer sounds five minutes later, Nancy waits a few seconds, straining to hear Alex's keys in the stairwell door.

She puts on her linen jacket before venturing from the nurses' station to open the terrace door for a woman in a brown suit with a pageboy haircut and a large briefcase.

"Hello, Ms. Foote, I'm Nancy Nicholson. Please come in." Nancy hates her welcome-to-my-parlor tone. She is trying to be professional and gracious, but it comes out sounding too personal. "Mr. Mullany's doctor, Dr. Vuckovic, will be right with you. If you'd like to wait here, I'll get him." As soon as the words are out of her mouth, Vuckovic materializes at her side.

"I'm Dr. Vuckovic. Nice to meet you." Vuckovic's tone is crisp. His blue gabardine suit and blue dress shirt seem to equalize the playing field between the doctor and lawyer, and Nancy feels weirdly grateful. "I don't know what you know about Mr. Mullany's condition, and privacy constraints prevent us from discussing his diagnosis or treatment. However, we can tell you that at the moment he is very agitated and poses a safety and flight risk. For this reason, we've had to physically restrain him and confine him to a quiet room." Vuckovic speaks as if explaining a filing system.

Two patients passing through the lounge area circle around the doctor and visitor and eye them suspiciously. The attorney looks official and ominous.

"His room is down the hall." Vuckovic guides the lawyer, and Nancy trails behind, glancing about, trying to see things with a stranger's eyes. A patient dozes in a corner chair and another stands at the medication room Dutch door. Frank appears, dressed in black jeans and a polo shirt, carrying a clipboard and striding confidently down the hall.

Diana MacKenzie, assigned to specials, sits outside the quiet room. Vuckovic asks a perfunctory "How's he doing?" as he pushes the door open, halfway, then wide.

"Matt, you have a visitor. I believe you're expecting her." Vuckovic steps aside to let the attorney approach the head of the bed and the patient. "If you have any questions, Ms. Foote, Nancy can help you, or I'll be glad to answer them. You can reach me at extension 317."

Half an hour later, Ms. Foote knocks timidly on the glass outside the nurses' station. Nancy smiles slightly, noticing for the first time how young the woman is. Barely thirty is her guess. The charge nurse also figures that this is her first time inside a psychiatric hospital. Nancy pulls out keys to unlock the terrace door.

"Everything go all right?" she asks expectantly as she walks toward the door.

"Frankly, I'm a little confused about what just transpired. Is there somewhere we can talk in private?"

"Certainly," Nancy says, and leads her to the tiny interview room off the hall.

The young woman sits in the molded plastic chair and positions her briefcase squarely on her lap.

"Matt seems quite upset. He feels he's being unfairly punished for minor infractions. I must admit, I was a little shocked to see him that way. He sounded rational and in control. Not that I'm questioning your treatment," she adds. "He wanted to submit a three-day notice."

Nancy's reaction is to object, but she checks herself. Despite a natural instinct to protest letting go of any patient who isn't markedly better, Matt's case might be the exception. Life on the Unit would vastly improve without him. She knows he doesn't belong on a psychotic disorders unit.

"I had to explain to him that he's here on a court order and he doesn't have that option," the lawyer continues. "He then told me he's been collecting evidence, that he's going to sue. He's taking notes, documenting everything. He says, boasts really, that he has a copy of his treatment record and that it proves that he's being abused." She sets her briefcase on the table, pops it open, and pulls out a piece of notebook paper filled with pencil scrawls. She flaps it dismissively.

"Then he told me he once robbed a liquor store with a water gun. I must confess, I really don't understand what's going on here." She consults her notes. "He claims he has attention deficit disorder and an antisocial personality disturbance. Could I ask you if that's true?"

"Those are recognized medical conditions," Nancy informs her. The charge nurse isn't going to discuss a diagnosis with anyone not sanctioned by the hospital or the patient, but she wishes she could explain them to this psychiatric sophomore and warn her of the dangers Matt presents.

Antisocial personality disorder is one of a handful of labels for a deep disturbance in a person's relationship with the world. Other names for it are psychopathy and sociopathic personality. Although it officially entered the psychiatric diagnostic manual in the early 1950s, it has been recognized as a mental illness since the 1800s. One of the first names used for it was "moral insanity," an accurate if somewhat incomplete characterization.

This is the classic criminal personality, and more controversy surrounds theories of its origin than arguments about the roots of any other psychiatric disturbance. While few thinkers in the field are naive enough to implicate only genetic or only environmental factors in its origins, the relative weight given to each position varies wildly.

The signs of the disorder are fairly clear-cut, beginning with restlessness, a short attention span, and indifference to authority or discipline. (Presociopathy may appear in children also diagnosed with attention deficit hyperactivity disorder, but the two do not necessarily run together.) A teenager showing signs of sociopathy has been regularly truant (the disorder is at least three times more prevalent among boys than girls); has run away from home a couple of times; may have been in fights, sometimes with a weapon; has vandalized property and may have become a deliberate fire setter; and lies easily.

As a person grows up, these symptoms infect the entire personality. The adult sociopath often can't hold a job and may move frequently, typically having no fixed address. His personal relationships are brief and stormy. He's impulsive, often irritable, and aggressive, regularly getting into fights and trouble with the law. The sociopath is a smooth, even pathological, liar. He doesn't believe that social norms apply to him, frequently ignoring debts and being physically reckless. And, he feels little remorse for his behavior or how he treats others. Substance abuse is almost invariably part of the profile.

The life of a sociopath is a rocky one. School difficulties usually launch him into the adult world without any skills. Often estranged from family, he may marry, though his relationships tend to be with equally disturbed and damaged partners. This is a phenomenon known as "assortative mating," and its implications are chilling for any child of these parents, regardless of whether one is of the nature or nurture school. Adoption studies of the biological parents of sociopaths reveal a higher than normal prevalence of alcoholism and antisocial behavior. Given their inclinations and behavior, sociopaths make up the bulk of the prison population and are regular participants in the mental health system.

The coupling of other psychiatric and some neurological deficits in these people has led doctors to speculate that the sociopath is merely the sum of his parts: a biological subgroup vulnerable to attention deficit and learning disability, often tortured by disturbed parents, unable to get life's early rewards at school and at home.

Treating a sociopath, once the disorder has existed for years or decades, is usually an exercise in frustration. One of the knottiest problems is that the patient takes no responsibility for his deeds and feels no motivation to change. He doesn't see a problem: it's society, family, police, and doctors who see illness and unacceptable behavior. Compounding his attitude is his regular presence before courts and law officers, leading the sociopath to retreat further into a victim mentality even as he continues to hurt others.

The young attorney shuts her briefcase and stands up. "It's hard to figure. Half the time, he seems to make sense, and then he launches into these tirades against the hospital and doctors and everyone." She buttons her jacket. "It's difficult, trying to assess whether his rights have been violated." She sighs, and asks the charge nurse to let her out.

Nancy smiles benignly, doubting if she'll ever hear from her again, and leads the lawyer down the hall.

Matt is out of restraints by afternoon and spends a quiet evening eating dinner on the Unit and watching TV. Every twenty minutes or so he appears at the nurses' station door asking for a light, but he doesn't make his usual complaints about the supervised flames ritual.

The next evening, as Vuckovic is leaving for the day, Matt waylays him by the terrace door. The patient appears unusually focused, making eye contact and not fidgeting as he speaks. He wears jeans and a T-shirt, and black high-top tennis shoes. Vuckovic remembers a note on his chart from the night nurse reporting that he had sat through an entire videocassette movie, and could recount the story line.

"Dr. Vuckovic, I'd like to make a request, sir," he says, no irony in his voice. "It's my wife's birthday tomorrow, and her sister's giving her a party. Would it be possible for me to get a town privilege so I could go?"

Matt shifts his weight back and forth; he looks tired, Vuckovic notes, and wonders if the Ritalin is preventing him from sleeping adequately.

"Matt, you were in four-points yesterday. Why on earth should we move along that fast?" Vuckovic pauses, remembering David Seltzer all too vividly. "What's changed?"

"I don't exactly know, sir, and I don't blame you for not

wanting to trust me, but I feel better, clearer, less angry. I read a magazine today, start to finish, and I could concentrate, remember it. I think I like your drug." He smiles slyly.

"That's good to hear," Vuckovic replies, not totally impressed. "If you can get your treatment team coordinator to approve your request, we'll talk about it more tomorrow. Also, don't forget the court still has an interest in our report on you." The psychiatrist wants to buttress whatever is happening to Matt neurochemically with a reminder of his precarious position in society.

Matt thanks Vuckovic profusely and retreats to the TV room.

The next morning, Vuckovic is again somewhat surprised to hear that Matt has taken his privilege request to Frank, of all people, and the mental health worker has no problem with approving off-grounds-with-family. His recent experience with David Seltzer still stinging, Vuckovic has an extensive discussion with both Frank and Nancy before writing the order.

Midmorning, at Jack Springer's suggestion, he has carefully read the court order that sent Matt to McLean and determined that it does not specify that the patient has to be restricted to the grounds. Before lunch, Matt's wife arrives to pick him up. Vuckovic spends several minutes with the couple, reminding both of the patient's restricted legal status.

By the early part of the afternoon, Matt's status is the last thing on Nancy's mind. Two admissions and two discharges keep the charge nurse scurrying between the telephone, scribbling reports, arranging for maintenance to clean rooms, and making nursing assignments. Friday admissions bear the extra pressure of immediately assembling all the pieces of insurance coverage and medical information because neither senior medical staff nor the patient accounts office personnel will be around to answer questions on the weekend.

One admission is a sad HIV-positive presurgical transsexual who is paranoid. He has lost his secondary male characteristics from hormone therapy and looks to the weary admitting resident like a pleasant, somewhat chunky matron. Insurance coverage for the final surgical procedure has been denied, however, and the resident is grateful that the patient refuses a physical, demanding authorization from the Central Intelligence Agency before allowing anyone near him. Vuckovic slips in and out of the Unit twice to log medication orders and to meet with John Graybill, who is seeing the second admission, a teenage boy transferred from Mass. General following a potentially lethal lithium overdose.

Matt returns to the Unit around 7:00 P.M. Diana MacKenzie lets him in through the staff and visitor door off the stairwell and hardly notices that he is sporting an exceptionally bulky jacket. He mumbles a greeting and disappears into his room.

Soon after, she sees a congregation of patients at the far end of the hall. They are standing in a circle, whooping and laughing, and she's pleased to see a bunch of usually taciturn people engaged in what looks like healthy socializing. She strolls down the hall toward them.

As she nears, the group opens up. At their feet, almost camouflaged by the beige tweed carpet, is a small white rabbit with a collar and leash. The end of the leash runs up to a loop around the wrist of a beaming Matt Mullany. The night nurse is speechless for a few seconds, then feels she has to say something, anything.

"That's a rabbit! Whose is it? It doesn't belong here!" She glares at Matt.

He smiles broadly. "Of course it's a rabbit, Diana. He's our new mascot, Crusader Rabbit. Is he a pip, or what?"

An image flashes through Diana's mind: she has read in Matt's history that as a child he liked to set live squirrels afire with a blowtorch.

"He's mine, but we'll be discussing walking privs; everyone will get their turn MESing with him. Step right up!" He scans the group with an innocent smile. Melissa Stanwyck, a large woman in a shapeless housedress who occupies Glenda's old room, giggles and yells, "Me, me, Matt!"

Everyone looks down at the white fur ball, which hops a few inches, depositing a half dozen dark pellets.

The nurse glares at Matt. "That rabbit doesn't belong here. It can't stay. It's unsanitary and against the rules." She pauses for a moment, unable to sort out the extent to which this requires immediate confrontation. Around her, the patients, mostly the chronically ill residents of the Unit, shuffle and titter. "You're going to have to give it up. We'll send it to the greenhouse, or —"

Matt shakes his head. "No way. This rabbit's mine. It's for us, the patients. Something we can love, and take care of." He yanks at the leash, briefly jerking the rabbit off the floor. Julie, who is standing beside Matt, sweeps the animal into her arms and cuddles it. Matt sidles closer to her. "I checked the rules. There's nothing about pets." He pulls from his back pocket a rolled-up copy of "Information for Families and Patients about the Psychotic Disorders Program" and waves it at the nurse. By now, the commotion has caught the attention of Kelly and Frank, who jog up the corridor and stand beside Diana.

"I've got a receipt," Matt continues smoothly. "This rabbit is legally mine. You people have lots of rules, but there's nothing about rabbits. Nothing for the patients. You're always telling us everything we can't do, never anything that's good for us. Crusader is good for us. What's wrong? You people afraid of a rabbit? Afraid we might feel something for it, something besides fear? Are you afraid of love and warmth?"

The patients edge close to Matt and Julie. Melissa keeps trying to pet the rabbit as Julie hugs it, blocking her. Rusty has joined the chorus of Matt's disciples, repeating his litany against the rules and laughing loudly.

"It's unsanitary. Pets don't belong on the Unit. Be reasonable, Matt," Kelly interjects. "We can't let patients have pets.

This place would be a smelly menagerie if we did. Give me the rabbit, and I'll make sure it goes to a good home."

"Nope, we're keeping it. It's time the patients had some say about what goes on here. This is one time your rules can't help you beat us down." He takes the rabbit from Julie, strokes its head, and hands it to Dave, a college student recently admitted for mania.

Julie steps forward. "Yeah, power to the patients!"

"This has nothing to do with patient rights," Diana declares. "The rabbit can't stay. It's against hospital rules. If you don't give me the rabbit, I'm going to have to call security. You leave me no choice." The rabbit is back in Matt's arms, and he doesn't budge. Diana, Kelly, and Frank look at each other and, defeated for the moment, start back to the nursing station.

It falls to Diana, the charge nurse for the evening, to enlist the senior psychiatrist to help her separate the rabbit from the patients. Calling security is a last resort; men in dark uniforms carrying walkie-talkies and nightsticks will only add ammunition to Matt's antiestablishment arguments.

Despite the late hour, Vuckovic is in his office seeing patients. Fifteen minutes later, he is on the Unit plotting strategy with MacKenzie. While the doctor and staff regroup, Matt marches the rabbit through the halls as other patients follow and plead for a turn with the animal. Dave proposes teaching the rabbit tricks, and Matt presides over the entreaties for his pet like a potentate. It sounds as if the circus has come to town. Patients scurry about on the heels of the procession and draw others from their rooms to join the fun. Frenetic laughter and overexcited shouting pierce the stale air.

Diana MacKenzie is distraught over the merriment; she is afraid that the manic patients will get too wound up, their sometimes hair-trigger emotions plunging them into tumult. The Unit needs quiet routine to function.

Feeling like a lion tamer entering a cage of unruly cats, Vuckovic ambles to the poolroom, where patients and rabbit have congregated. Matt is seated on the edge of the pool table, his pet hopping around on the green felt. Julie is beside him, holding his hand, although he ignores her. Patients stand around the table, taking turns petting the rabbit as Matt dictates when they can touch it.

Vuckovic walks up to Matt as if he is the only person in the room. He presses in close to the young man. Although Vuckovic's temper can flare, he has no experience dealing with physical violence beyond one three-hour in-service seminar with nursing staff, God knows how many years ago. However, he moonlit in many emergency rooms during residency and feels comfortable dealing with the unpredictable. He knows he is taking a calculated risk. The patient is only five nine, and the PIC towers over him, but Matt Mullany lifts weights and is streetwise. With luck, Vuckovic can hold him off in a physical confrontation long enough to yell for help. But he counts on Matt's recent evidence of improvement to help him out as well, along with the patient's knowledge of the stakes.

"Unit rules may say nothing about pets or animals, but hospital rules do," Vuckovic asserts, and reaches for the rabbit's leash. The patients around the pool table freeze, their eyes on Matt, who glares at Vuckovic but doesn't move. Julie lets his hand dangle.

"That rabbit is legally mine," Matt hisses into Vuckovic's face. "You touch it, and I'll have my lawyer here so fast your head will hurt!" He raises his hand as if to grab Vuckovic's arm, then makes a fist and slowly lays it on the pool table.

"This has nothing to do with legalities, Matt." Vuckovic scans the other patients. "I know having a pet is fun, but this is no place for one. This is a hospital, a place to get better. It's not like your home, and you can't make it that way." He looks at Melissa, whose eyes are beginning to water. "I'm sorry." Vuckovic tucks the white rabbit under his arm and leaves the poolroom.

As the door squeezes shut behind him, Vuckovic hears Matt's low voice: "He's gonna be sorry."

Inside the nurses' station, Vuckovic plops the rabbit on the carpeted floor, sighs, and sinks into an office chair. The animal turns to him and wiggles its nose. Vuckovic smiles as Kelly, Diana, and Frank look at him quizzically. His face crinkles as he breaks into a guffaw, slips off the chair, cannot stop laughing, slaps at the floor. The nursing station fills with the maniacal cackle of four voices yelping with poignant relief.

Matt refuses to participate in rounds the following Monday. Instead, he occupies the lounge area, loudly denouncing Vuckovic and hospital rules. He exhorts other patients to follow his example and not talk to the staff and students making their twice-weekly tour of the Unit. "Don't answer their questions!" he orders. "You don't have to do what they say. We're the paying customers here!"

Vuckovic holds rounds, regardless. The beleaguered staff huddles in the poolroom, reviewing Matt's case. The members of his treatment team — Vuckovic, the CNS, primary nurse, mental health worker, and social worker — pass around papers from his file, refreshing their memory of his psychiatric history.

"He's done this before, you know," Vuckovic points out. "At the Hall-Mercer Center when he was fourteen. Tried to organize the other children into defying curfew," he reads.

"Hall-Mercer's famous for its child riots," Jack Springer reminds the group. "They have more food fights, more uprisings, than an inner-city junior high. We get an emergency page from them asking for help in quelling some outburst at least twice a week."

"All those little boys, each one a demon in his own special way," Nancy remarks.

"They've got some pretty nasty girls over there too, Nancy," Vuckovic notes blandly. "Matt, however, has a history of being a ringleader. And I'm getting fed up exhausting our resources on this incorrigible sociopath. I think we'll agree that the Ritalin's working, but he has a lot more wrong with him than just ADD." He pauses. "By the way, anybody hear from his lawyer this morning? What was her name, Ms. Foote?"

Nancy shakes her head. "I did see Matt using the phone this morning and come storming out of the booth," she reports, then reflects optimistically. "Maybe she's no longer his lawyer. He does have a habit of bouncing checks."

"I bet that's what happened!" Kelly slaps the table.

Jack Springer squints thoughtfully at her. "Getting a little worked up, aren't we?" he teases.

The mental health worker rolls her head in exasperation. "I know this is countertransference, but I can't help it. He reminds me of my little brother, who was, is really, one of the most manipulative, amoral, conniving people I know. Mullany's phony charm drives me up a wall because I *know* he's up to something."

Vuckovic jumps in. "I think we're all overreacting to him, though for good reason. We take up valuable clinical time trying to deal with today's shtick or trying to preempt tomorrow's, and then don't have the time to help patients who actually want to be here. I know he's sick, and I know you guys know it too, but I truly don't know how to help someone like this." He throws his hands up in exasperation. "Does anyone else here know?" Vuckovic catches himself; he rarely vents, and the people around the table halt their paper shuffling and whispering to see how far he'll go.

Jack Springer puts the discussion back on track by neatly answering Vuckovic's question. "I've been thinking, looking at Matt's history here. He's got a serious substance abuse problem. How about shipping him to Appleton?"

Appleton is a three-story red-brick building on the very opposite corner of the McLean campus from the Unit. Appleton specializes in treating patients whose alcohol and drug abuse problems overshadow any other psychiatric illnesses. Many of its twenty-three beds are occupied by "dual diagnosis" patients whose addiction or alcoholism is so incapacitating or has so muddied their mental health that insurance carriers have agreed to hospitalization. Unlike the psychotic disorders units, Appleton applies a constant dose of individual and group psychotherapy as its primary weapon. Its staff is comfortable with, and somewhat blasé about, managing personality disorders.

"Very neat, I like it," Nancy opines. "But can it be done?"

Attention shifts to Vuckovic, who smiles slightly. "We're going to get a rep, you know: our unit can't hold on to its patients. No wonder our census is plummeting, people will say. We bounce patients out as soon as they arrive!" The group guffaws at the notion that they would deliberately shorten a patient's stay. If anything, they fight daily to hold on to patients who need further treatment but whose insurance carriers insist on discharge. The plunge in the average length of stay among patients is a scary topic around the hospital because staff feels patients are being sent off too soon.

"However, for this patient we'll risk it!" Vuckovic concludes. "I'll call the legal office to see if there's a problem, and if not I'll call Roger about it this afternoon." The nursing staff gives a quiet round of applause, a couple of grateful thank-yous, and turns its attention to the next patient. Vuckovic refrains from asking the obvious follow-up question: How on earth can this unmotivated man make use of a treatment program that requires a heck of a lot more of a commitment than popping a capsule each morning?

Matt is in his room, sitting legs akimbo on his bed, headphones on, palms pounding out the beat of Guns N' Roses on the mattress. Julie has just left when Vuckovic walks in to tell him the news.

"You have no right!" Matt bellows. "To mix me with all those druggies and alkies! I've got a psychiatric illness! You're just trying to punish me for the rabbit!"

He glares at Vuckovic, who is clearly caught off guard by

the young man's reaction. He thought Matt might welcome the opportunity to hone his skills on a group of staff unacquainted with his methods. Still, he says nothing; he isn't going to debate.

"Just like all the fucking foster homes! You don't like me, so you kick me out!" Matt heaves his Walkman at the wall. "You're gonna be sorry," he fulminates. "Get out of my room!"

The following afternoon, a "town meeting" at Pierce Hall in the Administration Building has siphoned off half the staff from the Unit. Normally town meetings are dull, sparsely attended events at which someone from the administration explains new policies or announced appointments. But that was before the cost-cutting frenzy that has spread from public to private insurers. McLean is changing every week: units close, outpatient services expand, budget deficits balloon. Town meetings are now better attended than the hospital Christmas party.

This afternoon, only a day after Vuckovic has told Matt of his impending move, the charge nurse feels stretched thin. She asks staff to double up for a couple of hours and juggle twice the usual write-ups along with checks, meds, specials, and other assignments. No one complains; the place is quiet. Melissa sits in a corner of the lounge, staring vacantly. Armando is chain-smoking and pops up at the nurses' station every ten minutes or so for a light. The occupational therapist is in the kitchen behind the lunchroom with Rusty and two other patients, engineering the assembly of an angel food cake.

Nancy stands at the fish tank behind the glass overlooking the Unit, watching Hector at the far end of the hall. He is sitting in the hallway, leaning against the wall, doing nothing. It strikes her as odd; it isn't where he usually hangs out. When she sticks her head around the glass partition to ask Hector if he is all right, she hears a faint noise that doesn't fit. It sounds like an animal far away; maybe the ducks on the pond outside the cafeteria are squawking. She listens, and feels rising panic. The noise sounds as if someone is hurt.

"Hector, do you hear that?" she asks as she strides down the hall toward him. Then she notices the other patients loitering about. Two sprawled across the floor in the bedroom opposite Hector's wall and one propped against the wall around the corner. All sit or stand nonchalantly, faces expressionless as the charge nurse sweeps by. "What's going on?" she demands, then listens again.

From the patient room on the very corner farthest away from the nursing station comes the distinct sound of a woman moaning. The tempo is picking up as well as the volume. There is no mistaking what is happening, nor whose room it is. Nancy grabs and twists the doorknob and though it moves easily for a half inch or so, it abruptly stops and she almost rams her chest into its smooth surface. The moaning grows louder, and the gaggle of patients moves in closer to the room.

The charge nurse yells down the hall for help, then aims her words at the barricaded door. "Matt, open up this minute!" She throws her shoulder against the door and it budges slightly. Frank appears at her side for the next go-around. The door slowly gives way, and with a final heave it swings open, sending the remnants of a chair into the empty twin bed.

Nancy's eyes, initially fixing on the bed, race around the room, then rest on Matt and Julie by the window. Julie is propped against the sill, rendered naked by her shift twisted around her neck. Matt is almost dressed, wearing a T-shirt and jeans, which are unbuttoned and hanging open around his hips.

Nancy is speechless, frozen. Frank barks at Matt, "That's it for you, you're outta here." He grabs Matt's arm.

As the mental health worker yanks him from Julie, who first grasps for him, then slumps into the harsh screen of the window, Matt turns to her. "Bitch! You made me do it!"

CHAPTER SIX

Trick or Treat

This 33yo married white lady, mother of three boys, is transferred to the Unit from AB-II because of an inability to contract for safety and participate in the AB-II milieu. The pt. is well known to AB-II from seventeen previous McLean admissions since age fifteen. Her diagnoses have included bipolar disorder NOS, borderline personality disorder, PTSD, OCD, schizoaffective illness, bulimarexia, with kleptomania, fibromyalgia, and cocaine abuse, the latter in remission.

Her most recent admission prior was September 12 thru Oct 2, precipitated by an overdose of six Ativan pills, apparently after being goaded by her husband to take them during a quarrel. The pt.'s husband did not allow her to return home, and she was discharged to a friend's house. However, she was apparently enraged as a result of not being able to visit her children.

At her friend's insistence, seven days following discharge, she was evaluated by me. I noted she had been sleepless for four nights, binging and vomiting large amounts of food nearly continuously into 33-

gallon plastic bags, and scratching at her forearms with a rusty fork. I admitted her to AB-II from my office.

During her week on AB-II, the pt. refused to take part in unit activities and isolated herself in her room, refusing to come out even for meals. She has been compliant with medication and has seen me and her therapist, Dr. Inger Hasselhoff, regularly but refused to communicate at all with AB-II staff. Yesterday, a body and belongings search initiated by nursing staff disclosed a supply of seven single-edged razor blades and fifty 8-mg Trilafon pills hidden in various locations in her room.

After a staff conference today, Dr. Hasselhoff and CNS Bonnie Bliss agreed that the patient was unsafe and that her behavior was compromising the treatment of the other patients. I suggested the Unit as best suited for the management of her complicated psychopharma-cologic regimen.

On admission, she was taking Depakote 500 mg bid, Trilafon 8 mg qhs, Zoloft 300 mg qAM, Ativan 1 mg qid prn anxiety, Motrin 600 mg tid prn muscle pain, Fioricet 2 tabs bid prn H/A, Spironolactone 25 mg qid prn premenstrual dysphoria, and Synthroid 0.2 mg qd as empirical mood stabilizer therapy. I began clomipramine 25 mg qhs on admission for better control of her bulimic and depressive symptoms. She apparently was *not* bulimic while on AB-II, and at present she does not look vegetatively depressed to me.

Past psychiatric history is well documented in previous records. However, it should be noted that the pt., the oldest of four sisters, was severely physically and sexually abused by her alcoholic father, an attorney, during her latency years. This was confirmed by DSS investigators. Mother suffered from severe bipolar disorder and was hospitalized recurrently.

Pt. ran away from home repeatedly in her early teens and began an approximately ten-year pattern of cocaine and alcohol abuse. She had four foster home placements, which were compromised by the patient's complaint of sexual abuse at the hands of all four foster fathers. However, only the first of these incidents was confirmed. The pt. began a pattern of psychiatric hospitalization with an aspirin overdose following that incident. She has had depressive episodes and several episodes of hypomania, though most of the latter appeared related to antidepressant therapy. She is prone to cutting and burning her wrists and arms in ritualistic ways.

She met her husband while both were students at the Arlington School at McLean. He has been treated for conduct disorder, depression, and rage attacks but is presently not in treatment. The relationship has been rocky.

Her longest period out of the hospital, approximately three years, occurred between the births of her second and third sons, beginning at age 25. Strikingly, she denies a history of postpartum depression. Her father died of a heart attack last September, and she has been hospitalized six times since then. She has been on multiple psychotropics, including lithium carbonate, Tegretol, multiple neuroleptics (though I question the reality of her self-reported psychotic symptoms), most tricyclics, Wellbutrin, Desyrel, Prozac, Klonopin, Vistaril, and at least one MAOI trial. She has either not tolerated or not responded to any of these, and her compliance has been suspect at times. She has not been tried on Clozaril; she has not had ECT. Her fibromyalgia diagnosis was established over the past year following the onset of severe lethargy and muscle pain; medical work-up revealed no clear etiology.

I've seen her for approximately two years; she fired her previous psychopharmacologist amidst charges of sexual abuse; the Massachusetts Board did not find them credible. So far, I have not been accused. She has never worked; her husband is a pediatrician.

I'll follow with you.

Sean Whelan, M.D.
Attending Psychiatrist

THE PATIENT AND DOCTOR are an incongruous sight, walking together across the grassy valley called the Upham bowl like a college couple on their way to a study date. Julie, petite, ghostly pale in yellow crewneck sweater, black jeans, and Top-Siders, has to step quickly to keep up with her companion. Sean Whelan is not a tall man; his build is bullish, and he walks in determined strides. Whelan had no objection when Julie asked for this meeting. He has heard all about the incident with Matt Mullany the day before and wonders what her version is. This stroll suits him; he believes walking to be a tonic for depression. And he prefers meeting this particular patient within the sight of others whenever possible.

The chilly spring sun slightly warms the walkers, and highlights Whelan's shaved pate. Far away, a keening cry emanates intermittently from the geriatrics unit on Proctor House I.

"So the Anafranil's agreeing with you?" Whelan looks straight ahead as he talks.

"Yes, I'm less depressed, but I don't feel like I'm getting the right treatment on the Unit. Dr. Vuckovic keeps adjusting the doses on my meds. I get the feeling he's unsure." She pauses as if weighing what to say next. "I don't think he knows how to treat me. He doesn't have your insight."

"You need to stop worrying about what your doctors are doing and pay more attention to your own behavior. Your episode with Mr. Mullany demonstrated either a striking lack of self-control, or a very calculated attempt to get ejected from the Unit." Whelan pulls himself short of the edge of personal, emotional issues. Not his specialty. "Whichever, I hope you're working with Dr. Hasselhoff on your self-control and acquiring some insight of your own."

"Sure, but it doesn't stick. I get so much more out of our sessions." She half smiles with a touch of shyness.

"You're being provocative *and* you're devaluing your therapist at the same time. Good trick." His cool voice turns stern. "Remember our treatment contract: I see you only if you take your therapy seriously. Dr. Hasselhoff does good work."

"Well, she doesn't say such nice things about you; I get

embarrassed when she says all you do is repeat my father's abuse by forcing pills down my throat."

Whelan stops and whirls to face his patient, his mouth pursed in annoyance. "Look, you really haven't heard me. I know Inger Hasselhoff well; you're not our only patient. I spoke with her last week and she told me *you* had said that to *her* about me."

A shadow seems to pass over Julie Swoboda. The liquid film over her eyes dulls and her face somehow tightens. Smile gone, she straightens her shoulders as she speaks in a deeper voice, an alto to her previous soprano.

"Julie didn't say it; I did."

Whelan says nothing. His mouth is now squeezed in distaste. The woman continues.

"She's telling you the truth. I was with Inger. I was pissed at you. I said it and meant it. Julie came back, and I guess Inger repeated it, so she thinks it, like, *came* from Inger, you know?"

"And who, may I ask, are you?" Whelan asks, spacing his words with a touch of sarcasm. They face each other, a foot apart, neither moving.

"I'm Will. Pleased to meet you." She sticks out her hand and Whelan simply looks at it.

"Let me guess. You're her alter." He half laughs, somewhere between a grunt and a sneer.

"Yeah, I think that's what the girls on AB-II say," the woman confidently retorts. "Actually, there's a bunch of us — Heather, Molly, a girl named Billie — but I'm in charge, though I can't really make any of the others do anything."

Whelan finally moves, crosses his arms. The woman does the same and cocks her head. A chill runs through the psychiatrist. Taking a weary breath, he says evenly, "I'd like to talk to Julie."

"I already told you I can't do that, asshole. Aren't you listening?" The voice chops the words like a blunt instrument, and Whelan envisions a wiry, angry young man. The inflection and rhythm of the speech is male. He squints against the sun.

"Well, then, let me pass a message to her through you, Will." His voice drips with exasperation and annoyance. "I don't treat people who call themselves multiple personalities. You're playing trick or treat with someone who doesn't believe in ghosts. When you see Julie, tell her that she needs a new psychopharmacologist."

Whelan wheels around and strides rapidly up the slope of the Upham bowl. Behind him, he hears a muffled sound, as of a haystack falling over in a strong wind. He turns to see Julie Swoboda raise her head from the ground, brown leaves sticking to the tears streaming down her cheeks.

"It's not me," she sobs, her voice higher-pitched, plaintive. "It's the others. I've been living with this terror for months, losing time, blacking out, not knowing what I did yesterday. I swear to you I'm not making it up. I tried to resist knowing, I didn't tell Dr. Hasselhoff about it. I don't want to lose you!" She collapses, head in her hands, and moans and rocks as the figure of Sean Whelan grows smaller and disappears over the lip of the small valley.

Nancy Nicholson fixes a steely gaze on Vuckovic as he enters the nursing station. The head nurse can't shake the image of where the checks nurse found Julie after two security guards delivered her back to the Unit. The fragile woman was huddled in her closet, wrapped in a blanket, clutching a stuffed walrus. Nicholson knew it would take days to coax her out.

"The wrong people have keys around here," she declares ominously. "I can't believe Sean Whelan. I've never seen a doctor behave so irresponsibly, so unprofessionally. Doesn't he care what happens to that woman!"

Vuckovic sits on a nearby chair, taken aback at this assault. He flicks a piece of lint from a gray serge suit. "You know, I just got this suit, and look at it. I think we should outlaw food in the rounds room, don't you?"

"I'm not kidding, Alex," Nancy seethes. "I'm going to have

a very hard time being civil to that man, and I'm thinking about making a formal complaint."

"Although I guess coffee might be OK," he continues, then realizes Nancy is beyond banter. "Very bad idea, Nancy. I know you're upset, but what Sean did was not as harmful as you think. Given her mental state, his action had a therapeutic purpose."

"Oh come on, Alex. He abandoned a patient! Who knows what she might have done! He's lucky she didn't pull a David Seltzer!"

Vuckovic tips back in his chair and glances at the wall clock. "Not likely. She was out to display her new personalities. If Sean had acknowledged the teaming hordes inside her, which undoubtedly includes a nasty character, a stock feature with multiples, then one of her so-called personalities might have gotten violent. But he didn't. He forced Julie to stay in charge."

Nancy takes a deep breath, as if girding herself for a verbal slugfest. "You don't believe in MPD, do you?"

"I don't even like the term 'multiple personality disorder,' " he declares disdainfully. "These aren't personalities. They're facets, fragments of a very active and skilled imagination."

"So you think it's all play-acting?" Nancy challenges. "What about the physical changes that take place in a multiple? These have been documented, Alex. An MPD whose eyesight changes from personality to personality; one with high blood pressure, another without. There have even been cases of multiples with brain scans that change with each personality! What about these?"

Nancy's voice rises through her tirade, and when she stops, she sees that staff outside the conference room is moving quietly, almost tiptoeing. But keeping distance; no one's going to help her in this skirmish. The subject of multiples is, at most, joked about but rarely debated. Opinions and feelings among staff and doctors run too strong to be discussed dispassionately.

The idea of multiple personalities occupying one body is like the theory of UFOs: either you believe or you don't.

Vuckovic emphatically shakes his head. "Doesn't wash. Sure, these things have been documented. Anecdotally. I've seen a multiple switch from a hardened prostitute, with all the body language of an experienced hooker, into a ten-year-old boy who really needed glasses and knew German. The patient had never studied or been to Germany. So how'd she do it?"

Vuckovic shakes his head in resignation, and continues. "She acquired the personalities through TV, tabloids, reading, casual conversations. Our culture is enormously rich — do you realize this is considered an American disorder? The British can count on one hand the number of cases reported there, while we're in the middle of an epidemic! I don't think multiples deliberately acquire personalities, but the raw material is all around and they soak it up unconsciously."

Nancy drums her fingers, ready to pounce. "If it wasn't deliberate, it can't be acting! That's what I'm saying. Multiple personalities grow and sprout on their own. They're real!"

"They're not consciously created by a patient," Vuckovic explains. "They're a product of a highly receptive individual exposed to a nurturing environment or to an individual who suggests the personalities."

Nancy musters up an expletive of sorts. "Bull crap! The 'therapy-nurtured' theory!"

"Swear all you like, Nance," Vuckovic teases, "but it's got a lot of validity. How else do you account for the fact that multiples cluster around the same therapists? Why are only a handful of therapists diagnosing this illness? Did you know that almost half of the known cases of MPD after the war and until the late sixties were reported by one psychiatrist? The same is true today: all the MPD specialists seem to find all the multiples."

"Alex, it makes no sense," Nancy chides. "Sean Whelan barely acknowledges his patients' own personalities, let alone suggests multiples."

Vuckovic chuckles. "You're right, but Sean's not the enabler here." He pauses. "It's Inger Hasselhoff. I adore the woman, think she's an exceptional psychiatrist, but she's one of these therapists who seems to have an inordinate number of MPDs in her waiting room. Julie's getting her cues from her, as well as from her pals on AB-II."

Nancy stands, gathering up binder and papers. She's not going to lose this one but will concede a draw. "So what do we do about Julie? Ignoring her, à la Sean, isn't going to help."

Vuckovic follows her through the nursing station toward the stairwell. They pause on the landing.

"I know, Nance." Vuckovic's voice is sadly resigned. "I may not believe in MPD, but I do believe in borderlines, and she's one of the sickest I've seen in a long while. That's what gets me. Treatment doesn't seem to help much. Whether meds or intensive therapy, it doesn't matter." His voice shifts. "And that's what pisses me off. Julie shouldn't be here. A hospital isn't the place for her kind of illness." He's interrupted by his beeper, which he momentarily stares at, then switches off. "Gotta run," he announces, and bounds up the stairs as Nancy disappears into the stairwell.

If medicine is a series of battles — the war on cancer, the fight against heart disease — then the controversy over multiple personality disorder is its Vietnam. The debate has raged since MPD was first identified around the turn of the century with shifting targets, dissension gripping both sides, and neither faction apparently capable of prevailing. The heart of the argument is whether the illness represents a unique, distinct sickness or if it is merely a variant of some other known mental illness.

The idea of one person harboring multiple personalities is as old as the Bible. The New Testament reports an encounter between Jesus and a man who declares, "My name is Legion, for we are many." Modern history traces the development of multiple personalities to demonic possession and, in the nineteenth century, to the widespread practice of using hypnosis to explore and treat mental illness. Dr. Morton Prince, writing around the turn of the century, is sometimes referred to as the "father of multiple personality syndrome" because of his observation that the symptoms of "double personality" bore a striking resemblance to those of hysteria. The theory of multiple personalities gained medical credibility from the French psychologist Pierre Janet, whose research into hysteria produced the theory of dissociation, which is a patient's capacity to separate parts of herself, also known as splitting her personality.

In the early twentieth century, MPD was largely ignored as Freudian theories gained popularity. Freud's dismissal of hypnosis as a useful medical tool and his lack of belief in the reality of childhood abuse ensured that the idea of multiple personalities would not be given much attention. Until the 1970s, only a smattering of cases appeared, including the 1954 case reported by therapists Corbett Thigpen and Hervey M. Cleckley which became the basis of their book, *The Three Faces of Eve*. Even as recently as the 1970s, multiple personality was not included as a separate disorder in the psychiatric diagnostic manual. The illness was a subcategory of dissociative disorders, namely a form of hysterical neurosis.

For a host of reasons, known and unknown, the number of reported cases of multiple personality disorder surged in the 1970s. The authoritative book *Multiple Personalities, Multiple Disorders* by Carol North, Jo-Ellyn Ryall, Daniel Ricci, and Richard Wetzel notes that in 1960, fewer than 30 cases had ever been documented. Then in the 1970s, that number jumped to around 80, and in the 1980s, reported cases skyrocketed to more than 630. Accounts of MPD, the authors conclude, have now reached "epidemic" proportions. According to *Multiple Personalities, Multiple Disorders,* a psychiatrist noted in 1986 that more cases had been reported in the past five years than in the previous two centuries.

This surge in cases has not diminished the controversy over

the disorder. In many ways, the tidal wave of cases has fueled the debate. While controlled studies of MPD are rare, the sheer number of cases has greatly added to psychiatrists' knowledge of the illness. Some of this information adds substance to the idea of the illness as a distinct disorder, some calls it into question. For instance, as the number of cases has multiplied, so has the number of personalities reported by a single patient. Originally thought to be a disorder of dual personalities, MPD has acquired more and more potential identities over the years. Eve in 1957 had three personalities (she later developed more), and the famous Sybil in 1973 had sixteen. Ten years later, accounts were being published about patients with hundreds of personalities. One report tells of a thousand inhabitants of a single patient's brain. This multiplication of selves is also mirrored in individual patients. *Multiple Personalities, Multiple Disorders* reports that researchers have found that initially MPD patients in therapy display two personalities, then proceed to add to their coterie, with eight being the average number of ultimate identities. Treatment methods also flame the controversy: hypnosis and intensive exploratory psychotherapy continue to be the most common methods psychiatrists use to address multiple personalities. But many experts believe these treatments may well encourage the creation of additional personalities.

As cases have proliferated, experts have identified characteristics and symptoms common to multiple personality disorder. MPD patients are mainly women in their thirties, although the illness is said to first appear in childhood, and men with MPD are not unknown. The vast majority of the women report childhood abuse, usually sexual. Aside from the most obvious symptom of alternate personalities, other common signs are a history of suicide attempts, amnesia or fugue, headaches, and what's referred to as "hysterical conversion," which is a physical symptom, such as paralysis of an arm or localized pain, with a psychological origin. The multiple personality patient rarely has just MPD; other mental illnesses almost always accompany it. These illnesses include affective disorders, anxiety disorders, anorexia nervosa, post-traumatic stress disorder, and somatization disorder. This last illness, known years ago as hysteria and now also called Briquet's syndrome, is often the alternative diagnosis for someone showing multiple personalities. This disorder begins early in life with chronic complaints of ailments with no verifiable medical basis. The complaints usually center on an organ system and may include abdominal pain, dizziness, painful menstruation, joint pain, or difficulty swallowing, and are usually recounted in dramatic, vague, or exaggerated ways. Personality disorders — namely borderline personality, histrionic personality, or antisocial personality — are also regularly paired with MPD, and the overlap between them and the behavior of multiples has led many doctors to believe that they are, more or less, the same illness.

Personality disorders occupy a special section of psychiatric illnesses. The *Diagnostic and Statistical Manual of Mental Disorders (DSM)* defines illnesses according to one of five categories or axes. The Axis I disorders are most like the medical illnesses that strike the rest of the body. They have beginnings, middles, ends: manic episodes, depressions, panic attacks. These disorders invade a personality; they are intruders, seemingly from without, into the previously comfortable life of the psyche. Regardless of country or culture, they are similar.

Personality disorders, however, which are chronic patterns of deviant behavior and thinking which begin early in life, are lumped into Axis II. The predominantly male sociopathic or antisocial personality disorder has a twin in the mainly female borderline personality disorder. Both disorders share features, including an ability to charm, that probably contribute to their survival from generation to generation. Other features are less appealing: a lifelong tendency to impulsiveness and difficulty in delaying gratification, an inability to maintain meaningful relationships because of a lack of empathy for others, with a resulting tendency to manipulate those who get in the way, and an absolute absence of responsibility for the consequences of behavior.

A degree of personal violence is also part of their make-up, although the antisocial and borderline personalities diverge in the direction of their violence. The sociopath steals from and injures others while the borderline attacks herself. Consequently, the men often end up in the criminal justice system, and the women wander through therapists' offices and in and out of psychiatric hospitals.

Theories about suspected origins of these disorders and MPD share many similar characteristics. The theories not only help explain why the behavior is so unruly and destructive, but also indicate to some psychiatrists that the differences between the illnesses are a matter of degree, and that MPD is in truth a type of personality disorder.

One school of thought believes that personality disorders are predetermined at birth by genetic or other inborn tendencies. A popular variety of this theory sees tendencies in some children which make them vulnerable to emotional injury in such a way as to create a social invalid for life. One two-year-old may be oblivious to a parent away for a weekend while another may be permanently scarred by the experience and become intolerably anxious whenever Mom leaves. Thus, one person may be born more impressionable than another. Experiences of abandonment at crucial times in a child's developmental years may push a person into a pattern of lifetime mental illness. An accumulation of such internal injuries, even without overtly traumatic life events, can lead to adult personality disorder.

Other observers believe the disorders are imposed on awholly unformed infant or child by trauma, which may be as private as sexual or physical abuse or as culturally pervasive as violence on TV. These researchers consider self-destructive behavior to be the understandable product of severe sexual, physical, or emotional abuse. The patient is unable to form trusting relationships as a result of the abuse and the resulting self-loathing, and turns her anger onto herself. This particular theory linking abuse and illness is widely accepted as the basis of yet another syndrome, post-traumatic stress disorder. PTSD is a complex collection of painful memories, sleep disturbance, anxiety, and emotional turmoil; it is also an Axis I disorder, meaning it is not a personality disorder but an illness with a distinct medical basis.

The role of sexual abuse in all these disorders, and questions about the validity of reports of it, are at the heart of the debate surrounding multiple personality disorder.

Sexual abuse has long been underreported. Depending on how strictly it is defined, as many as twenty to thirty percent of all children may be subjected to it to some degree as they grow up. The great majority of these people do not develop any psychiatric disorders. However, fifty to seventy-five percent of patients suffering from borderline personality report such a history. And upward of ninety-eight percent of reported MPDs say they were sexually abused. In most of these accounts, parents, stepparents, siblings, and strangers are reported to have indulged in often complex and perverse behavior with the patient. Sadism, masochism, and random violence abound in these stories. The complexity of the story seems to correspond to the severity of the patient's illness. The sickest, and presumably the most seriously abused, of the borderline patients can exhibit symptoms that look like multiple personality disorder.

It is at this point in the progression of illnesses, however, that some psychiatrists become skeptical. The problem with a history of sexual abuse as a basis for diagnosis is that it is usually an uncorroborated account by the patient. Many of the experiences cannot be verified, and this questionable credibility leads many doctors to conclude that the experiences are fabricated and that the personalities that seem to emanate from them are also fictitious.

The correct diagnosis for someone with a history of verifiable sexual trauma, skeptics insist, is post-traumatic stress disorder. In its list of symptom criteria for various illnesses, the *DSM-III-R* includes exposure to a traumatic event "outside the range of usual human experience" under post-traumatic stress, not borderline personality and not MPD.

The difficulty accepting MPD as a genuine, distinct illness, say the disbelievers, is that the symptoms are so subjective. The *DSM-III-R* criteria for MPD are remarkably few and general: "The existence within a person of two or more distinct personalities or personality states. At least two of these personalities or personality states recurrently take full control of the person's behavior."

Believers in MPD acknowledge that there is very little, if any, scientific or empirical data to verify the existence of the disorder. Yet the counterargument also makes sense: the absence of proof does not automatically mean that something does not exist.

The argument over which diagnostic category MPD belongs in is more than psychiatric hairsplitting. The precise diagnosis of an illness, particularly MPD, in large part determines how it is treated. Simply put, psychiatrists who consider a patient's multiple personalities to be secondary to a personality disorder or somatization disorder may well apply a certain "benign neglect," and ignore the MPD signs while addressing the behavioral problems of the primary personality disorder. On the other hand, psychiatrists who are confident and comfortable assigning a primary diagnosis of multiple personality disorder concentrate their efforts on integrating the various personalities.

The "success rate" for treating borderline personalities and multiple personality disorder is among the worst in psychiatry The outcome for patients with these illnesses, and the usual constellation of accompanying disorders, is often compared with schizophrenia; that is, it develops into a lifelong illness requiring repeated hospitalizations. This is what many psychiatrists believe, but detailed follow-up studies of people diagnosed with borderline personality or MPD personalities are sparse. Part of the problem is that borderlines and multiples are troublesome patients. As inpatients, they often complain, defy rules, and object to regulations. As outpatients, they typically make unreasonable demands on their therapists, regularly threaten suicide, and are verbally abusive.

A psychiatrist quoted in *Multiple Personalities, Multiple Disorders* sums up the problem in dealing with multiples. Integration of personalities, he believes, is "a minor miracle but it is hardly the end. Patients do regress, the problems of life do not vanish." The book's authors conclude about the prospects for patients with personality disorders: "These conditions are notoriously chronic and recalcitrant to all psychiatric interventions, and are severe and disabling in their own right."

The controversy over MPD does not end with the question of diagnosis or treatment methods. Even established treatment centers, like the AB-II unit at McLean, encounter strong opinions as to the appropriateness of their treating milieu. This is because MPD patients are normally grouped with personality disorder patients, an environment ripe for patients to compare notes and, suggest doubters, to swap and create memories of abuse.

The director of AB-II, Dr. James Chu, has no doubts about the legitimacy of MPD: "This is not a fun problem. It causes extraordinary distress. Patients don't use switches into other states as a way of escaping difficulties; they switch when feeling overwhelmed. It's involuntary." He concludes, "It's like being able to stop throwing up. You can't prevent it for long. It will soon come."

The atmosphere on AB-II feels much different from that on the Unit. Most of the twenty-three beds are taken by women. The patients act differently; they are not suffering from psychotic disorders that produce irrational outbursts or disjointed thinking, but from emotional upheavals. They may spend much of their time isolated in their rooms in the grip of painful memories. Nights may be hard for some, and sleeplessness, or more accurately a fear of sleep and nightmares, may cause patients to walk the halls at all hours. Ninety-five percent of the patients on the unit, says Chu, report "gross abuse." Much of the day here is devoted to individual psychotherapy, very specialized group therapy, and one-on-one exchanges with staff. Nevertheless, medication is standard fare on the unit because many of the patients also suffer from other illnesses. It's also frequently used for tranquilizing and blunting feelings from horrific flashbacks so that therapy can have an effect.

The immediate goal of treatment on the unit is, says Chu, "to stabilize their symptoms." Typically, patients are admitted in a crisis. They may be actively suicidal or self-mutilating. Often, memories of abuse have produced uncontrollable feelings of hopelessness, depression, self-destruction, and anger. They also may trigger a roller coaster of extreme emotional reactions, what Chu calls "switching." He explains: "A patient who's been abused by her father learns how to assume different states — one to function, one for sadness, one for rage." In the MPD patient, switching is the process of bringing a new personality to the forefront and happens suddenly, in a matter of seconds or minutes.

When patients feel disconnected from themselves or from reality, Chu and his staff teach what are called "grounding techniques." This is behavioral therapy to learn how to control painful flashbacks by emphasizing the patient's present reality, the here and now. It may consist of a therapist telling a patient in the throes of a flashback, "Feel this wall, feel this carpet, you are in the hospital and nowhere else." Simple devices like a watch with a regular alarm may help a patient to anchor herself in her surroundings.

The final treatment goal of the unit is to help patients become competent and functional in their daily lives. Treating their underlying traumas, whether it involves trying to mesh dozens of personalities or helping them refrain from mutilating themselves whenever they feel abandoned, is beyond the resources and time available on AB-II. The "ticking time bombs," as Chu calls patients with grotesque histories of abuse and emotional difficulties, are treated on an outpatient basis and require years to defuse. As on the Unit, the average stay here is two to three weeks, and patients are discharged not healed, but patched up.

Nancy Nicholson purposefully enters the empty, fluorescent-lit conference room on AB-III. She pulls her white sweater tightly about her shoulders, walks to the thermostat on the opposite wall, and turns up the temperature, then sits at the corner of an oak table. She surveys the room, eyes lighting on the gigantic old-fashioned blackboard nearly covering the far wall. Its grayish surface is covered with scribblings and schematic diagrams of neurons, receptors, and drug names.

The door swings open and Vuckovic walks in, carefully balancing a yellow porcelain mug. He circles the table and sits next to her, placing the mug in front of him and inhaling its vapors for a moment. Turning to smile at Nancy, he brings himself up and shambles over to the thermostat. "Hot in here," he declares as he lowers the temperature. Then, "You're still upset."

"Darn right I am. That narcissistic drip Whelan should have his privileges taken away. You say his dramatic exit had therapeutic value. Tell that to Julie. She did a good job cutting herself this morning. Abandonment is a rather touchy subject with patients like her, Alex."

"How'd she cut herself?" Vuckovic asks casually, as if inquiring about a recipe.

"She used the metal tip from her cowboy boots." Nancy

lightens up for a moment. "I gotta hand it to her, she's resourceful."

Sensing he's coming across as too disinterested, Vuckovic gravely adds, "Yeah. It's too bad she can't apply that wonderfully creative mind of hers to the healing process."

Vuckovic takes a sip from his mug and gratefully waves to Art Wiggins as the social worker walks in and sits on the opposite side of the table.

"How's it hanging, Alex?" Wiggins asks cheerfully. Looking at Nancy, he purses his lips. "We'll sort it all out here, right, sweetie?"

"You two think everything's funny, don't you?" she says sternly. "It would've been quite a yuk if she'd taken off and gotten run over by the commuter train."

Before either man can respond, the tiny figure of Dr. Inger Hasselhoff enters the room. She is an attractive, light-complected woman of indeterminate age with precise features. She is known at McLean for taking on the toughest cases, the most severe and seemingly intractable personality disorders. She spent a decade in a convent before leaving her order and getting her Ph.D. in psychology, and the self-discipline and concern for others which defined her first vocation shine through in her personal demeanor. She is respected by McLean's therapy community as well as by the psychopharm crowd. Today, her blond, nearly white hair is pulled back into a bun, offset by a crisply pressed black suit around a white blouse with a high collar. She sits at the table between Wiggins and the other two.

"Hi, Alex." She smiles, placing a manila folder bulging with papers in front of her. "Should I be looking forward to this?"

"Absolutely." Vuckovic's eyes crinkle. "Inger, I think you know Nancy, and this is Art Wiggins, who's been working with the family."

"It's nice to meet you after all our phone conversations," the therapist remarks to the social worker.

"*Enchanté,* doctor," Wiggins replies with a mixture of

charm and respect. A silence ensues as Hasselhoff opens her folio and arranges her notes.

The figure of Ross Baldessarini appears at the door. "Is this the place?" he asks, arching thick eyebrows. The researcher has arrived in his capacity as program director and professor of psychiatry to unravel another mess.

"It is, and you're most welcome," Vuckovic replies. The senior psychiatrist sweeps into the room and sits next to Wiggins, pulling his chair away from the table and toward the blackboard.

"I think slate exerts a magnetic pull on you, Dr. B," Wiggins remarks, and everyone laughs. Baldessarini is renowned for obsessively scribbling the facts of a case on the board as they are presented, usually until the entire surface is near white with chalk. Vuckovic looks at his watch.

"Should we begin? It's a complicated case, and I'm sure Sean will be —" Before the words are entirely out of his mouth, a clatter arises and a breathless Sean Whelan bursts into the room, followed by an equally winded John Graybill. Graybill closes the door shut behind them.

"Sorry, people. John here was helping me with my new research project and the time got away from us." He nods gravely at Baldessarini, somehow suggesting a special collegiality with the director.

"Thanks for coming, Sean," Vuckovic inserts. "Inger was just about to present the case."

All eyes turn to the diminutive Hasselhoff, who speaks in a precise and soft voice.

"We are all familiar with the details of this case. Dr. Baldessarini, you had a chance to go over my summary, I hope?"

She looks toward the senior researcher, who has taken up a position in front of the blackboard and is busily sweeping its surface with a dirty gray eraser.

"Every remarkably thorough page." He smiles. "You shot my Tuesday night bingo game."

"Thank you," the psychologist continues. "I would like to limit my remarks to recent developments in the case, which are both striking and troubling.

"As most of you know, Mrs. Swoboda, who was admitted here in the context of a family crisis and, after a chronic course of characterologic and affective symptomatology unresponsive to intensive therapy and various medications, has revealed to me the presence of at least four and perhaps more separate alter personalities within herself."

She is interrupted by a snort from the opposite end of the table. "You'll have your turn, Sean. I believe the formulation of a multiple personality is the most parsimonious explanation for her treatment resistance and the multiplicity of previous diagnoses. I challenge anyone in this room" — she pauses and fixes Whelan with a steely gaze — "to provide an alternate diagnosis that cuts through the questions and capsulizes this case as clearly."

"Fine," Whelan snaps. "The primary diagnosis is borderline disorder, along with a secondary bipolar II disorder. Her intimate encounters with the patients on AB-II — along with the enabling effect of your own credulity — have resulted in her concoction of these phantasms."

Inger Hasselhoff's face turns blush red and she speaks in a controlled whisper. "I have treated several hundred patients with characterologic problems, many far sicker than this woman, in my two decades as a clinician, Sean. We've shared some of these cases, and I've always listened to your perspective. We may have disagreed at times, but I have never called you a credulous fool!"

Whelan dramatically wipes his forehead and closes his eyes. "Look, Inger, don't you think you're overreacting here? I'm simply giving Ross the medical perspective on her condition." Whelan intones condescendingly.

Baldessarini steps away from the blackboard, where he has written two words, each about ten inches high, one on top of another: DIAGNOSIS and TREATMENT. "Let me give it a shot, why don't you?" Relief sweeps over the room.

"You'll notice I've limited my handwork today," he begins, gesturing toward the board with his chalky right jacket sleeve. "I fear ten boards would be insufficient to resolve the problems defined in those two words as they pertain to this case, and to you two dedicated clinicians. When in doubt, stick to the facts. I've found this a worthwhile motto."

Baldessarini's lecturing style, while chatty, is never patronizing. His words have a ring of legitimate candor. "Dr. Hasselhoff, you do agree that the patient fulfills *DSM-III-R* criteria for borderline personality disorder and bipolar disorder, not otherwise specified?"

"Yes I do, but that's not my point," the psychologist answers impatiently.

Baldessarini raises his hand like a crossing guard. "I understand." He turns to the other side of the table.

"Dr. Whelan, *you* will agree that the patient today fulfills criteria for *DSM-III-R* multiple personality disorder." It is not a question. Whelan, not taking his eyes off Baldessarini, nods almost imperceptibly.

"Thus in a very short time we have addressed the first of our dilemmas, at least to the extent that they are addressable in a mutually agreeable vocabulary. Now, on to job two!"

Vuckovic's face betrays no particular reaction, but he feels like a silent neophyte fiddler at a virtuoso cello performance.

Baldessarini crisply proceeds to the next issue. "Let me ask the other clinicians to contribute to the issue of the lady's management. Nancy, can you tell us how Mrs. Swoboda has appeared to the line staff?"

"Sure," the charge nurse begins. "We were surprised that the patient was instantly cooperative with the evaluation and routine of the Unit, especially as she had been described as near catatonic on AB-II. However, she's been labile, sometimes tearful, sometimes giddy, *very* manipulative, and self-mutilating. We've seen no obvious personality shifts. Frankly, she looks and acts like a borderline." Whelan leans his chair back, arms folded in back of his head, and smiles.

"The patient has staff grumbling about the appropriateness of treating her on this unit. However," the nurse goes on, "we've been absolutely mortified by the casual, dare I say indifferent, attitude of some treatment team members to issues of her safety."

Whelan's expression is now stony, as he interrupts. "This is exactly why I don't treat these patients!" he declares, as if someone has asked him to take on an entire unit of personality disorders. "The treatment milieu and professional alliances are completely compromised. They split doctors and staff, pit doctors against doctors, and make treatment conferences unnecessarily contentious," he dispassionately concludes.

"Nancy," Inger Hasselhoff interjects, "you, Sean, and I go way back. I know he'd never endanger a patient willingly, and so do you. Maybe he let his judgment slip for a second." Hasselhoff nods at Whelan with a sympathetic expression, but he betrays no response. She continues, "I do agree with you, Sean, that we're seeing her pathology intrude in this room."

"Shall we move on?" The upbeat voice of Alexander Vuckovic fills the momentarily silent room. "Art, the family?"

"Not much to say, Alex," the social worker responds. "I think Bud has more or less given up on the relationship. As you know, he's got his own issues, and he feels overwhelmed by this situation. He came to the office the other day and told me he was going ahead with divorce proceedings; he's mainly worried for the kids."

"Great," Vuckovic remarks. "Nothing like another loss for this woman. Would she have a place to stay if she had to leave a hospital setting?"

"I suspect her friend and recent roommate may feel a bit burned out by now. As you know, Julie is totally estranged from those members of her family we can locate. And I'm not sure about financing for a halfway house. Bud says he's stretched thin with day care for three kids. And he's a pediatrician, not a cardiac surgeon. He says the bucks ain't there."

Vuckovic directs the discussion to the end of the table. "Well, Dr. Baldessarini, can you solve the treatment dilemma as cleanly as you've addressed the diagnostic issue?"

The program director shakes his head ruefully. "How about a hundred blackboards? Seriously, let's look at the facts again. Sean, you made a note in the chart to the effect that Mrs. Swoboda's affective pathology is under relatively good control."

"Indeed," says Whelan, always the assured clinician. "I believe her bulimic exacerbation and near catatonic depressive state lifted as a direct result of the addition of clomipramine to her antidepressant regimen. I know she responded quickly."

"So quickly," Hasselhoff interrupts, "that her bulimic behavior cleared before her first dose. Come on, Sean. The woman has a marital crisis and may lose her kids. That accounts for all her recent symptoms, including the sudden emergence of her alters."

"Ladies and gentlemen," Baldessarini says wearily, "we're speculating again. Irrespective of the causes, it sounds very much as if her issues today are related to borderline and dissociative pathology. It also sounds as if she's got no safe place to go and she's too unstable for a less structured unit. May I suggest, in the immediate term, that she move back to AB-II, where she can better resolve those difficulties? And where she can be given a second chance to repair the torn relationship with her family — whoops, treaters." He smiles broadly, as does Nancy Nicholson. Whelan remains serious, unsure whether to be offended.

"Two problems, boss," Vuckovic interjects. "One is that unless he's changed his mind in the last half hour, my friend Sean has taken himself off the case."

"That's right," Whelan concurs.

Baldessarini looks ingenuously at the PIC. "Well, Dr. Vuckovic, it appears you've bought yourself a psychopharm patient.

Unless we want to subject her to the ministrations of a total stranger, unaccustomed to her ways. And the second problem?"

Vuckovic allows himself a small shrug. If this is the price of pacifying his staff and charge nurse, so be it. He has treated tougher patients. "Problem two is, What if they don't want her back? She seems to have burned her bridges rather thoroughly."

"I think they can be persuaded," Baldessarini allows, "assuming Mrs. Swoboda is willing to participate in their program. Why don't we see the patient?" He looks questioningly at Vuckovic, who reaches for the telephone on the floor behind him.

Within five minutes, a knock on the door of the conference room announces the arrival of Julie Swoboda, escorted by Frank. Wiggins opens the door, and the patient, blond hair flowing around her small face, sits next to Vuckovic as he stands to motion her welcome.

"Mrs. Swoboda, I think you know everyone around this table except Dr. Baldessarini." The patient looks about, frowning. "He's our senior consultant, and he has some ideas about your treatment given the difficult events of the last few days. I hope you don't mind if he asks you a few questions."

Baldessarini smiles warmly. "Thank you for coming to talk with us, Mrs. Swoboda. I know it isn't easy with all these people around."

The woman at Vuckovic's side shrinks into her chair. "That's two of you called me that," she breathes heavily. "Who's this Slobova? My name's Louise, and you people are scaring me. I'm gettin' outta here!"

As if in slow motion, the wisp of a woman next to Vuckovic kicks back her chair, bounds across the conference table past the arms of a lunging Frank, and vaults from the table's end through the open door.

Half following the pandemonium of jumping, yelling people around him, Vuckovic grabs the phone and punches in the extension for hospital security, muttering to himself, "Sure . . . she'd love to participate."

Security easily catches up with Louise as she huddles in plain view under the gnarled oak outside the DeMarneffe cafeteria. By the time she is hustled to the Unit between two burly security personnel, she is Julie again and puzzled at her restricted status and at the grass stains on her best dress. Her husband and Vuckovic arrive simultaneously, and the psychiatrist spends a confusing hour explaining what had happened that morning to two people, both of whom apparently were not there.

Julie seems pleased about a transfer back to AB-II, but immediately saddens, mentioning the friends she made on Vuckovic's unit. She then coolly declares to her husband that she's very sorry for the pain she has caused him, but that she needs to deal with her problems without him. He leaves the room, sobbing, with Vuckovic's arm around his shoulder.

Thursday greets Alexander Vuckovic with a thunderstorm, and he sprints from the parking lot to the Admissions Building. Inger Hasselhoff has asked for a breakfast meeting to talk about the duet they will be performing as Julie's psychopharmacologist and psychotherapist.

She's waiting at a table near the window of the cafeteria and looks up from a cup of coffee as Vuckovic approaches with his twelve-ounce mug, decorated with the logo BELMONT HIGH CLASS OF '77.

"Hi, Alex. Do they let you carry that weapon into the cafeteria line?"

"Present from the wife. The nice lady at the coffee machine looks the other way while I pour and the really nice lady at the cash register lets me pass for a buck. And, how about you, Inger? Survive our jolly treatment conference?"

The therapist laughs softly. "Sean certainly can come on a little strong! Every now and then he gets to me, but he's emotionally honest, and a brilliant psychopharmacologist, so I'm happy to put up with his unique personality," she asserts diplomatically.

"We've never shared a patient before," Hasselhoff goes on amiably, "so I want to make sure that we both understand what each other's doing."

Vuckovic grins. "You make it sound as if we're going to be roommates!"

The former nun laughs. "Not quite, more like sharing a horse's suit, you know, like in the school play. Am I right in assuming that you've never treated a multiple before? Except, of course, on your unit."

"Let's just say, never for any length of time and never voluntarily. But, be that as it may, I'm not going to be medicating Mrs. Swoboda's multiples." Vuckovic shifts uncomfortably in the molded plastic chair and notices the rain pelting the patio furniture outside.

"Alex, please, drop the sword. I'm really not here to duel over diagnostic disagreements. Each of our perspectives is much needed with this patient. I just want to warn you that Julie can be exceedingly manipulative. I can't count the number of midnight calls I've gotten from her, claiming she's going to swallow a pile of Elavils or a container of antifreeze, and what am I going to do about it?" The therapist throws up her hands in exasperation.

Vuckovic shakes his head in camaraderie. "At least on AB-II she won't be able to get to the phone any time of day or night!" He continues in a more serious tone. "It's possible that the combined antidepressants and mood stabilizers may reduce her impulsivity. However, I can't take the actress out of her."

"I think that issue comes under my umbrella," Hasselhoff remarks ruefully, as if it's all too familiar. "While you're going after the affect, I'll be wrestling with the weird transference."

Vuckovic raises an eyebrow. "What, not finding the core personality, not integrating the alters?"

The psychotherapist shifts her eyes toward the wet patio, then scans the tables around them, as if stalling or making a decision. She lowers her voice. Although the cafeteria is largely empty, three patients occupy a table nearby. "Julie Swoboda does not have true MPD."

"Does not have true MPD," Vuckovic repeats.

"I believe she has factitious MPD," Hasselhoff declares, and sips her coffee.

"Factitious MPD." Vuckovic pauses. "You understand my problem with this, Inger. Since I believe MPD to be a factitious disorder, you're telling me she has a factitious factitious disorder. Does that mean you think she has a *true* disorder? Or is that only for me to believe, since you think her factitious disorder is true?"

"Alex, I knew you'd respond like this. Look, you have true psychosis and factitious psychosis. It's analogous. You wouldn't give neuroleptics to someone with factitious psychotic disorder, right? Well, we feel similarly. She's a severe borderline and she's faking her MPD."

"How can you tell?" Vuckovic's gaze is stern.

"What do you mean?"

"Factitious psychosis is different in reproducible, observable ways. It's briefer, responds to reassurance or placebo, is fantastic in its content — Smurfs dancing on your belly. How can you tell her personalities are fake and the other fourteen bodies times twenty souls are real?"

"Jesus, Alex, you just can. I've been doing it for years. It's a feeling."

"How's this going to affect her treatment? What do the people on AB-II think?"

"In all honesty," Hasselhoff admits, "not much. AB-II knows the situation, but their concern is helping Mrs. Swoboda to the point where she can function outside, return to her family."

Vuckovic nods in agreement. "Borderline, multiple. It really doesn't make much of a difference, does it? She is still going to be a very sick lady for a very long time."

CHAPTER SEVEN

Leaving the Unit

KIESHA THOMAS: DISCHARGE SUMMARY

■ *Hospital Course:* Pt. was initially grossly psychotic and refused therapy. She was highly agitated and required restraint during her first four hospital days. Following the administration of haloperidol as a chemical restraint, she became cooperative with treatment and was stabilized on haloperidol 2 mg po bid. She experienced a significant resolution of her symptoms and acknowledged that she had been ill. Prior to discharge, an ultrasound demonstrated the viability of her fetus. Condition on discharge was moderately improved, as the patient remained mildly euphoric and tangential. She was aware of the risk of tardive dyskinesia from haloperidol therapy and took the medication willingly. Activity and diet were ad lib.

■ *Discharge Diagnosis:* Axis I: Bipolar Disorder, Manic Episode, Psychotic, in Partial Remission.

■ *Aftercare:* Pt. was discharged to her husband's care on haloperidol 2 mg po bid, to be followed at the Massachusetts Mental Health Center's Outpatient Clinic.

A. Vuckovic, M.D., PIC

Kiesha Thomas had a healthy seven-pound boy, after which she started lithium carbonate therapy. Haldol was tapered and discontinued. She sent a card to "My Friends on the Unit" announcing the birth and thanking the staff and Vuckovic for their "kindly attention." Since her discharge, she hasn't had a recurrence of her mania in over a year.

DAVID SELTZER: DISCHARGE SUMMARY

■ *Hospital Course:* Pt. was initially admitted to the Unit in a depressed, delusional, and actively suicidal state. He believed he smelled bad and engaged in hand- and foot-washing rituals. He was placed on haloperidol 4 mg bid and clomipramine 100 mg qd but was intolerant of side effects, including tremor, myoclonus, constipation, and urinary retention. Medications were discontinued and the patient agreed to a course of ECT. He received seven bilateral square wave electroconvulsive treatments and experienced minimal cognitive disturbance. At the beginning of the ECT series, the patient attempted suicide by hanging, but was fortunately discovered in time to prevent any lasting injury. After a brief period of medical evaluation at Mass. General Hospital, he returned to the Unit to complete his series of treatments. Following treatment five, the pt.'s depressive symptoms remitted dramatically. However, persistent washing rituals resulted in a transfer to the Cognitive and Behavioral Treatment Unit, where Dr. Roz Goldstein engaged him in individual behavioral psychotherapy and he took part in the group contract meeting for two weeks. Consultation with Dr. Vuckovic led to the initiation of fluoxetine therapy at 20 mg qd, which the pt. tolerated with latency insomnia as the only significant side effect. This was well controlled with triazolam 0.25 mg qhs. The pt. was moderately improved on discharge with persistence of some foot washing and continuing remission of depressive symptoms. Activity and diet: as tolerated.

■ *Discharge Diagnosis:* Axis I: Major Depression, Recurrent, with Psychotic Features, in Remission; Obsessive Compulsive Disorder, in Partial Remission. Axis II: None.

■ *Aftercare:* Pt. was discharged home. He will see Dr. Goldstein in weekly psychotherapy and Dr. Vuckovic in monthly medication management. Medications as above.

Harold Benjamin, Ph.D.
Psychologist-in-Charge, CBTU

David Seltzer joined a friend in purchasing a franchise selling home water filter systems. He continued to take his antidepressant and met monthly with Vuckovic, and he saw his behaviorist weekly. His foot washing decreased to four times daily. Seltzer became active in the National Depressive and Manic Depressive Association and was a vocal supporter of shock therapy. About three months after discharge, David and his wife, Carol, divorced.

SUSAN BEEKMAN: DISCHARGE SUMMARY

■ *Hospital Course:* Pt. was originally admitted to the Unit suffering from an exacerbation of restrictive and purging eating behavior. After several days on the Unit, the pt.'s eating disorder symptoms worsened despite an increase in her Zoloft dosage to 150 and then 200 mg qd. She was transferred to the CBTU to establish an individual and group behavioral therapy regimen. Dr. Roz Goldstein engaged her in individual therapy and Dr. Whelan consulted on medication issues. The pt. made good use of a behavioral schedule, initiated in a quiet room setting, and was able to gain four pounds within her first ten days at Upham/Appleton House. However, her surreptitious binging and vomiting behavior persisted to a troubling degree. A psychotherapy consultation was requested from Dr. Inger Hasselhoff. Dr. Hasselhoff met with the pt. in three one-hour consultative sessions and was able to elicit from the pt. previously repressed memories of repeated childhood sexual abuse at the hands of a male relative. She made a recommendation for intensive individual psychotherapy. The pt. and family took exception to the recommendation and the pt. filed a three-day note of intent to leave the hospital. In the absence of suicidal ideation or psychosis, we felt compelled to discharge the pt. against medical advice the following day, in a mildly improved condition. Activity and diet were as tolerated.

■ *Discharge Diagnosis:* Axis I: Anorexia Nervosa, Bulimia, Post-Traumatic Stress Disorder. Axis II: None.

■ *Aftercare:* Pt. was discharged to her parents' home, taking Zoloft 200 mg qam. She was to be followed by Dr. Sean Whelan for pharmacotherapy and declined further psychotherapy.

Harold Benjamin, Ph.D.
Psychologist-in-Charge, CBTU

After leaving McLean, Susan Beekman moved in with a man she knew from school and became engaged to him. She returned to school to study psychology, and got a job conducting telephone surveys for a polling company. Six months following her discharge, she suffered a major episode of clinical depression and was hospitalized at Upham/Appleton House.

GLENDA BELLINI: DISCHARGE SUMMARY

■ *Hospital Course:* Ms. Bellini had an extremely gratifying course. She was initially grossly disorganized, experiencing near continuous hallucinosis, paranoid delusions, and significant orofacial and buccal movements consistent with tardive dyskinesia. Reinstitution of her haloperidol therapy did not adequately control her symptoms and the pt. gave informed consent to the initiation of clozapine therapy. Within a week of treatment quickly titrated to 75 mg qd, the pt. showed remarkable improvement in affect, activities of daily living, and organization of her thinking. Her TD symptoms decreased significantly as well. She was discharged in a markedly improved condition. Her activity and diet were ad lib.

- *Discharge Diagnosis:* Axis I: Schizophrenia, Paranoid Type, Chronic with Acute Exacerbation.
- *Aftercare:* Pt. was discharged to her boarding house on clozapine 75 mg po qhs and lorazepam 0.5 mg po tid prn anxiety. She will be followed by Dr. Jeffries through the clozapine clinic and the McLean OPC.

A. Vuckovic, M.D., PIC

Glenda Bellini stopped taking clozapine a month after she left McLean, suffered a psychotic relapse, and was admitted to East House II for a week. She refused another trial of clozapine and was put on Prolixin decanoate intramuscular therapy. Her rooming house refused to take her back and a Cambridge shelter was listed as her discharge destination. Vuckovic occasionally sees her among the homeless around Boston Common.

MATT MULLANY: DISCHARGE SUMMARY

- *Hospital Course:* Pt. had a rough course. He was admitted on a Section 15C from Waltham District Court for evaluation and treatment and showed signs of irritability, distractibility, and antisocial behavior, but showed no psychotic symptoms. He was assaultive to nursing staff and required restraint on several occasions. Because of a clinical picture consistent with residual attention deficit disorder, he was begun on methylphenidate SR 20 mg po bid. He responded dramatically to this therapy within a week, with decreased irritability and significant resolution of his dysphoria. His behavior remained grossly inappropriate and provocative, however. Following an incident of sexual acting out with another pt., he was briefly restricted to the Unit. He became quite cooperative after this and was given a group privilege. On his first trip to the cafeteria with a group, the pt. eloped. He was placed on escape status and his family and appropriate police and court agencies were notified. McLean Hospital legal counsel and the

District Court have informed me that at this point it is appropriate to discharge the pt. formally and to place him on persona non grata status. His condition is unchanged. Activity, diet, and aftercare status are moot.

■ *Discharge Diagnosis:* Axis I: Attention Deficit Hyperactivity Disorder, Residual Type. Axis II: Antisocial Personality Disorder.

■ *Aftercare:* Unknown.

A. Vuckovic, M.D., PIC

Matt Mullany was picked up by police within days of his escape from the Unit. He is in jail awaiting trial. He is not taking Ritalin.

JULIE SWOBODA: DISCHARGE SUMMARY

■ *Hospital Course:* Pt. was initially admitted to AB-II following an escalating pattern of dysphoria, sleeplessness, and bulimic behavior. While compliant with her regimen of valproate, perphenazine, sertraline, and thyroxine, and with the addition of a low dose of clomipramine, the pt. was uncooperative with the AB-II treatment program. She was transferred to the Unit, where she showed no clear affective symptomatology but was labile, impulsive, and frequently manipulative. Following an incident of sexual acting out with another pt., the pt. reported that she was experiencing dissociation into several discrete personality states. A case conference with Dr. Ross Baldessarini as consultant was held. At this conference, Dr. Baldessarini agreed that the pt. was newly exhibiting symptoms of a multiple personality disorder and suggested a transfer to a more appropriate milieu. She was transferred back to AB-II and later discharged to the halfway house and day treatment components of Codman III. Her condition was mildly improved on discharge. Activity and diet were ad lib.

■ *Discharge Diagnosis:* Axis I: Bipolar Disorder NOS, in remission; Multiple Personality Disorder. Axis II: Borderline Personality Disorder.

- *Aftercare:* Pt. to be followed at CH-III by Dr. Hasselhoff in individual psychotherapy, and by myself in pharmacotherapy. She remains on perphenazine 8 mg po qhs, sertraline 300 mg po qam, thyroxine 0.2 mg po qd, clomipramine 25 mg po qhs, spironolactone 25 mg po qid prn, ibuprofen 600 mg po tid prn, and lorazepam 1 mg po tid prn. She was aware of the risk of tardive dyskinesia on perphenazine therapy.

A. Vuckovic, M.D., PIC

Three days following her discharge to Codman House III, Julie Swoboda escaped to her home and took her youngest son with her to the Greyhound bus station in Boston, explaining to the baby sitter that she was meeting her husband. Police arrested her in Providence, and the boy was returned, unharmed, to his father's custody. Julie is in the Worcester State Hospital, spending much of her time as Will, who takes full responsibility for the kidnapping of her child.

On a Friday in June, a couple of months after the last of these patients was discharged, the Unit lost its light, airy space and moved to the dark, cramped second floor of East House.

The move itself was probably the least traumatic part of the reorganization. Two days before, staff and patients packed their things into cartons labeled with the name and room number of their new home. On moving day, the floridly psychotic patients were housed on another locked unit while the more coherent patients spent the day in the gym with the staff. By 4:00 P.M., the new residents of East House II were unpacking their clipboards and clothing.

Settling into EH-II has required adjustments. With smaller rooms, narrower halls, and no spacious lounge areas, patients live closer together. Nurses are more on guard for flare-ups over intrusions into personal space. The staff has also lost room, with fewer places to escape stressful encounters. There's less hanging out in the EH-II nurses' station, fewer opportunities to swap snippets of information or flashes of humor.

The smaller quarters of East House II accommodate fewer patients and staff. Although the unit officially houses twenty patients, it has lost a quiet room. A mental health worker has been bumped to another unit and two nurses have taken positions elsewhere in the hospital.

The Unit's metamorphosis into EH-II is part of a major consolidation at McLean. The adult inpatient population of the entire hospital has slipped to around 180, and rumors of the prospect of entire units being closed float widely. "Flexibility" has become the code word for this massive change in McLean Hospital. In the face of a plummeting patient population, survival dictates that McLean find another way to offer treatment. The hospital is on its toes, ready to jump any number of ways, depending on what type and how many patients come to its doors. One possibility is turning units into halfway houses or converting them into residential housing for part of the year.

The reconstructed EH-II is next on the hit list of units to be closed if patient numbers continue to fall. The "census watch" has become a regular activity for the Unit. Every day, the staff and doctors note how many patients have entered and left McLean's psychotic disorders program. The single day when twenty-five patients departed sent a shudder through everyone. Dr. Alexander Vuckovic is still the psychiatrist-in-charge, but his frustration with the shrinking resources and uncertainty about the future of his unit is taking its toll. He's snapping at, and apologizing more to, his charge nurse, and wonders if he's getting an ulcer.

Summertime is a predictably quiet season for McLean, a few months when patients, for a host of reasons, stay away. So the doctors and staff of EH-II are holding their breath, hoping their institution can make it to fall when, just maybe, their special brand of medicine will be in demand again.

Medical Terms and Abbreviations

ADHD: attention deficit hyperactivity disorder

affective disorder: a mental illness in which changes in mood, usually depression and mania, are the primary symptoms

Anafranil: trade name of an antidepressant drug also used to treat obsessive-compulsive disorder

anhedonic: an inability to experience normal pleasure

Apgar: a rating scale for testing basic physiological responses in newborn infants

appy: appendectomy

Ativan: trade name of an antianxiety drug

atropine: generic name for a drug containing barbiturates

Axis I: part of a system for diagnosing mental illnesses according to the *Diagnostic and Statistical Manual of Mental Disorders, Third Edition, Revised;* this category includes major illnesses such as schizophrenia, mood disorders, and anxiety disorders

Axis II: second part of *DSM-III-R* diagnostic system; this category covers developmental disorders and personality disorders

Axis III: third part of *DSM-III-R* diagnostic system; this category covers any accompanying physical disorders and conditions

Axis IV: fourth part of *DSM-III-R* diagnostic system; this category covers any accompanying psychosocial stresses

Axis V: fifth part of *DSM-III-R* diagnostic system; this category includes a score for global assessment of functioning

bid (abbr): twice a day

bipolar disorder: manic depression; an illness of affect or mood that includes depression and mania

borderline personality disorder/grand hysteria: illness characterized by difficult personal relationships, anger, mood swings, self-destructive tendencies, impulsiveness, feelings of emptiness, an inability to be alone, and identity confusion

buccal: related to the mouth

Chr Par Sz: chronic paranoid schizophrenic

clang association: the pairing of words that sound similar but have no relationship in meaning; e.g., "sing" and "bing." A symptom of mania

clomipramine: generic name of an antidepressant drug also used to treat obsessive-compulsive disorder

Clozaril: trade name of an antipsychotic drug used to treat schizophrenia

CNS: clinical nurse supervisor; central nervous system

Cogentin: trade name of a drug used to treat Parkinsonian side effects of other drugs, particularly tremor and muscular rigidity

cp: cerebral palsy

d/c: discontinue

decanoate: long-acting form of certain drugs

Depakote: trade name of an anticonvulsant drug also used to treat psychosis and mania

Desyrel: trade name of an antidepressant drug

dx: diagnosis
dysphoria: a state of extreme unhappiness or unpleasant mood

Elavil: trade name of an antidepressant drug
elision: the omission of the initial or final sound in pronunciation
endocrine: a test of the thyroid and related glands
EtOH: ethanol, alcohol, liquor

fibromyalgia: a debilitating disorder causing fatigue and muscular
    pain
Fioricet: trade name of a drug that contains a barbiturate and
    caffeine and is used for tension headache
fluoxetine: generic name of the antidepressant drug Prozac
fugue: state of confusion during which a patient is conscious but
    afterward has no memory of it

GAF: Global Assessment of Functioning; a scale from 90 (highest)
    to 1 (lowest) indicating a patient's level of functioning
gravida: pregnant
gustatory: relating to the sense of taste

H/A: headache
Haldol: trade name of an antipsychotic drug
haloperidol: generic name of the antipsychotic drug Haldol
HLOC: hospital level of care
hs: bedtime dose
hx: history
hypercholesterolemia: excess cholesterol in the blood
hysterical neurosis: a dated term for conversion disorder that is
    characterized by a loss of physical functioning that reflects a
    psychological conflict

IM: intermuscular
imipramine: generic name of an antidepressant drug also used to
    treat panic disorder and obsessive-compulsive disorder

Klonopin (sometimes Clonopin): trade name of an anticonvulsant drug also used to treat anxiety

LA: long-acting
labile: frequently or regularly changing; emotionally unstable
latency insomnia: inability to fall asleep
lithium carbonate: a naturally occurring mineral salt used to treat mania and manic depression
LOC: loss of consciousness
loxapine: generic name of an antipsychotic drug also used to treat psychotic depression

MAOI: monoamine oxidase inhibitor, a class of antidepressant drugs
Mellaril: trade name of an antipsychotic medication also used to treat borderline personality
MHA: mental health aide
mood-congruent psychotic features: hallucinations or delusions that match a person's mood; e.g., ominous or scary sights or sounds and a depressed mood
myoclonus: involuntary contraction of a muscle

NAD: no acute distress
Navane: trade name of an antipsychotic drug
NKDA: no known drug allergy
nortriptyline: generic name of an antidepressant drug
NOS: not otherwise specified

OCD: obsessive-compulsive disorder
OPC: outpatient clinic
oppositionality: a personality style characterized by constant disagreeing, arguing, and defying authority
organic delusional syndrome: delusions associated with medical, surgical, or neurological disorders, or with drug intoxications
orobuccal: toothless

orofacial: relating to the mouth and face

PCN: penicillin
pemoline: generic name of a drug used to treat attention deficit
    hyperactivity disorder and treatment-resistant depression
PIC: psychiatrist-in-charge
po (abbr): per oral; taking medication by mouth
prn: as needed *(pro re nata)*
Prolixin: trade name of an antipsychotic drug
prostatitis: inflammation of the prostate
Prozac: trade name of an antidepressant drug
pt.: patient
PTSD: post-traumatic stress disorder

q: with
qam: once in the morning
qd: every day
qhs: at bedtime
qid: four times a day
qpm: in the afternoon

R/O: rule out
RPR: a test for syphilis
Rxist: therapist

schizoaffective disorder: a depressive or manic syndrome that in-
    cludes psychosis; shares some symptoms with schizophrenia
    and some symptoms with mood disorders
Serentil: trade name of an antipsychotic drug
sh/fl: sharps and flames
SI/HI: suicidal ideation/homocidal ideation
s/p: status post, after
SR: slow release
SSRI: selective serotonin reuptake inhibitor, a type of antidepres-
    sant medication

sup: supervised

Sustacal: trade name of a dietary supplement

Sx: seizure; schizophrenic

T & A: tonsillectomy and adenoidectomy

Taractan: trade name of an antipsychotic drug

Tegretol: trade name of an anticonvulsant medication also used to treat manic depression

terminal insomnia: insomnia at the end of the night

TFT: thyroid function test

Thorazine: trade name of an antipsychotic drug

three spheres: oriented to time, place, and person

tid (abbr): three times a day

trazadone: generic name of an antidepressant drug also used to treat anxiety

tricyclics: a class of antidepressant drugs

Trilafon: trade name of an antipsychotic drug also used to treat borderline personality disorder

valproate: a salt of valproic acid, which is an anticonvulsant drug used to treat psychosis

Vistaril: trade name of a drug used as a sedative

VS: vital signs

Wellbutrin: trade name of an antidepressant drug

WNL: within normal limits

w/u: medical work-up

Xanax: trade name of an antianxiety drug also used to treat depression

Zoloft: trade name of an antidepressant drug

INDEX

Mailman Research Center. *See*
  McLean Hospital
Mania, 11
  clang association in, 256
  ECT and, 86, 87, 88
  seasonal, 21
Manic depression (bipolar disorder),
  119, 256
MAOI, defined, 258
Massachusetts General Hospital, 57,
  73, 109, 209
Medicaid. *See* Insurance coverage
Medical students, 44–46
  case reports, 32, 178
  prescription of medication by, 45–
  46, 48, 56, 64, 136–37
Medicare. *See* Insurance coverage
Medication: Anafranil, 221, 255
  anticonvulsant, 258, 260
  antidepressant, 20, 84, 88, 119,
  185, 191, 256–60 *passim*
  antipsychotic, 20, 57, 68–72, 140–
  42, 256–60 *passim*
  aporphines, 75–78
  Ativan, 16, 199, 255
  chlorpromazine, 68–69
  clomipramine, 84, 256
  clozapine (Clozaril), 49–50, 70,
  140–45, 158, 250, 256
  Cogentin, 256
  Depakote, 256
  Desyrel, 256
  and drug abuse, 59, 91, 214–15
  Elavil, 257
  Fioricet, 257
  haloperidol (Haldol), 65, 66, 67,
  76, 84, 113, 140, 141, 147, 188,
  257
  "handedness" of, 77
  imipramine, 191, 257
  Klonopin (Clonopin), 258
  licensing of, 78
  lithium carbonate, 48, 52–53, 54–
  55, 56, 256
  loxapine, 258
  Mellaril, 258
  Metrazol, 88
  Navane, 258

nortriptyline, 258
pemoline, 16, 259
Prolixin, 50, 250, 259
Prozac, 130, 183, 191, 257, 259
reserpine, 68
Ritalin, 188, 190, 197, 207, 213,
  251
Serentil, 259
side effects of, 17, 38, 69–71, 77,
  84, 88, 113, 140, 141, 145, 256
Tegretol, 260
Thorazine, 69, 161, 260
trazadone, 17, 260
Trilafon, 260
valproate, 260
Vistaril, 199, 260
Wellbutrin, 260
Xanax, 18, 260
Zoloft, 118, 260
Medication nurse, 18–19
Medication therapy: administration
  of, 19
  cognitive behavior therapy vs., 125
  ECT combined with, 26
  ECT preferred over, 88
  judicial decision in, 56–57
  Medicaid and, 50
  for MPD, 234
  noncompliance with (recurrent), 8,
  139, 144
  prescription of, 12, 16, 38
  by medical students, 45–46, 48,
  56, 64, 136–37
  for night admissions, 5
  for pregnant patient, 38, 44,
  53, 54
  psychoeducational approach
  combined with, 20
  and psychopharmacology, 2, 38
  psychotropic, 67
  research in, 28–29, 67–78
  for schizophrenia, 140–41, 142
Meduna, Ladislas, 87
Mellaril, 258. *See also* Medication
Mental health aide (MHA), 64–65,
  143, 213
  leads group therapy, 146–48
  and privileges, 208, 210–11